DATE DUE

DEC 6-06			

DEMCO 38-296

ROSALIND

Major Literary Characters

**THE ANCIENT WORLD THROUGH
THE SEVENTEENTH CENTURY**

ACHILLES
Homer, *Iliad*

CALIBAN
William Shakespeare, *The Tempest*
Robert Browning, *Caliban upon Setebos*

CLEOPATRA
William Shakespeare, *Antony and
    Cleopatra*
John Dryden, *All for Love*
George Bernard Shaw, *Caesar and
    Cleopatra*

DON QUIXOTE
Miguel de Cervantes, *Don Quixote*
Franz Kafka, *Parables*

FALSTAFF
William Shakespeare, *Henry IV, Part I,
    Henry IV, Part II, The Merry Wives
    of Windsor*

FAUST
Christopher Marlowe, *Doctor Faustus*
Johann Wolfgang von Goethe, *Faust*
Thomas Mann, *Doctor Faustus*

HAMLET
William Shakespeare, *Hamlet*

IAGO
William Shakespeare, *Othello*

JULIUS CAESAR
William Shakespeare, *Julius Caesar*
George Bernard Shaw, *Caesar and
    Cleopatra*

KING LEAR
William Shakespeare, *King Lear*

MACBETH
William Shakespeare, *Macbeth*

ODYSSEUS/ULYSSES
Homer, *Odyssey*
James Joyce, *Ulysses*

OEDIPUS
Sophocles, *Oedipus Rex, Oedipus
    at Colonus*

OTHELLO
William Shakespeare, *Othello*

ROSALIND
William Shakespeare, *As You Like It*

SANCHO PANZA
Miguel de Cervantes, *Don Quixote*
Franz Kafka, *Parables*

SATAN
The Book of Job
John Milton, *Paradise Lost*

SHYLOCK
William Shakespeare, *The Merchant
    of Venice*

THE WIFE OF BATH
Geoffrey Chaucer, *The Canterbury
    Tales*

**THE EIGHTEENTH AND
NINETEENTH CENTURIES**

AHAB
Herman Melville, *Moby-Dick*

ISABEL ARCHER
Henry James, *Portrait of a Lady*

EMMA BOVARY
Gustave Flaubert, *Madame Bovary*

DOROTHEA BROOKE
George Eliot, *Middlemarch*

CHELSEA HOUSE PUBLISHERS

Major Literary Characters

DAVID COPPERFIELD
Charles Dickens, *David Copperfield*

ROBINSON CRUSOE
Daniel Defoe, *Robinson Crusoe*

DON JUAN
Molière, *Don Juan*
Lord Byron, *Don Juan*

HUCK FINN
Mark Twain, *The Adventures of Tom Sawyer, Adventures of Huckleberry Finn*

CLARISSA HARLOWE
Samuel Richardson, *Clarissa*

HEATHCLIFF
Emily Brontë, *Wuthering Heights*

ANNA KARENINA
Leo Tolstoy, *Anna Karenina*

MR. PICKWICK
Charles Dickens, *The Pickwick Papers*

HESTER PRYNNE
Nathaniel Hawthorne, *The Scarlet Letter*

BECKY SHARP
William Makepeace Thackeray, *Vanity Fair*

LAMBERT STRETHER
Henry James, *The Ambassadors*

EUSTACIA VYE
Thomas Hardy, *The Return of the Native*

TWENTIETH CENTURY

ÁNTONIA
Willa Cather, *My Ántonia*

BRETT ASHLEY
Ernest Hemingway, *The Sun Also Rises*

HANS CASTORP
Thomas Mann, *The Magic Mountain*

HOLDEN CAULFIELD
J. D. Salinger, *The Catcher in the Rye*

CADDY COMPSON
William Faulkner, *The Sound and the Fury*

JANIE CRAWFORD
Zora Neale Hurston, *Their Eyes Were Watching God*

CLARISSA DALLOWAY
Virginia Woolf, *Mrs. Dalloway*

DILSEY
William Faulkner, *The Sound and the Fury*

GATSBY
F. Scott Fitzgerald, *The Great Gatsby*

HERZOG
Saul Bellow, *Herzog*

JOAN OF ARC
William Shakespeare, *Henry VI*
George Bernard Shaw, *Saint Joan*

LOLITA
Vladimir Nabokov, *Lolita*

WILLY LOMAN
Arthur Miller, *Death of a Salesman*

MARLOW
Joseph Conrad, *Lord Jim, Heart of Darkness, Youth, Chance*

PORTNOY
Philip Roth, *Portnoy's Complaint*

BIGGER THOMAS
Richard Wright, *Native Son*

CHELSEA HOUSE PUBLISHERS

Major Literary Characters

ROSALIND

Edited and with an introduction by
HAROLD BLOOM

CHELSEA HOUSE PUBLISHERS
New York ◇ Philadelphia

Rosalind

e Hepburn as Rosalind in the 1950
ɔu Like It (Billy Rose Theatre Collection,
New York Public Library). *Inset:* First page of *As You Like It*
from the First Folio (1623) (The Folger Shakespeare Library).

Chelsea House Publishers

Editor-in-Chief Remmel T. Nunn
Managing Editor Karyn Gullen Browne
Picture Editor Adrian G. Allen
Art Director Maria Epes
Manufacturing Director Gerald Levine

Major Literary Characters

Senior Editor S. T. Joshi
Associate Editor Richard Fumosa
Designer Maria Epes

Staff for ROSALIND

Picture Researcher Ellen Barrett
Assistant Art Director Noreen Romano
Production Manager Joseph Romano
Production Coordinator Marie Claire Cebrián

First Printing

1 3 5 7 9 8 6 4 2

Library of Congress Cataloging-in-Publication Data

Rosalind / edited and with an introduction by Harold Bloom.
        p.   cm.—(Major literary characters)
        Includes bibliographical references and index.
        ISBN 0-7910-0927-0.—ISBN 0-7910-0982-3 (pbk.)
        1. Shakespeare, William, 1564–1616. As you like it.
    2. Shakespeare, William, 1564–1616—Characters—Rosalind.
    3. Rosalind (Fictitious character)   I. Bloom, Harold.   II. Series.
                PR2803.R67   1991
                822.3'3—dc20
                    91-9051
                    CIP

CONTENTS

THE ANALYSIS OF CHARACTER

Harold Bloom

"Character," according to our dictionaries, still has as a primary meaning a graphic symbol, such as a letter of the alphabet. This meaning reflects the word's apparent origin in the ancient Greek *charactēr,* a sharp stylus. *Charactēr* also meant the mark of the stylus' incisions. Recent fashions in literary criticism have reduced "character" in literature to a matter of marks upon a page. But our word "character" also has a very different meaning, matching that of the ancient Greek *ēthos,* "habitual way of life." Shall we say then that literary character is an imitation of human character, or is it just a grouping of marks? The issue is between a critic like Dr. Samuel Johnson, for whom words were as much like people as like things, and a critic like the late Roland Barthes, who told us that "the fact can only exist linguistically, as a term of discourse." Who is closer to our experience of reading literature, Johnson or Barthes? What difference does it make, if we side with one critic rather than the other?

Barthes is famous, like Foucault and other recent French theorists, for having added to Nietzsche's proclamation of the death of God a subsidiary demise, that of the literary author. If there are no authors, then there are no fictional personages, presumably because literature does not refer to a world outside language. Words indeed necessarily refer to other words in the first place, but the impact of words ultimately is drawn from a universe of fact. Stories, poems, and plays are recognizable as such because they are human utterances within traditions of utterances, and traditions, by achieving authority, become a kind of fact, or at least the sense of a fact. Our sense that literary characters, within the context of a fictive cosmos, indeed are fictional personages is also a kind of fact. The meaning and value of every character in a successful work of literary representation depend upon our ideas of persons in the factual reality of our lives.

Literary character is always an invention, and inventions generally are indebted to prior inventions. Shakespeare is the inventor of literary character as we know it; he reformed the universal human expectations for the verbal imitation of personality, and the reformation appears now to be permanent and uncannily inevitable. Remarkable as the Bible and Homer are at representing personages, their characters are relatively unchanging. They age within their stories, but their habitual modes of being do not develop. Jacob and Achilles unfold before us, but without metamorphoses. Lear and Macbeth, Hamlet and Othello severely modify themselves not only by their actions, but by their utterances, and most of all through *overhearing themselves,* whether they speak to themselves or to others. Pondering what they themselves have said, they will to change, and actually do change, sometimes extravagantly yet always persuasively. Or else they suffer change, without willing it, but in reaction not so much to their language as to their relation to that language.

I do not think it useful to say that Shakespeare successfully imitated elements in our characters. Rather, it could be argued that he compelled aspects of character to appear that previously were concealed, or not available to representation. This is not to say that Shakespeare is God, but to remind us that language is not God either. The mimesis of character in Shakespeare's dramas now seems to us normative, and indeed became the accepted mode almost immediately, as Ben Jonson shrewdly and somewhat grudgingly implied. And yet, Shakespearean representation has surprisingly little in common with the imitation of reality in Jonson or in Christopher Marlowe. The origins of Shakespeare's originality in the portrayal of men and women are to be found in the *Canterbury Tales* of Geoffrey Chaucer, insofar as they can be located anywhere before Shakespeare himself. Chaucer's savage and superb Pardoner overhears his own tale-telling, as well as his mocking rehearsal of his own spiel, and through this overhearing he is emboldened to forget himself, and enthusiastically urges all his fellow-pilgrims to come forward to be fleeced by him. His self-awareness, and apocalyptically rancid sense of spiritual fall, are preludes to the even grander abysses of the perverted will in Iago and in Edmund. What might be called the character trait of a negative charisma may be Chaucer's invention, but came to its perfection in Shakespearean mimesis.

The analysis of character is as much Shakespeare's invention as the representation of character is, since Iago and Edmund are adepts at analyzing both themselves and their victims. Hamlet, whose overwhelming charisma has many negative components, is certainly the most comprehensive of all literary characters, and so necessarily prophesies the labyrinthine complexities of the will in Iago and Edmund. Charisma, according to Max Weber, its first codifier, is primarily a natural endowment, and implies a primordial and idiosyncratic power over nature, and so finally over death. Hamlet's uncanniness is at its most suggestive in the scene of his long dying, where the audience, through the mediation of Horatio, itself is compelled to meditate upon suicide, if only because outliving the prince of Denmark scarcely seems an option.

Shakespearean representation has usurped not only our sense of literary character, but our sense of ourselves as characters, with Hamlet playing the part of the largest of these usurpations. Insofar as we have an idea of human disinterestedness, we tend to derive it from the Hamlet of Act V, whose quietism has about it a ghostly authority. Oscar Wilde, in his profound and profoundly witty dialogue, "The Decay of Lying," expressed a permanent insight when he insisted that art shaped every era, far more than any age formed art. Life imitates art, we imitate Shakespeare, because without Shakespeare we would perish for lack of images. Wilde's grandest audacity demystifies Shakespearean mimesis with a Shakespearean vivaciousness: "This unfortunate aphorism about art holding the mirror up to Nature is deliberately said by Hamlet in order to convince the bystanders of his absolute insanity in all art-matters." Of *Hamlet's* influence upon the ages Wilde remarked that: "The world has grown sad because a puppet was once melancholy." "Puppet" is Wilde's own deconstruction, a brilliant reminder that Shakespeare's artistry of illusion has so mastered reality as to have changed reality, evidently forever.

The analysis of character, as a critical pursuit, seems to me as much a Shakespearean invention as literary character was, since much of what we know about how to analyze character necessarily follows Shakespearean procedures. His hero-villains, from Richard III through Iago, Edmund, and Macbeth, are shrewd and endless questers into their own self-motivations. If we could bear to see Hamlet, in his unwearied negations, as another hero-villain, then we would judge him the supreme analyst of the darker recalcitrances in the selfhood. Freud followed the pre-Socratic Empedocles, in arguing that character is fate, a frightening doctrine that maintains the fear that there are no accidents, that overdetermination rules us all of our lives. Hamlet assumes the same, yet adds to this argument the terrible passivity he manifests in Act V. Throughout Shakespeare's tragedies, the most interesting personages seem doom-eager, reminding us again that a Shakespearean reading of Freud would be more illuminating than a Freudian exegesis of Shakespeare. We learn more when we discover Hamlet in the Freudian Death Drive, than when we read *Beyond the Pleasure Principle* into *Hamlet*.

In Shakespearean comedy, character achieves its true literary apotheosis, which is the representation of the inner freedom that can be created by great wit alone. Rosalind and Falstaff, perhaps alone among Shakespeare's personages, match Hamlet in wit, though hardly in the metaphysics of consciousness. Whether in the comic or the modern mode, Shakespeare has set the standard of measurement in the balance between character and passion.

In Shakespeare the self is more dramatized than theatricalized, which is why a Shakespearean reading of Freud works out so well. Character-formation after the passing of the Oedipal stage takes the place of fetishistic fragmentings of the self. Critics who now call literary character into question, and who proclaim also the death of the author, invariably also regard all notions, literary and human, of a stable character as being mere reductions of deeper pre-Oedipal desires. It becomes clear that the fortunes of literary character rise and fall with the prestige of normative conceptions of the ego. Shakespeare's Iago, who wars against being, may be the first deconstructionist of the self, with his proclamation of "I am not what I am." This constitutes the necessary prologue to any view that would regard a fixed ego as a virtual abnormality. But deconstructions of the self are no more modern than Modernism is. Like literary modernism, the decentered ego came out of the Hellenistic culture of ancient Alexandria. The Gnostic heretics believed that the psyche, like the body, was a fallen entity, mechanically fashioned by the Demiurge or false creator. They held however that each of us possessed also a spark or pneuma, which was a fragment of the original Abyss or true, alien God. The soul or psyche within every one of us was thus at war with the self or pneuma, and only that sparklike self could be saved.

Shakespeare, following after Chaucer in this respect, was the first and remains still the greatest master of representing character both as a stable soul and a wavering self. There is a substance that endures in Shakespeare's figures, and there is also a quicksilver rendition of the unsettling sparks. Racine and Tolstoy, Balzac and Dickens, follow in Shakespeare's wake by giving us some sense of pre-Oedipal sparks or drives, and considerably more sense of post-Oedipal character and personality, stabilizations or sublimations of the fetish-seeking drives. Critics like Leo Bersani and René Girard argue eloquently against our taking this mimesis as the only proper work of literature. I would suggest that strong fictions of the self, from the Bible through Samuel Beckett, necessarily participate in both modes, the sublimation of desire, and the persistence of a primordial desire. The mystery of Hamlet or of Lear is intimately invested in the tangled mixture of the two modes of representation.

Psychic mobility is proposed by Bersani as the ideal to which deconstructions of the literary self may yet guide us. The ideal has its pathos, but the realities of literary representation seem to me very different, perhaps destructively so. When a novelist like D. H. Lawrence sought to reduce his characters to Eros and the Death Drive, he still had to persuade us of his authority at mimesis by lavishing upon the figures of *The Rainbow* and *Women in Love* all of the vivid stigmata of normative personality. Birkin and Ursula may represent antithetical and uncanny drives, but they develop and change as characters pondering their own pronouncements and reactions to self and others. The cost of a non-Shakespearean representation is enormous. Pynchon, in *The Crying of Lot 49* and *Gravity's Rainbow*, evades the burden of the normative by resorting to something like Christopher Marlowe's art of caricature in *The Jew of Malta*. Marlowe's Barabas is a marvelous rhetorician, yet he is a cartoon alongside the troublingly equivocal Shylock. Pynchon's personages are deliberate cartoons also, as flat as comic strips. Marlowe's achievement, and Pynchon's, are beyond dispute, yet they are like the prelude and the postlude to Shakespearean reality. They do not wish to engage with our hunger for the empirical world and so they enter the problematic cosmos of literary fantasy.

No writer, not even Shakespeare or Proust, alters the available stock that we agree to call reality, but Shakespeare, more than any other, does show us how much of reality we could encounter if only we retained adequate desire. The strong literary representation of character is already an analysis of character, and is part of the healing work of a literary culture, which implicitly seeks to cure violence through a normative mimesis of ego, *as if it were stable,* whether in actuality it is or is not. I do not believe that this is a social quest taken on by literary culture, but rather that we confront here the aesthetic essence of what makes a culture *literary,* rather than metaphysical or ethical or religious. A culture becomes literary when its conceptual modes have failed it, which means when religion, philosophy, and science have begun to lose their authority. If they cannot heal violence, then literature attempts to do so, which may be only a turning inside out of the critical arguments of Girard and Bersani.

I conclude by offering a particular instance or special case as a paradigm for the healing enterprise that is at once the representation and the analysis of literary character. Let us call it the aesthetics of being outraged, or rather of successfully representing the state of being outraged. W. C. Fields was one modern master of such representation, and Nathanael West was another, as was Faulkner before him. Here also the greatest master remains Shakespeare, whose Macbeth, himself a bloody outrage, yet retains our imaginative sympathy precisely because he grows increasingly outraged as he experiences the equivocation of the fiend that lies like truth. The double-natured promises and the prophecies of the weird sisters finally induce in Macbeth an apocalyptic version of the stage actor's anxiety at missing cues, the horror of a phantasmagoric stage fright of missing one's time, of always reacting too late. Macbeth, a veritable monster of solipsistic inwardness but no intellectual, counters his dilemma by fresh murders, that prolong him in time yet provoke him only to a perpetually freshened sense of being outraged, as all his expectations become still worse confounded. We are moved by Macbeth, however estrangedly, because his terrible inwardness is a paradigm for our own solipsism, but also because none of us can resist a strong and successful representation of the human in a state of being outraged.

The ultimate outrage is the necessity of dying, an outrage concealed in a multitude of masks, including the tyrannical ambitions of Macbeth. I suspect that our outrage at being outraged is the most difficult of all our affects for us to represent to ourselves, which is why we are so inclined to imaginative sympathy for a character who strongly conveys that affect to us. The Shrike of West's *Miss Lonely-hearts* or Faulkner's Joe Christmas of *Light in August* are crucial modern instances, but such figures can be located in many other works, since the ability to represent this extreme emotion is one of the tests that strong writers are driven to set for themselves.

However a reader seeks to reduce literary character to a question of marks on a page, she will come at last to the impasse constituted by the thought of death, her death, and before that to all the stations of being outraged that memorialize her own drive towards death. In reading, she quests for evidences that are strong representations, whether of her desire or her despair. Such questings constitute the necessary basis for the analysis of literary character, an enterprise that always will survive every vagary of critical fashion.

EDITOR'S NOTE

This book brings together a representative selection of the best criticism, old and new, that has been devoted to the Rosalind of Shakespeare's *As You Like It*, considered as a major literary character. The critical extracts and essays are reprinted here separately, each in the chronological order of their original publication. I am grateful to Richard Fumosa for his skill and devotion in assisting my editing of this volume.

My introduction centers upon two perspectives for appreciating Rosalind: the contrast, within the play, between her and those false wits, Jaques and Touchstone; and beyond the play, between her and two equally formidable masters of wit, Falstaff and Hamlet.

The critical extracts begin with William Hazlitt's portrait of Rosalind, and proceed through such notable views as those of Shaw, Chesterton, Stoll, and Iser, to conclude with a group of estimates by our contemporary scholars of Shakespeare.

Harold C. Goddard, my favorite Shakespeare critic, begins the full-scale critical essays with his charming celebration of Rosalind's precise mode of wit. We are then given C. L. Barber's superb sense of Rosalind's mastery of perspectives, after which Walter R. Davis investigates the source for Shakespeare's Rosalind in Thomas Lodge's.

Edward I. Berry returns us to the contrast between Lodge's and Shakespeare's Rosalinds, while Charles R. Forker develops Barber's emphasis upon perspectives. R. Chris Hassel, Jr., emphasizes the sophistication that the love-games of Rosalind and Orlando demand from the audience. Another sophistication, the audience's skepticism as to the possibility of gender transformations, is the subject of William C. Carroll. Devon L. Hodges similarly explores Rosalind's, and the play's skepticism, as to whether it is wise to break out of the orders, forms, and structures that at once confine us yet also protect us against chaos.

The issue of Shakespeare's own skepticism as to the bounds of gender is discussed by Barbara J. Bono, while Marjorie Garber celebrates Rosalind as a prefiguration of *The Tempest*'s Prospero, after which the formidable Camille Paglia, visionary of sexual personae, concludes this book with a Dionysian perspective upon Rosalind.

INTRODUCTION

Many of us have had a particular reading experience, one that is rather difficult to describe or categorize, in which we pass from a protracted immersion in Shakespeare's plays to a perusal of some other author, old or new. Even if that author is one of Shakespeare's few peers, say Chaucer or Cervantes or Tolstoy, we are still highly conscious that the transition away from reading Shakespeare involves a difference both in degree and in kind. The difference is a falling away in what seems the persuasiveness in representing what we want to call reality, particularly the reality of a self with which we can identify. We have a sense that Shakespeare portrays human inwardness not only far better than anyone else, but in a way that partakes of the inwardness, indeed augments the inwardness. My language is of course impressionistic; it lacks the concern for materiality, race, gender, social history, and all those other indubitable verities of what I am asked to believe is a New Historicism, without which no current studies of Shakespeare can be politically correct. But then Shakespeare, rather sublimely, is not politically correct, and is anything but an historicist. You can go hunting for what is vital in John Marston or George Chapman, armed with your Foucaultian bow and Marxist arrow, but you will return from the Forest of Arden with nothing to show for your enlightened zeal.

Be old-fashioned with me, as archaic as Dr. Johnson and William Hazlitt, and start again with Shakespeare's characters, abysses of inwardness. How exactly do they differ from literary characters before them, and why do the most intense of them continue to surpass all characters since? Shakespeare's greatest originality, as I have ventured before, is that his characters overhear themselves, ponder what they themselves have said, and on that basis frequently resolve to change and subsequently do change. In the Hebrew Bible, characters change, but not because they have overheard and pondered their own asides or soliloquies. The J Writer's principal character, Yahweh himself, changes profoundly at Sinai, and behaves very badly indeed in the Wilderness, but his changes are not Shakespearean, as a close comparison with his literary descendant, King Lear, will demonstrate. Lear learns humility by learning his own violent nature, because he is struck by his own

I

utterances. Yahweh is not capable of overhearing himself, and so learns nothing, and remains therefore always violent, always unpredictable.

A preference among Shakespearean protagonists, where there is so bewildering a plenitude, almost always will have a subjective element, and yet it is a commonplace to affirm the superior, indeed the heroic wit of three figures in particular: Rosalind, Falstaff, Hamlet. Of these, Rosalind's wit is the most balanced, the most proportionate to the pragmatics of everyday existence, and clearly the most capable of harmony, of what Yeats liked to call Unity of Being. Like Falstaff in the two parts of *Henry IV*, and like Hamlet, Rosalind is larger than her play, and restores our sense of the overwhelming reality of literary character. In ways almost too subtle for critical description to encompass, Rosalind could be judged as Shakespeare's supreme representation of a possible human personality. Her clearest rival is Hamlet, but he is too strong for any context, and reaches so far beyond us that we cannot always apprehend him. Rosalind, a miracle of wit, is closer to us and requires no mediation between ourselves and her role.

C. L. Barber catches one of the several senses in which Rosalind touches the limits of Shakespearean representation:

> The dramatist tends to show us one thing at a time, and to realize that one thing, in its moment, to the full; his characters go to extremes, comical as well as serious; and no character, not even a Rosalind, is in a position to see all around the play and so be completely poised, for if this were so the play would cease to be dramatic.

Let us repeat Barber's point, but in the other direction: more than any other Shakespearean character, more even than Falstaff or Hamlet, Rosalind is almost completely poised, nearly able to see all around the play. What Barber names as a poise that transcends perspectivizing, I would rather term heroic wit, a stance that comprehends both skepticism and a vitalistic exuberance. Falstaff darkens because his educational and paternal love is rejected; in losing his pupil, he loses himself, having invested too much of his wit in Hal. Hamlet darkens because he is Hamlet, and is too supremely intelligent for any context or any action available to him. Rosalind, best balanced of all Shakespearean figures, does not darken though, like Falstaff and Hamlet, immense wit compels her to change, however subtly, each time she speaks. Her difference from Falstaff and from Hamlet, otherwise her peers, lies in the nature of her will. Like them, she has a will to power over the interpretation of her own play, and like them she is a dramatist, forever devising fresh scenes and skits. But Rosalind never seeks to express her will, as Hamlet and Falstaff do, in different but complementary ways. Her quest is to express her energy and joy, her sense of more life. Falstaff has a contest to win, against both time and the interests of the state. Agonistically, Falstaff's energy and joy are superbly activated, yet his will necessarily is contaminated by his two great antagonists. Hamlet's mighty opposite is hardly the wretched Claudius, but is himself, since another of the Prince of Denmark's great originalities is that he inaugurates the great trope that Freud appropriated, the civil war in the psyche in which each of us is her own worst enemy. In our hearts there is a kind of fighting that will not let us sleep, but such is not the heart of Rosalind.

The touchstones for Rosalind's spirit are Jaques and Touchstone himself, both of them fundamentally rancid beings, though Shakespeare scholars see Jaques for what he is, while they are weirdly charmed by Touchstone. I exempt only Harold Goddard, Shakespeare's best critic since Hazlitt, for Goddard sees Touchstone precisely as Rosalind sees this vicious wit, a Fool who will be rotten ere he is ripe. Here is Touchstone's vision of human reality:

And so, from hour to hour we ripe and ripe,
And then from hour to hour we rot and rot.

Historicists, whether Old or New, tend to be reductionists: they all are would-be Touchstones. The late Helen Gardner, Old Historicist, was enchanted by Touchstone: "In everything that Touchstone says and does gusto, high spirits and a zest for life ring out. Essentially comic, he can adapt himself to any situation in which he may find himself. Never at a loss, he is life's master." Gardner goes on to tell us that Jaques is Touchstone's opposite: "He is the cynic, the person who prefers the pleasures of superiority, cold-eyed and cold-hearted."

Rosalind has even less esteem for Touchstone than she does for Jaques, but then Rosalind is anything but an historicist, let alone a politically correct master of sexual politics. Like the nurse in *Romeo and Juliet,* Touchstone is popular with our modern groundlings, and like the nurse Touchstone has vicious elements in his nature. Rosalind, heroically free of the Death Drive, repudiates every intimation of sadism with her astonishing wit, perhaps the only wit in all Western literature that has affection at its core. Speaking as Ganymede playing Rosalind, Rosalind playfully denies her lover Orlando, who resorts to grand hyperbole, and is answered by the only prose in Shakespeare that is equal to Falstaff's, a prose that here mocks Christopher Marlowe, who is so strange a presence-by-absence throughout *As You Like It:*

ROSALIND: Well, in her person, I say I will not have you.

ORLANDO: Then, in mine own person, I die.

ROSALIND: No, faith, die by attorney. The poor world is almost six thousand years old, and in all this time there was not any man died in his own person, videlicet, in a love cause. Troilus had his brains dashed out with a Grecian club; yet he did what he could to die before, and he is one of the patterns of love. Leander, he would have lived many a fair year though Hero have turned nun, if it had not been for a hot midsummer night; for, good youth, he went but forth to wash him in the Hellespont, and being taken with the cramp, was drowned; and the foolish chroniclers of that age found it was "Hero of Sestos." But these are all lies. Men have died from time to time, and worms have eaten them, but not for love.

How many of us, suffering the agonies of passion, requited *or* rejected, have been aided by Rosalind's amiable wisdom: "Men have died from time to time, and worms have eaten them, but not for love." That competes with several of Falstaff's for the eminence of being the best sentence in the language. Rosalind, as much in love as anyone else in Shakespeare, or in what we call reality, teaches Orlando, herself, and her audience the limits of love. Would that we could die by proxy, but even then, the cause would not be love. Troilus, paradigm of the true lover, is obliterated by Rosalind's double jest: his dignified death by the spear of Achilles is transformed into having "his brains dashed out with a Grecian club," and the metaphysical agonies he will undergo a year or two later in *Troilus and Cressida* are reduced to masochism, "yet he did what he could to die before." Rosalind, least Marlovian of all stage protagonists whatsoever, joins in the general mockery of poor Marlowe that rather strangely runs all through *As You Like It* as an undersong. Touchstone, directly before defining the truest poetry as the most feigning, and love as another feigning, throws away Shakespeare's astonishing epitaph for his truest precursor: "When a man's verses cannot be understood, nor a man's good wit seconded with the forward child, understanding, it strikes a man more dead than a great reckoning in a little room." The "great reckoning in a little room" was the disputed tavern bill that supposedly caused Ingram Frizer to strike Marlowe dead, with a dagger-thrust through the poet's eye. Phebe the shepherdess, smitten with love for Rosalind disguised as Ganymede, is employed for a mockery of the most famous line in Marlowe's *Hero and Leander:*

> Dead shepherd, now I find thy saw of might,
> "Who ever loved that loved not at first sight."

Marlowe, permanently esteemed as the poet of the lyric, "The Passionate Shepherd to His Love," is not only the dead shepherd of *As You Like It,* but he is the spirit of the negation that the play repudiates in rejecting the viciousness of Touchstone and the rancidity of Jaques. Marlowe (and Chapman) are the last of the "foolish chroniclers" who gave the verdict that the cause of Leander's cramp and subsequent drowning was Hero of Sestos. Rosalind's amiable skepticism is the cure for Marlowe's Ovidian eroticizing of human failings and accidents into the Death Drive. Just as *Twelfth Night* is a comedy in part directed against Ben Jonson, with Malvolio a displaced Jonsonian moralist, so *As You Like It* stages an implicit polemic against Marlovian hyperboles of desire. There is something of Rosalind in Emily Dickinson, and Dickinson can give us the apt phrase for Rosalind: "adequate desire." The mystery of Rosalind's character centers upon the astonishing poise with which Shakespeare has endowed her. How do we describe an intellect that has faith both in itself and in language? Hamlet, who has faith in neither, is incommensurate with us, and so requires the mediation of Horatio's love. No one mediates Rosalind for us, except perhaps Touchstone and Jacques, who accomplish that by negation.

All that Rosalind asks for her will is that it not be violated or usurped; she has no will to power over others. She is the ancestor of that grand tradition of fictive heroines of the Protestant Will that includes Jane Austen's Elizabeth Bennet and

Emma Woodhouse. The tradition, which goes from Richardson's Clarissa Harlowe through Austen and George Eliot and George Meredith, has its American representatives in Hawthorne and James, and reverberates still in the heroines of Forster and Woolf, and in the Brangwen sisters of Lawrence. Like Rosalind, these figures concentrate upon the giving and receiving of esteem, a very different dialectical exchange from the Marlovian agon of rhetoric, in which the will to power over other souls is always at the center. Rosalind's wit is heroic because it struggles against every invidious quality that could debase or compromise it.

Shakespeare chose never to bring his grandest negations and his most heroic wits onto the same stage. One's imagination plays with the possible confrontations: duels of intellect between Iago and Falstaff, or Edmund and Hamlet. But one cannot imagine Rosalind in the cosmos of the great Shakespearean villains, and not just because her context is the Forest of Arden. Her freedom is that of a wholly normative personality: mature, without malice, needing to turn aggressivity neither against herself nor against others. We rejoice in her because no other figure in Western literature, not even in Shakespeare, is at once so accomplished in wit, and so little interested in the power that great wit can bring if properly exercised. No one else, in Shakespeare or any other author, is so free of resentment while yet retaining all of the natural human endowments of curiosity, vitality, and desire. We intensely welcome her company, because no other fictive presence is at once so naturalistically refreshing, or less insistent upon appropriating for herself.

—H. B.

CRITICAL EXTRACTS

WILLIAM HAZLITT

Rosalind's character is made up of sportive gaiety and natural tenderness: her tongue runs the faster to conceal the pressure at her heart. She talks herself out of breath, only to get deeper in love. The coquetry with which she plays with her lover in the double character which she has to support is managed with the nicest address. How full of voluble, laughing grace is all her conversation with Orlando—

> In heedless mazes running
> With wanton haste and giddy cunning.

How full of real fondness and pretended cruelty is her answer to him when he promises to love her 'For ever and a day!'

> ROSALIND: Say a day without the ever: no, no, Orlando, men are April when they woo, December when they wed: maids are May when they are maids, but the sky changes when they are wives: I will be more jealous of thee than a Barbary cock-pigeon over his hen; more clamorous than a parrot against rain; more new-fangled than an ape; more giddy in my desires than a monkey; I will weep for nothing like Diana in the fountain, and I will do that when you are disposed to be merry; I will laugh like a hyen, and that when you are inclined to sleep.
> ORLANDO: But will my Rosalind do so?
> ROSALIND: By my life she will do as I do.

The silent and retired character of Celia is a necessary relief to the provoking loquacity of Rosalind, nor can anything be better conceived or more beautifully described than the mutual affection between the two cousins:—

> We still have slept together,
> Rose at an instant, learn'd, play'd, eat together,

7

And wheresoe'r we went, like Juno's swans,
Still we went coupled and inseparable.

—WILLIAM HAZLITT, *Characters of Shakespeare's Plays*
(London: C. H. Reynell, 1817)

H. N. HUDSON

It is something uncertain whether Jaques or Rosalind be the greater attraction: there is enough in either to make the play a continual feast; though her charms are less liable to be staled by use, because they result from health of mind and symmetry of character; so that in her presence the head and the heart draw together perfectly. I mean that she never starts any moral or emotional reluctances in our converse with her: all our sympathies go along with her freely, because she never jars upon them, or touches them against the grain.

For wit, this strange, queer, lovely being is fully equal to Beatrice, yet nowise resembling her. A soft, subtile, nimble essence, consisting in one knows not what, and springing up one can hardly tell how, her wit neither stings nor burns, but plays briskly and airily over all things within its reach, enriching and adorning them; insomuch that one could ask no greater pleasure than to be the continual theme of it. In its irrepressible vivacity it waits not for occasion, but runs on for ever, and we wish it to run on for ever: we have a sort of faith that her dreams are made up of cunning, quirkish, graceful fancies; her wits being in a frolic even when she is asleep. And her heart seems a perennial spring of affectionate cheerfulness: no trial can break, no sorrow chill, her flow of spirits; even her sighs are breathed forth in a wrappage of innocent mirth; an arch, roguish smile irradiates her saddest tears. No sort of unhappiness can live in her company: it is a joy even to stand her chiding; for, "faster than her tongue doth make offence, her eye doth heal it up."

So much for her choice idiom of wit. But I must not pass from this part of the theme without noting also how aptly she illustrates the Poet's peculiar use of humour. For I suppose the difference of wit and humour is too well understood to need any special exposition. But the two often go together; though there is a form of wit, much more common, that burns and dries the juices all out of the mind, and turns it into a kind of sharp, stinging wire. Now Rosalind's sweet establishment is thoroughly saturated with humour, and this too of the freshest and wholesomest quality. And the effect of her humour is, as it were, to *lubricate* all her faculties, and make her thoughts run brisk and glib even when grief has possession of her heart. Through this interfusive power, her organs of play are held in perfect concert with her springs of serious thought. Hence she is outwardly merry and inwardly sad at the same time. We may justly say that she laughs out her sadness, or plays out her seriousness: the sorrow that is swelling her breast puts her wits and spirits into a frolic; and in the mirth that overflows through her tongue we have a relish of the grief with which her heart is charged. And our sympathy with her inward state is the more divinely moved, forasmuch as she thus, with indescribable delicacy, touches it through a masquerade of playfulness. Yet, beneath all her frolicsomeness, we feel that there is a firm basis of thought and womanly dignity; so that she never laughs away our respect.

It is quite remarkable how, in respect of her disguise, Rosalind just reverses the conduct of Viola, yet with much the same effect. For, though she seems as much at home in her male attire as if she had always worn it, this never strikes us otherwise than as an exercise of skill for the perfecting of her masquerade. And on the same principle her occasional freedoms of speech serve to deepen our sense of her innate delicacy; they being manifestly intended as a part of her disguise, and springing from the feeling that it is far less indelicate to go a little out of her character, in order to prevent any suspicion of her sex, than it would be to hazard such a suspicion by keeping strictly within her character. In other words, her free talk bears much the same relation to her character as her dress does to her person, and is therefore becoming to her even on the score of feminine modesty.—Celia appears well worthy of a place beside her whose love she shares and repays. Instinct with the soul of moral beauty and female tenderness, the friendship of these more-than-sisters "mounts to the seat of grace within the mind."

> We still have slept together;
> Rose at an instant, learn'd, play'd, eat together;
> And wheresoe'er we went, like Juno's swans,
> Still we went coupled and inseparable.

The general drift and temper, or, as some of the German critics would say, the ground-idea of this play, is aptly hinted by the title. As for the beginnings of what is here represented, these do not greatly concern us; most of them lie back out of our view, and the rest are soon lost sight of in what grows out of them; but the issues, of which there are many, are all exactly to our mind; we feel them to be just about right, and would not have them otherwise. For example, touching Frederick and Oliver, our wish is that they should repent, and repair the wrong they have done, in brief, that they should become good; which is precisely what takes place; and as soon as they do this, they naturally love those who were good before. Jaques, too, is so fitted to moralize the discrepancies of human life, so happy and at home, and withal so agreeable, in that exercise, that we would not he should follow the good Duke when in his case those discrepancies are composed. The same might easily be shown in respect of the other issues. Indeed I dare ask any genial, considerate reader, Does not every thing turn out just *as you like it?* More-over there is an indefinable something about the play that puts us in a receptive frame of mind; that opens the heart, soothes away all querulousness and fault-finding, and makes us easy and apt to be pleased. Thus the Poet here disposes us to like things as they come, and at the same time takes care that they shall come as we like. The whole play indeed is *as you like it.*

Much has been said by one critic and another about the improbabilities in this play. I confess they have never troubled me; and, as I have had no trouble here to get out of, I do not well know how to help others out. Wherefore, if any one be still annoyed by these things, I will turn him over to the elegant criticism of the poet Campbell: "Before I say more of his dramatic treasure, I must absolve myself by a confession as to some of its improbabilities. Rosalind asks her cousin Celia, 'Whither shall we go?' and Celia answers, 'To seek my uncle in the Forest of Arden.' But, arrived there, and having purchased a cottage and sheep-farm, neither the daughter nor niece of the banished Duke seem to trouble themselves much to inquire about either father or uncle. The lively and natural-hearted Rosalind discovers no impatience to embrace her sire, until she has finished her masked courtship with Orlando. But Rosalind was in love, as I have been with the comedy these forty years; and love is blind; for until a late period my eyes were never couched so as to see this objection. The truth however is, that love is *wilfully* blind; and now that my eyes are opened, I shut them against the fault. Away with your best-proved improbabilities, when the heart has been touched and the fancy fascinated."

—H. N. HUDSON, *Shakespeare: His Life, Art, and Characters*
(Boston: Ginn & Co., 1872 [4th ed. 1882], Vol. I, pp. 344–47

GEORGE BERNARD SHAW

The popularity of Rosalind is due to three main causes. First, she only speaks blank verse for a few minutes. Second, she only wears a skirt for a few minutes (and the dismal effect of the change at the end to the wedding dress ought to convert the stupidest champion of petticoats to rational dress). Third, she makes love to the man instead of waiting for the man to make love to her—a piece of natural history which has kept Shakespeare's heroines alive, whilst generations of properly governessed young ladies, taught to say "No" three times at least, have miserably perished.

—GEORGE BERNARD SHAW, "Toujours Shakespeare," *Saturday Review* (London),
December 5, 1896, p. 586

GEORG BRANDES

The two cousins, Rosalind and Celia, seem at first glance like variations of the two cousins, Beatrice and Hero, in the play Shakespeare has just finished. Rosalind and Beatrice in particular are akin in their victorious wit. Yet the difference between them is very great; Shakespeare never repeats himself. The wit of Beatrice is aggressive and challenging; we see, as it were, the gleam of a rapier in it. Rosalind's wit is gaiety without a sting; the gleam in it is of "that sweet radiance" which Oehlenschläger attributed to Freia; her sportive nature masks the depth of her love. Beatrice can be brought to love because she is a woman, and stands in no respect apart from her sex; but she is not of an amatory nature. Rosalind is seized with a passion for Orlando the instant she sets eyes on him. From the moment of Beatrice's first appearance she is defiant and combative, in the highest of spirits. We are introduced to Rosalind as a poor bird with a drooping wing; her father is banished, she is bereft of her birthright, and is living on sufferance as companion to the usurper's daughter, being, indeed, half a prisoner in the palace, where till lately she reigned as princess. It is not until she has donned the doublet and hose, appears in the likeness of a page, and wanders at her own sweet will in the open air and the greenwood, that she recovers her radiant humour, and roguish merriment flows from her lips like the trilling of a bird.

Nor is the man she loves, like Benedick, an overweening gallant with a sharp tongue and an unabashed bearing. This youth, though brave as a hero and strong as an athlete, is a child in inexperience, and so bashful in the presence of the woman who instantly captivates him, that it is she who is the first to betray her sympathy for him, and has even to take the chain from her own neck and hang it around his before he can so much as muster up courage to hope for her love. So, too, we find him passing his time in hanging poems to her upon the trees, and carving the name of Rosalind in their bark. She amuses herself, in her page's attire, by making herself his confidant, and pretending, as it were in jest, to be his Rosalind. She cannot bring herself to confess her passion, although she can think and talk (to Celia) of no one but him, and although his delay of a few minutes in keeping tryst with her sets her beside herself with impatience. She is as sensitive as she is intelligent, in this differing from Portia, to whom, in other respects, she bears some resemblance, though she lacks her persuasive eloquence, and is, on the whole, more tender, more virginal. She faints when Oliver, to excuse Orlando's delay, brings her a handkerchief stained with his blood; yet has sufficient self-mastery to say with a smile the moment she recovers, "I pray you tell your brother how well I counterfeited." She is quite at her ease in her male attire, like Viola and Imogen after her. The fact that female parts were played by youths had, of course, something to do with the frequency of these disguises.

Here is a specimen of her wit (iii. 2). Orlando has evaded the page's question what o'clock it is, alleging that there are no clocks in the forest.

ROSALIND: Then, there is no true lover in the forest; else sighing every minute, and groaning every hour, would detect the lazy foot of Time as well as a clock.

ORLANDO: And why not the swift foot of Time? had not that been as proper?

ROS.: By no means, sir. Time travels in divers paces with divers persons. I'll tell you, who Time ambles withal, who Time trots withal, who Time gallops withal, and who he stands still withal.

ORL.: I pr'ythee, who doth he trot withal?

ROS.: Marry, he trots hard with a young maid, between the contract of her marriage, and the day it is solemnised: if the interim be but a se'nnight, Time's pace is so hard that it seems the length of seven years.

ORL.: Who ambles Time withal?

ROS.: With a priest that lacks Latin, and a rich man that hath not the gout; for the one sleeps easily, because he cannot study; and the other lives merrily, because he feels no pain . . .

ORL.: Who doth he gallop withal?

ROS.: With a thief to the gallows; for though he go as softly as foot can fall, he thinks himself too soon there.

ORL.: Who stays it still withal?

ROS.: With lawyers in the vacation; for they sleep between term and term, and then they perceive not how Time moves.

She is unrivalled in vivacity and inventiveness. In every answer she discovers gunpowder anew, and she knows how to use it to boot. She explains that she had an old uncle who warned her against love and women, and, from the vantage-ground of her doublet and hose, she declares—

I thank God, I am not a woman, to be touched with so many giddy offences, as he hath generally taxed their whole sex withal.

ORL.: Can you remember any of the principal evils that he laid to the charge of women?

ROS.: There were none principal: they were all like one another, as half-pence are; every one fault seeming monstrous, till his fellow fault came to match it.

ORL.: I pr'ythee, recount some of them.

ROS.: No; I will not cast away my physic but on those that are sick. There is a man haunts the forest, that abuses our young plants with carving Rosalind on their barks; hangs odes upon hawthorns, and elegies on brambles; all, forsooth, deifying the name of Rosalind: if I could meet that fancy-monger, I would give him some good counsel, for he seems to have the quotidian of love upon him.

Orlando admits that he is the culprit, and they are to meet daily that she may exorcise his passion. She bids him woo her in jest, as though she were indeed Rosalind, and answers (iv. 1):—

ROS.: Well, in her person, I say—I will not have you.

ORL.: Then, in mine own person, I die.

ROS.: No, 'faith, die by attorney. The poor world is almost six thousand years old, and in all this time there was not any man died in his own person, *videlicet*, in a love-cause. Troilus had his brains dashed out with a Grecian club; yet he did what he could to die before, and he is one of the patterns of love. Leander, he would have lived many a fair year, though Hero had turned nun, if it had not been for a hot midsummer night; for, good youth, he went but forth to wash him in the Hellespont, and, being taken with the cramp, was drowned, and the foolish chroniclers of that age found it was—Hero of Sestos. But these are all lies: men have died from time to time, and worms have eaten them, but not for love.

What Rosalind says of women in general applies to herself in particular: you will never find her without an answer until you find her without a tongue. And there is always a bright and merry fantasy in her answers. She is literally radiant with youth, imagination, and the joy of loving so passionately and being so passionately beloved. And it is marvellous how thoroughly feminine is her wit. Too many of the witty women in books written by men have a man's intelligence. Rosalind's wit is tempered by feeling.

She has no monopoly of wit in this Arcadia of Arden. Every one in the play is witty, even the so-called simpletons. It is a festival of wit. At some points Shakespeare seems to have followed no stricter principle than the simple one of making each interlocutor outbid the other in wit (see, for example, the conversation between Touchstone and the country wench whom he befools). The result is that the piece is bathed in a sunshiny humour. And amid all the gay and airy wit-skirmishes, amid the cooing love-duets of all the happy youths and maidens, the poet intersperses the melancholy solos of his Jaques:—

I have neither the scholar's melancholy, which is emulation; nor the musician's, which is fantastical; nor the courtier's, which is proud; nor the soldier's, which is ambitious; nor the lawyer's, which is politic; nor the lady's, which is nice; nor the lover's, which is all these; but it is a melancholy of mine own, compounded of many simples, extracted from many objects . . .

This is the melancholy which haunts the thinker and the great creative artist; but in Shakespeare it as yet modulated with ease into the most engaging and delightful merriment.

—GEORG BRANDES, *William Shakespeare: A Critical Study*, tr. William Archer
(London: William Heinemann, 1898), Vol. I, pp. 266–69

G. K. CHESTERTON

In numberless modern novels and magazine stories, the heroine is apparently complimented by being described as "boyish". Doubtless there will soon be another fashion in fiction, in which the hero will always be described as girlish. Fettered as we are with an antiquated Victorian prejudice of the equality of the sexes, we cannot quite understand why one should be a compliment any more than the other. But, anyhow, the present fashion offers a much deeper difficulty. For the girl is being complimented on her boyishness by people who obviously know nothing at all about boys. Nothing could possibly be more unlike a boy than the candid, confident, unconventional and somewhat shallow sylph who swaggers up to the unfortunate hero of the novel à la mode. So far from being unconventional and shallow, the boy is commonly conventional because he is secretive. He is much more sullen outside and much more morbid inside. Who then is this new Pantomime Boy, and where did she come from? In truth she comes out of a very old pantomime.

About three hundred years ago William Shakespeare, not knowing what to do with his characters, turned them out to play in the woods, let a girl masquerade as a boy and amused himself with speculating on the effect of feminine curiosity freed for an hour from feminine dignity. He did it very well, but he could do something else. And the popular romances of today cannot do anything else. Shakespeare took care to explain in the play itself that he did *not* think that life should be one prolonged picnic. Nor would he have thought that feminine life should be one prolonged piece of private theatricals. But Rosalind, who was then unconventional for an hour, is now the convention of an epoch. She was then on a holiday; she is now very hardworked indeed. She has to act in every play, novel or short story, and always in the same old pert pose. Perhaps she is even afraid to be herself: certainly Celia is now afraid to be herself.

We should think it rather a bore if all tragic youths wore black cloaks and carried skulls in imitation of Hamlet, or all old men waved wands and clasped enormous books in imitation of Prospero. But we are almost as much tied to one type of girl in popular fiction today. And it is getting very tiresome. A huge human success is banking up for anybody bold enough to describe a quiet girl, a girl handicapped by good manners and a habit of minding her own business. Even a sulky girl would be a relief.

The moral is one we often draw; that the family is the real field for personality. All the best Shakespearian dramas are domestic dramas; even when mainly concerned with domestic murders. So far from freedom following on the decay of the family, what follows is uniformity. The Rosalinds become a sort of regiment; if it is a regiment of vivandières. They wear uniform of shingled hair and short skirts; and they seem to stand in a row like chorus girls. Not till we have got back within the four walls of the home shall we have any great tragedy or great comedy. The attempts to describe life in a Utopia of the future are alone enough to prove that there is nothing dramatic about an everlasting picnic.

Men and women must stand in some serious and lasting relation to each other for great passions and great problems to arise; and all this anarchy is as bad for art as it is for morals. Rosalind did not go into the wood to look for her freedom; she went into the wood to look for her father. And all the freedom; and even all the fun of the adventure really arises from that fact. For even an adventure must have an aim. Anyhow, the modern aimlessness has produced a condition in which we are so bored with Rosalind that we almost long for Lady Macbeth.

—G. K. CHESTERTON, "The Repetition of Rosalind" [1932], *Chesterton on Shakespeare,* ed. Dorothy Collins (Henley-on-Thames: Darwen Finlayson, 1971), pp. 100–101

E. E. STOLL

Rosalind is the heartiest, the most abundant and exuberant ⟨of Shakespeare's maidens⟩. In her, for once, Aphrodite, goddess of love and laughter, flew up into the North, and by her if not by others the 'laureate of love' wins his laurels. Beatrice when most moved contracts to seriousness; Rosalind unfolds and expands. For her wit has no trace of a sting in it—like her frown, which Orlando fears would kill him,—'By this hand,' she, in her disguise, reassures him, 'it will not kill a fly.' Wit and humour are both the mask and the indirect utterance of her passion, the effervescence of her happiness. Indeed, love and merriment are in her fairly inseparable, even when happiness is still in doubt. 'But is all this for your father?' Celia asks her cousin when after the first sight of Orlando she is in the dumps.

No, some of it is for my child's father,

which in Elizabeth Bergner's screen version has been sentimentally blunted and flattened into 'my father's child.' And this glorious, romantic reunion of love and laughter Shakespeare has facilitated by the conventions of disguise and impersonation. As Rosalind and Orlando pretend that in her man's clothing she is Rosalind, she plays only a part that she feels, and eagerly notes as he woos her how much—and says mockingly, how little—he feels the part he plays. Fact and fiction here merge, and her joy in the fact overflows in her merriment over the fiction.

This is a remarkable case of an improbable convention being employed to enrich the situation, to broaden the emotional range; for it is the high ambition and privilege of art not to reproduce reality but without conspicuously offending against it to enlarge its confines. Her disguise is like the feigning of Hamlet, whereby, under the cover of madness, he can, as he bides his time, say out what he thinks and feels. It is like the convention of calumny credited, whereby the spirit of jealous vengeance coils round Othello's trustful love. And there, and often elsewhere in art, the end justifies the means. As we have seen already, the spirit of wit and humour, and the taking of the initiative by a newly enamoured but sweet and innocent young woman, though rightly treated, they heighten the romantic effect, decidedly imperil it; but here both are given full warrant by a device that is improbability itself. Orlando, for whom to see her was to love her, a day or two ago, would surely know her in any costume conceivable, to their days' end. But without the armour of disguise Rosalind could not profit by full knowledge on her part or by ignorance on his; and, certain of his love though she has not yet received a proposal, she would not be in a position, as she is, to coax him into making it, under the mocking eyes of Celia, in words that are enough to pull the soul out of his body:

> Come, woo me, woo me: for now I am in a holiday humour and like enough to consent. What would you say to me now, an I were your very very Rosalind?

Spoken in skirts and stomacher, at a time when, off the stage, women no more laid bare their hearts than they then did their bodies, such words would never do.

Spoken in disguise or without, by the enlightened and enfranchised female of today, they would do well enough but lack their startling charm. They would lend themselves to psychology, not drama.

—E. E. STOLL, "The Maidens of Shakespeare's Prime," *Shakespeare's Young Lovers* (New York: Oxford University Press, 1937), pp. 70–72

JAY L. HALIO

In *As You Like It* Shakespeare exploits timelessness as a convention of the pastoral ideal along with other conventions taken from pastoralism, but unlike his treatment, say, of Silvius and Phebe, his treatment of time is not so thoroughly satirical. Though neither will quite do, timelessness in Arden (on the whole) contrasts favorably to the time-consciousness of court and city life which Touchstone, for example, brings to the forest. In addition, timelessness links life in Arden with the ideal of an older, more gracious way of life that helps regenerate a corrupt present.

⟨. . .⟩ Rosalind's awareness of time, however related to the preoccupation imported from the "outside" world, is different from Touchstone's obsession with "riping and rotting." It is, partly, the awareness of a girl in love and impatient for the attentions of her lover, a healthy consciousness that recalls Juliet's except as it is undarkened by tragic fate. But her awareness has further implications. When she and Orlando first met in the forest, their dialogue, appropriately enough, is itself about time. Rosalind's question, "I pray you, what is't o'clock?", although banal, suits the occasion; for despite her boast that she will speak like a saucy lackey, she is momentarily confused by confronting Orlando and scarcely knows how to begin. What follows in her account of Time's "divers paces" (III.ii.317–351), however, is something more than a verbal smokescreen to help her collect her wits, detain her lover, and make sure he keeps coming back: it is a development of Jaques' Seven Ages speech with important thematic variations. Jaques' speech describes a man in his time playing many parts and suggests that his speed, or "pace," will vary along with his role; the series of vignettes illustrates the movement of a person *in* time. Rosalind not only adds appreciably to Jaques' gallery, but showing profounder insight, she shifts the emphasis from the movement of a *person,* to the movement of *time* as apprehended, for example, by the young maid "between the contract of her marriage and the day it is solemniz'd. If the interim be but a se'ennight, Time's pace is so hard that it seems the length of seven year." In this way, she more thoroughly accounts for *duration,* or the perception of time, which, unlike Jaques' portrait of our common destiny, is not the same for everyone.

Naturally, Rosalind is most concerned with the perception of time by the lover, and here her behavior is in marked contrast to Orlando's. Quite literally— and like any fiancée, or wife—she is Orlando's timekeeper. When he fails to keep his appointments, she suffers both pain and embarrassment (III.iv) that are relieved only by the greater follies of Silvius and Phebe that immediately follow. When he finally does turn up an hour late—as if to dramatize his belief that "'there's no clock in the forest" (III.ii.319)—Rosalind rebukes him severely:

ROSALIND: Why, how now, Orlando? Where have you been all this while? You a lover? An you serve such another trick, never come in my sight more.

ORLANDO: My fair Rosalind, I come within an hour of my promise.

ROSALIND: Break an hour's promise in love? He that will divide a minute into a thousand parts and break but a part of the thousand part of a minute in the affairs of love, it may be said of him that Cupid hath clapp'd him o' th' shoulder, but I'll warrant him heart-whole.

ORLANDO: Pardon me, dear Rosalind.

ROSALIND: Nay, an you be so tardy, come no more in my sight. I had as lief be woo'd of a snail.   (IV.i.38–52)

Rosalind's time-consciousness goes beyond the mere moment: she knows the history of love—witness her speech on Troilus and Leander (IV.i.94–108)—and she predicts its future, as she warns Orlando of love's seasons after marriage (IV.i.143–149). Her ardent impulse is thus in comic juxtaposition with her realistic insight, just as Orlando's "point-device" attire and time-unconsciousness comically contrast with his rimes and other protestations of love.

In this fashion we arrive at the theme's center, or balance. If Orlando, as we have seen, is an agent of regeneration, he appears through his forgetfulness of time to be in some danger of not realizing his function. He might like Silvius, were it not for Rosalind, linger through an eternity of unconsummated loving; certainly, like the Duke, he feels in the forest no urgency about his heritage—at least not until he comes upon his brother sleeping beneath an ancient oak tree and menaced by a starved lioness (the symbolism is obvious). Oliver's remarkable conversion after his rescue and his still more remarkable engagement to Celia pave the way for Rosalind's resolution of the action, for under the pressure of his brother's happiness, Orlando can play at games in love no longer. And despite the play's arbitrary finale—Duke Frederick's conversion and the end of exile, in all of which she has had no hand—nevertheless, it is again Rosalind who has had an important share in preparing the principals for this chance. Like her less attractive counterpart Helena in All's Well That Ends Well, she remains a primary agent for the synthesis of values that underlies regeneration in Shakespeare's comedy. At the very outset we see her, the daughter of Duke Senior at the court of Duke Frederick, as a link between two worlds, not unlike Orlando's representative linking of two generations. In love, she is realistic rather than cynical, but not without a paradoxical—and perfectly human—romantic bias. So, too, with regard to time she moves with Orlando to a proper balance of unharried awareness. For all of these functions—as for others—the timeless world of the forest, with its complement of aliens, serves as a haven; but more importantly, it serves as a school.

Neither the extremes of idealism nor those of materialism, as they are variously represented, emerge as "the good life" in As You Like It. That life is seen rather as a mean of natural human sympathy educated—since that is a major theme in the play—by the more acceptable refinements of civilization (II.vii) and the harsh realities of existence ("winter and rough weather"). The "antique world" stands for a timeless order of civilization still in touch with natural human sympathy that, under the "new" regime (while it lasted), had been forced underground. To the forest, the repository of natural life devoid of artificial time barriers, the champions of regeneration repair in order to derive new energy for the task before them. There they find refuge, gain strength, learn—and return.

—JAY L. HALIO, "'No Clock in the Forest': Time in *As You Like It*,"
Studies in English Literature 1500–1900 2, No. 2 (Spring 1962):
197, 204–7

RICHARD KNOWLES

Previous to *As You Like It* there had been many light-hearted Shakespearean references to Hercules as a great lover: Armado, for instance, takes comfort that even the mighty Hercules fell to loving, and Berowne asks, "For valor, is not Love a Hercules,/Still climbing trees in the Hesperides?" In *As You Like It* Shakespeare seems to model his hero largely on the Hercules in love whom Sir Philip Sidney had declared an ideal subject for comedy.

Rosalind easily turns the young Herculean wrestler into "a quintain, a mere lifeless block" (I.ii.263), and he soon cries, "O poor Orlando, thou art overthrown!/ Or Charles or something weaker masters thee" (I.ii.271–272). Thereafter he forgets wrestling altogether and becomes "Signior Love" (III.ii.310), shaken with the "quotidian of love" (III.ii.384), writing love-sonnets on trees, and subjecting himself to Ganymede's mockery. From time to time Rosalind herself seems to think of Orlando as a young Hercules. When Celia reports finding him under a tree "like a dropped acorn" (III.ii.248), Rosalind, knowing that the oak was sacred to Jove, answers, "It may well be called Jove's tree when it drops forth such fruit" (III.ii.250–251). What she may mean is that Jove's tree ought to produce a man like Hercules, who was in fact the "scion of the seed of Jove." In this scene she herself has been associated with Diana (III.ii.4), and behind her remark at Orlando's hunter's furnishings—"Oh, ominous! He comes to kill my heart" (III.ii.260)—may be a punning allusion to Hercules' third labor, the capture in Arcadia of Diana's sacred stag. Later, after the battle with the lion, she may be referring to Hercules' weakness before love when she says to Orlando about Oliver and Celia, "Clubs cannot part 'em."

The other mythological names in the play have less comprehensive implications, though the allusions are significantly more apt and consistent than in Lodge. The four references to Cupid are merely conventional, indicating the mischievous force of love. Rosalind is associated with Helen and Atalanta (III.ii.153–156), Diana (III.ii.2–4; IV.i.154), Juno (I.iii.77; V.iv.147), and Ganymede (I.iii.126–127 et passim); all of these personages were notable for their beauty and (except for Helen) chastity. There is no such consistency in Lodge, where Rosalind is compared in addition with Apollo, Aurora, Daphne, the Graces, Phaeton, the Phoenix, and Venus. W. Schrickx has noticed a continuous association of Celia with Jupiter; since all but one of Rosalind's uses of the names Jupiter and Jove may be spoken directly to Celia, they are probably at least a playful pretense that Celia must be the father of the gods if Rosalind is Ganymede, Jove's cupbearer.

—RICHARD KNOWLES, "Myth and Type in *As You Like It,*" *ELH* 33, No. 1 (March 1966): 8–9

JAN KOTT

Rosalind assumed the name of Ganymede when she escaped to the Forest of Arden. Shakespeare adopted this from Lodge's story which served him as material for the plot of *As You Like It.* The choice and assumption of this name was not a matter of chance.

> I'll have no worse a name than Jove's own page,
> And therefore look you call me Ganymede.   (*As You Like It,* I, 3)

Rosalind, disguised as a boy, meets Orlando in the Forest of Arden. Orlando is in love with her and she is in love with him. But Orlando does not recognize Rosalind in the shape of Ganymede. Rosalind woos him with intensity, but she does it as a boy, or rather as a boy who in this relationship wants to be a girl for his lover. Rosalind plays Ganymede who in turn plays Rosalind:

> ORLANDO: I would not be cured, youth.
> ROSALIND: I would cure you, if you would but call me Rosalind and come every day to my cote and woo me.
> . . . .
> ORLANDO: With all my heart, good youth.
> ROSALIND: Nay, you must call me Rosalind.   (III, 2)

This is just the beginning. These scenes belong to the finest and most re-fined among Shakespeare's love dialogues and (but for the fact that the term "mannerism" has a certain traditional pejorative flavour) they should be recognized as a masterpiece of mannerism. On the surface of the dialogue, on the higher level of a disguise, identical with that of *Twelfth Night,* two youths, Ganymede and Orlando, play a love game. On the intermediate level we have Rosalind and Orlando in love with each other. But the real Rosalind happens to be a disguised boy.

The borderlines between illusion and reality, between an object and its reflection, are gradually lost. Once more one has to recall the theatrical aesthetics of Genet. The theatre represents in itself all human relationships, but not because it is their more or less successful imitation. The theatre is the image of all human relationships because it is based on falseness—original falseness, rather like original sin. The actor plays a character he is not. He is who he is not. He is not who he is. To be oneself means only to play one's own reflection in the eyes of strangers.

There are no whites and blacks existing separately. Negroes are black only for white men, just as white men are white only for Negroes. The "real" Negroes are white men who play blacks; just as "real" whites are blacks who play whites. But Negroes and white men exist together, and so they infect each other with their images, just as mirrors placed at certain angles repeat the reflection of each object an infinite number of times. The "real" girl is a disguised boy.

In the love scenes of Arden Forest, just as in those of Illyria, the theatrical form and the theme completely correspond with and penetrate each other, on condition, that is, that female parts are played, as they were on the Elizabethan stage, by boys. An actor disguised as a girl plays a girl disguised as boy. Everything is real and unreal, false and genuine at the same time. And we cannot tell on which side of the looking glass we have found ourselves. As if everything were mere reflection.

> GANYMEDE: And I am your Rosalind.
> CELIA: It pleases him to call you so; but he hath a Rosalind of a better leer than you.
> GANYMEDE: Come, woo me, woo me! for now I am in a holiday humour and like enough to consent. What would you say to me now, an I were your very very Rosalind? (IV, I)

Rosalind plays Ganymede who plays Rosalind. She plays herself being married to Orlando. At that wedding ceremony Celia will play the priest. The amazing poetics of these scenes has not yet been demonstrated. As if our contemporary theatre had no proper instrument! And yet these scenes contain Genet's theatre to the same degree that Beckett's theatre is contained in *King Lear,* except that they are sur-Genet, just as the quartet of madmen, real and feigned, in the third act of *Lear,* is sur-Beckett.

The love scenes in the Forest of Arden have the logic of dreams. Planes, persons, tenses—past, present, future—are intermingled; so is parody with poetry.

> GANYMEDE: . . . Come, sister, you shall be the priest and marry us. Give me your hand, Orlando. What do you say, sister?
> ORLANDO: Pray thee marry us.
> CELIA: I cannot say the words.
> GANYMEDE: You must begin, 'Will you, Orlando,'—
> CELIA: Go to. Will you, Orlando, have to wife this Rosalind?
> ORLANDO: I will.
> GANYMEDE: Ay, but when?
> ORLANDO: Why now, as fast as she can marry us.
> GANYMEDE: Then you must say, 'I take thee, Rosalind, for wife.'

ORLANDO: I take thee, Rosalind, for wife.
GANYMEDE: I might ask you for your commission; but I do take thee, Orlando,
    for my husband. There's a girl goes before the priest, . . .   (IV, I)

—JAN KOTT, "Shakespeare's Bitter Arcadia," *Shakespeare Our Contemporary*,
            tr. Boleslaw Taborski (Garden City, NY: Doubleday & Co., 1964
                                    [rev. ed. 1966]), pp. 269–72

HUGH M. RICHMOND

Rosalind is Shakespeare's most delightful heroine, and her sexual experience anticipates the vagaries of our own age closely. Shakespeare's other female characters
may be more passionate or heroic, more deeply moving to the audience, but
Rosalind experiments most successfully with the range of amatory relationships
open to both sexes. Her capacity for bisexuality seems to impress Shakespeare
greatly, for he never shows her less than creatively alert and responsive to all the
nuances of amatory feeling and action that surround her. By the end of *As You Like
It,* her sexual insights are so potent that she anticipates Prospero's magical dominion
over his environment: "Believe then . . . that I can do strange things . . . and yet not
damnable . . . though I say I am a magician" (V. ii. 63ff.). However, she is never
tyrannical in her authority over others' emotions. By comparison even Portia has a
strain of the termagant (one might even say of the racist) in her contemptuous
attitude to her foreign suitors, not to mention her cat-and-mouse treatment of
Shylock and Bassanio. When Rosalind finally resolves all the emotional tangles which
have grown up around her because of her fascination for both sexes, it is without
false rhetoric or drastic action. Simply because she is able when she wishes to
present herself as what she most conveniently should be, all the problems evapo-
rate into mere absurdity. As a catharsis of incompetence in her victims this is one
of the least painful in the comedies. Rosalind is thus all a woman can ever hope to
be. Emotionally committed to femininity yet sexually experienced in both male and
female attitudes, she remains witty and skeptical enough never to be trapped in an
inexpedient role. She thus deserves our closest attention as the most successful
model for women in Shakespeare.

She is the more impressive in that her proficiency is less artificial than that
shown in the manipulations of any of the earlier comedies. In Petruchio we encountered a fascinating but enigmatic figure whose therapeutic operations on Katharina's responses obviously depend directly on Shakespeare's own sophisticated
awareness. Unfortunately there is no more attempt to explain how Petruchio might
have acquired this invaluable finesse than to justify the extraordinary intellectual
superiority of Biron over his more academic companions in *Love's Labour's Lost.*
By contrast, it is true that the peculiar marital settlement imposed on Portia by her
father's will offers a strengthening challenge to her personality, which may help to
explain her dominion over her companions in *The Merchant of Venice.* But the
evolution of Portia's personal awareness is far less evident and instructive than

Shakespeare's delicate exposition of Rosalind's maturation. Far from centering on clever permutations of the pastoral mode, *As You Like It* is concerned to explore the crystallization of personality by building up a scintillating constellation of human types centered on Rosalind's own kaleidoscopic identity. Here for the first time we see a womanly figure plausibly capable of attaining St. Paul's heroic ideal of "being all things to all people."

At the start of the play Rosalind displays a gifted character in equipoise. Despite her dependent position since the exile of the duke, her father, she has learned how to accept her misfortunes "as one, in suffering all, that suffers nothing" (*Hamlet*, III. ii. 71). Indeed, the superiority this gives her to her friend Celia, daughter of the usurper, soon so infuriates the envious father that he banishes Rosalind for her very merits:

> She is too subtle for thee; and her smoothness,
> Her very silence and her patience
> Speak to the people, and they pity her.   (I. iii. 79–81)

She herself was previously so aware of the perfected stasis of her way of life that she coolly considered the idea of deliberately losing emotional balance for the fun of it. Seeking to "devise sports" to distract her mind, her first inquiry is: "What think you of falling in love?" (I. ii. 27). Love for her is thus to be the same kind of testing game that wrestling physically is for her more naive lover, Orlando.

We therefore find her even keener than Juliet to respond to the cleverly varied claims on her sympathy with which Shakespeare endows the conventionally romantic figure of Orlando. Her surrender to love is more consciously explicit and candid than any other heroine's:

> He calls us back: my pride fell with my fortunes;
> I'll ask him what he would. Did you call, sir?
> Sir, you have wrestled well and overthrown
> More than your enemies.   (I. ii. 264–267)

For the less experienced and humorous young women in most of Shakespeare's plays, such a surrender leads directly to disaster. With Juliet, Hero, Cressida, or Desdemona, the frank avowal of love for a genuinely respectable man brings about their ruin. Nor is the exile of Rosalind immediately thereafter an exceptional release from pressure. Most of Shakespeare's romantic heroes escape their beloved's presence with the assistance of authority (though all find themselves inconveniently restored to their ladies' company earlier than they might have wished, at least subconsciously). Rosalind really escapes disaster more creatively, and the way she does so takes us back to the theme of Sonnet 94, the capacity to keep one's deepest feelings to oneself. Rosalind's flight in male disguise is her salvation, even though she still risks the paradoxical misfortunes of Helena and Hermia by sharing her lover's refuge in the forest. Fortunately he is too intoxicated with passion to identify her accurately. Her own drastic reversal of sexual roles serves by contrast to crystallize fully her awareness of the arbitrariness of the human lot, which the play commemorates so schematically in Jaques' speech about "the ages of man." Far more than Jaques, Rosalind is forced to surrender her established identity whole-sale to the demands of threatening circumstances. Jaques merely affects to don the clown's motley, which his whimsical egotism has anyway largely earned him. But by disguising herself as a boy, Rosalind has to give up that very sexual pattern to which she has just committed herself in her avowal to Orlando.

It is this chastening of her sexual identity which makes Rosalind so interesting to moderns, for whom her ambivalent experience has become increasingly familiar in both sexes. We now are accustomed to trousered women and effeminate males. Rosalind's experiments as a male are an early prefiguration of Jung's sense of the creative possibilities of at least some awareness of bisexuality. In her exchange of sex we see how a maturation of personality like Katharina's or Isabella's might be achieved without the arbitrary intervention of a magician like Petruchio or Duke Vincentio. Nor is this tempering process merely a latent theme in the play. Intending us to recognize fully how Rosalind attains that dazzling sexual finesse which finally allows her to secure the happiness not only of herself but of all the lovers in the play, Shakespeare permutes the sexual roles of Rosalind with a virtuosity exceeding that of a Petronius, or a Boccaccio, or even a Proust.

These roles of Rosalind require her portrayer to be a youthful Proteus, for her changes of identity are paradoxical in the extreme. We must start from the inescapable fact for an Elizabethan audience (as with a recent authentic London production of the play): they are watching here a boy actor playing a girl's part, a fact Shakespeare insists on our recognizing also in Rosalind's Epilogue ("If I were a woman . . ."). Thus the play cannot invite us to see a realistic display of how women behave, with all their conventional lapses into human fallibility (such as Chekhov's *Three Sisters* shows us). Rather, it presents a girls' role boldly illuminated, height-ened, even transcended, by exploitation of the unconventional vigor and wit that a boy must almost inevitably bring to it. Shakespeare's comic heroines (and Rosalind *par excellence*) thus map out the way for truly emancipated modern women to behave, precisely because these roles were *not* originally to be acted by women but by unusually vivacious males. The parts necessarily lack the easy sentimentality and the merely physical eroticism which all too often resulted from the introduction upon the stage of actresses (and hence of traditional ideals of femininity) in facile roles of the kind sometimes evident in the plays of Dryden, or even Wycherley.

Moreover, in *As You Like It* the boy originally playing Rosalind appears physi-cally costumed as a girl only three brief times in the play. For Shakespeare's tact usually disdains to exploit any direct demonstrations of sexuality. All the physically erotic passages in his presentation of amatory themes are retrospective, and often second-hand. The physiological fascinations and sexual capacities of such women as Cleopatra or Imogen are necessarily narrated, often by other characters than their lovers (such as Enobarbus or Iachimo). Still more than theirs, Rosalind's role as a young woman is deliberately deprived of even a retrospective physiological inter-est: she is costumed as a boy and "her" maleness is even finally acknowledged openly in the play's epilogue. By means of such devices "Rosalind" is forced to adopt a pattern of purely mental or inward femininity (which is, after all, true to the discipline of the actor playing the part). Further, the actor is obliged to sustain "her" feminine nature while continually performing in situations more appropriate to male virility, such as responding to the blunt erotic advances of the nymph Phoebe or playing a sexually jaded Mercutio to Orlando's sentimental Romeo.

The surface form of this latter relationship of Rosalind with Orlando marks one of the most bizarre extremes of Shakespeare's sophistication of personality: the boy actor here plays a girl who is continually playing at being a boy, who in turn has to humour Orlando and "pretend" to be the girl (Rosalind) that he is supposed, by the conventions of the play, actually to be. The role of Rosalind thus dissolves into a chromatic spectrum of personae. As a boy actor she speaks as a male in the Epilogue; as avowedly a girl she speaks to Orlando in Act I, scene ii, only for a few moments; as a supposed male she masquerades as Ganymede thereafter, except when she "falsely" affects to be feminine for Orlando's instruction. Shakespeare produces many interesting results from this detachment of rational mind from its wildly oscillating sexual identity. He suspends Rosalind's awareness precariously between the two poles of human eroticism formed by the conventional roles of men and women. As a maturing person, Rosalind eagerly investigates both sexual potentialities; and Shakespeare shows us this process with an assurance modern writers have only recovered since Jung asserted the presence of both the female-oriented persona (or anima) and the male animus in all human personalities, whatever their local physiological attributes.

From a very early moment Rosalind begins to analyze her relationship to her various sexual roles. She even starts out briskly by claiming many of the physical capacities of a male:

> Were it not better,
> Because that I am more than common tall,
> That I did suit me all points like a man?
> A gallant curtle-axe upon my thigh,
> A boar-spear in my hand; and—in my heart
> Lie there what hidden woman's fear there will—
> We'll have a swashing and a martial outside,
> As many other mannish cowards have
> That do outface it with their semblances.   (I. iii. 116–124)

The choice is a common one for Shakespeare's women, always with tragic results if it is made without Rosalind's cool suspicion of affected virility. St. Joan and the Duchess of Gloucester (in *Henry VI*) both mistake the toughness and bellicosity of the male for absolute virtues, an error far more subtly developed in the character of Lady Macbeth. Rosalind, by contrast, does not ape the male out of envy, but through mere necessity. And in masquerading as a man she comes to recognize that what conventionally passes for virility is often little more than her own masquerade.

By virtue of that disguise she also acquires an insight into male psychology uncolored by the effects of sexual excitement. She can speak to Jaques, Silvio, and Orlando with the privileged bluntness of a fellow man when she sees their behavior uncensored by awareness of a female observer. Even more instructively, she is forced to recognize and cope with the classic aberrations of women's sexual behavior without the advantage of a softening screen of male sentimentality. She discovers not only much to reproach in the perverseness of her lover Phoebe, but also in herself. Moreover, her own wayward instincts can find no release with Orlando beyond their own censure in her objective exposition of women's responses to courtship (III. ii. 360ff.). Rosalind's detachment from her identities is a magnificent school for self-awareness, as well as a unique pedagogic opportunity in her dealings with others. As with Prospero's feigned tempest, Rosalind is able to stage-manage a storm of emotional entanglements, confident of her power to resolve them because she is sharply aware of their artificiality and arbitrariness.

Phoebe is thus brought down from her role as Silvio's cruel deity by public proof that she is so indiscriminate as to focus her own sexual interests on Ganymede, a person not only physically unequipped to meet them, but indeed scarcely actual in any way at all. Orlando is purged of a lover's sentimental affectations by relentlessly authoritative instruction in female unpredictability. Paradoxically, he comes to know the nature of his mistress fully just because for a time he fails to recognize her as other than a discriminating friend. But of course the play's most creative display of personality development lies in showing what all this complication does to Rosalind and what she makes of the result, for she alone in the play (except, perhaps, for Jaques) knowingly develops her own nature by deliberate choices.

Early on in the forest her responses oscillate, and her estimates of her own nature are quite contradictory. On the one hand she asks: "Do you not know I am a woman? When I think, I must speak" (III. ii. 263) and on the other, she asserts to Orlando: "Me believe it! you may as soon make her that you love believe it; which, I warrant, she is apter to do than to confess she does" (III. ii. 406–408). The latter passage has the ingenious dramatic irony so characteristic of Shakespeare. A mere two hundred lines of dialogue have advanced Rosalind from sentimental confusion at the approach of her lover ("Alas the day! what shall I do . . .") to wry self-judgment. The fatuous example of Pheobe's treatment of Silvio further increases her detachment from the conventional role of a mistress, while the whimsical egotism of Jaques' humor ("a melancholy of mine own . . . in which my often rumination wraps me in a most humorous sadness" IV. i. 15ff.) serves as a further awful example of the dangers of complacency.

Thus, in affecting to flirt maliciously with Orlando, Rosalind attains a dual catharsis: enjoying perhaps a vestigial and harmless delight in female waywardness, yet also dramatizing for herself a role that she sees to be frivolous if not contemptible. As one such scene develops, one notes how its tone delicately evolves. Rosalind's contempt for her lover's rhetoric becomes explicit: "These are all lies: men have died from time to time and worms have eaten them, but not for love" (IV. i. 106–108). But at the same time, she progresses from affected flirtation to a far less flippant rehearsal of the marriage ceremony (with the comment, "There's a girl goes before the priest; and certainly a woman's thought runs before her actions" IV. i. 139–141). Obviously Rosalind is no longer simply illustrating attitudes which she plans to reject, she is also experimenting with the as yet merely hypothetical marriage contract which she will soon be ready to carry out in practice. In her play she is preparing for a role which she will soon adopt in full earnest, even though surely never at the expense of her liveliness ("the wiser, the waywarder" IV. i. 162).

As in all Shakespeare's comedies, the surface humor of *As You Like It* rises from the ridiculous behavior produced by intense emotions untempered by good sense. But more than most, the play organizes these eccentricities into a complex investigation of the interaction of the conscious mind with its emotional drives and the physiological equipment with which it finds itself arbitrarily endowed. The other characters in the play are merely the resultants of exterior pressures triggering predictable responses. They are "but stewards of their excellence," ultimately guided to their own well-being largely by the will of Rosalind. She alone explores her own identity, faculties, and roles with creative intelligence.

Just as interesting is her healthy respect for danger. Knowing the limitations of herself and others, she has a practical caution that her naive lover Orlando cannot attain. When he optimistically tries a fall with Fate in the person of the wrestler Charles, his brother has insured that the stakes are life and death; Rosalind risks only an emotional pang when she risks a fall with Love. She arrives in the forest well provided and is soon comfortably established in a cottage. Orlando arrives penniless and starving: he has to demand food at sword's point from the outlaws, again no very wise proceeding. Later he also attacks a hungry lioness. For all the witty lectures he receives from Rosalind, Orlando shows no clear symptoms of maturity. Indeed, his own sexual desire is largely a conventional reflection of Rosalind's spontaneous interest in him.

If, as I believe, the distinction of drama lies in its capacity to show broadly meaningful changes in situations and characters, then *As You Like It* depends for its importance almost entirely on the role-changing of Rosalind. And in this it is a work of consummate virtuosity, for Shakespeare manages to convince us thoroughly of the plausibility of her emotional growth to womanhood, from her initial unawakened state, through casual sexual excitement, to wry self-awareness and tough recognition of her lover's conventionality, to which she reconciles herself in marriage. If I had my way the play would be required reading for every teenage girl, not as a charming pastoral fantasy about outlaws and country pleasures, but for this successful exposition of what the sexual maturing of feminine temperament ideally should be. The rest of the play may be charming or merely clever, but as a whole its richness and importance depend on its principal female role.

Rosalind's career shows that young women who emulate the roles of their male contemporaries can only learn the inadequacy of such models. We see the greater richness of a realistic feminine perspective which is undistorted by sexual envy of the male with all his greater capacities for physical folly. However, any modern mass attempt to imitate Rosalind may well still favor coeducation—not as a means of assimilating the sexes, but as an occasion to dramatize their intrinsically contrasting natures. A boyish girl may well be amusing for a time and learn from her experience, but if she matures into a mannish woman she risks becoming a monster—not because women cannot compete with men, but because the conventional Anglo-Saxon ideal of male excellence is an inferior type of personality in itself.

> —HUGH M. RICHMOND, "Rosalind, Helene and Isabella: The Descent to Sexual Realities," *Shakespeare's Sexual Comedy: A Mirror for Lovers* (Indianapolis: Bobbs-Merrill, 1971), pp. 137–46

GORDON LELL

Imagine a modern theatre production of Shakespeare's *As You Like It* in which the role of Rosalind-"Ganymede" is played by a boy. Such a boy would doubtless be chosen for his feminine features, delicate physique, and girlish voice. Since he would be spending a major part of his time on stage in a boy's costume as "Ganymede," he would need to adopt some effeminate mannerisms and gestures to remind the audience that he is "really" a girl. This is essentially the situation that existed on the Elizabethan stage, where *all* women's roles were played by boys. On the modern stage, however, such casting would very likely draw loud boisterous guffaws from liberated sophisticates relishing the overt suggestions of homosexuality, especially in III.ii. and IV.i. where Orlando first courts and then "marries" Ganymede. Using a boy in a modern production might be criticized as a distortion of Shakespeare, since modern theatregoers are unfamiliar with, if not completely unaware of, the Elizabethan convention of using boy-actors in girls' roles. It might also be argued that modern permissiveness in attitudes toward sex and even exploitation of sex have engendered responses toward homosexuality that are simply inapplicable to Shakespearean drama. A brief look at Elizabethan attitudes toward homosexuality and the use of boy-actors would suggest, however, that Shakespeare's audience may have been quite capable of responding to the boy "Rosalind" in a manner somewhat like that of the modern audience presented with a boy in the role.

Elizabethans were not completely naive concerning suggestions of homosexuality. Included in that large body of ideas associated with the new humanistic learning of the Renaissance were striking new attitudes toward sex. Not only were classical texts filled with wanton and erotic tales involving heterosexual love, but there were also literary and historical traditions involving homosexual relationships, in particular the tradition of paederasty or Greek love, the love of an older man for a youth. This tradition is found in the writings of Plato, the Greek and Roman historians, and various classical poets and satirists. The Greek-love tradition was first introduced in Elizabethan literature in sixteenth century English translations from the classics. One of the most important works in this respect was Ovid's *Metamorphoses,* which contains the story of Orpheus' introduction of Greek love in Thrace and the tradition of a paederastic relationship between Jupiter and his cupbearer Ganymede. The tradition involving Ganymede as partner in a homosexual union is particularly interesting since "Ganymede" is the name Rosalind assumes in *As You Like It* when she disguises herself as a boy. Arthur Golding's translation of Ovid appeared in 1565; his version of the story of Orpheus follows:

> And *Orphye* (were it that his ill successe hee still did rew,
> Or that he vowed so too doo) did utterly eschew
> The womankynd, Yit many a one desyrous were too match
> With him, but he them with repulse did all alike dispatch.
> He also taught the *Thracian* folke a stewes of Males to make
> And of the flowring pryme of boayes the pleasure for to take.   (X.87–92)

Stories of the loves of Phoebus for Cyparisse and Hyacinth follow (X.113–147, 168–233). In this section concerning "prettie boyes / That were the derlings of the Gods" (X.157–158), Golding provides a brief account of the abduction of Ganymede:

> The king of Goddes did burne erewhyle in love of *Ganymed*
> The *Phrygian,* and the thing was found which *Jupiter* that sted
> Had rather be than that he was. Yit could he not beteeme
> The shape of any other Bird than Aegle for too seeme.
> And so he soring in the ayre with borrowed wings trust up
> The *Trojane* boay who still in heaven even yit dooth beare his cup,
> And brings him nectar though against Dame *Junos* will it be.   (X.161–167)

Further on, Golding mentions "Fayre *Ganymed* who Jupiter did ravish as his joy" (XI.871). Other important early translations related to this tradition were *The Golden Ass* of Apuleius, translated by William Adlington (1566), which contains an extended account of a band of effeminate priests, and Thomas North's translation of Plutarch's *Lives,* which contains several episodes from the Greek-love tradition, including the story of the Sacred Band of Thebes (which consisted entirely of pairs of Greek lovers) and an account of the stormy affair between Plato and Dionysius. ⟨. . .⟩

The most complex of all such situations in Shakespeare occurs in *As You Like It,* where Rosalind, disguised as "Ganymede" is wooed by Orlando. On the Elizabethan stage this situation would involve a handsome young actor (Orlando) wooing, and actually wedding, in a mock ceremony, an effeminate boy (the boy-actor playing Rosalind disguised as a boy). When Rosalind decides to disguise herself as a boy, she says, "I'll have no worse a name than Jove's own page; / And therefore look you call me Ganymede" (I.iii.122–123). The name "Ganymede" must have caused many playgoers to recall the wanton relationship of Jove and Ganymede celebrated both in contemporary poetry and on the stage in Marlowe and Nashe's *Dido.* The adoption of the name of Ganymede occurs in Shakespeare's source, Thomas Lodge's *Rosalynde,* but Rosalind's reference to the Jove-Ganymede story does not occur in Lodge's tale. It must be remembered too that since Lodge's *Rosalynde* is a prose tale rather than a drama, the possible Greek-love reference to the Jove-Ganymede tradition is based solely on the disguise of a real girl and has none of the additional suggestions that the boy-actor of drama would provide. Lodge does have one curious passage concerning the potential that boys might have for surpassing feminine beauty. Rosalynde (as Ganymede) says, "Who knowes not, but that all women have desire to tie soverein to their peticoats, and ascribe beautie to themselves, where if boyes might put on their garments, perhaps they would prove as comely; if not as comely, it may be more courteous." Quite possibly, this suggestion that boys exploit their beauty, along with the very choice of the name Ganymede for the disguised girl, may have suggested to Shakespeare the possibility of exploiting the inherent Greek-love aspects of Lodge's tale.

There are still other subtle references in *As You Like It* that may have Greek-love implications. Rosalind as Ganymede tells how she cured a young man of love:

> He was to imagine me his love, his mistress; and
> I set him every day to woo me: at which time would
> I, being but a moonish youth, grieve, be effeminate,
> changeable, longing and liking; proud, fantastical,
> apish, shallow, inconstant, full of tears, full
> of smiles; for every passion something and for
> no passion truly any thing, as boys and women are
> for the most part cattle of this colour: would
> now like him, now loathe him; then entertain him,
> then forswear him; now weep for him, then spit at
> him; that I drave my suitor from a mad humour of
> love to a living humour of madness.   (III.ii.394–406)

Here a boy-actor tells how he acted effeminate in a make-believe situation. The passage, "as boys and women are for the most part cattle of this colour," literally suggests that boys and women are both objects of courtship by men and that their actions during courtship are similar. And Celia at one point tells Rosalind she has "misused our sex" in her mock-courtship with Orlando (IV.i.188–189). At this point it is difficult to determine *which* sex is being misused: if Ganymede (as a boy) is using exaggerated feminine mannerisms and speech in the mock-courtship with Orlando, then it is actually the *male* sex that is being abused. The impression that Ganymede is really a boy is strengthened when Phebe falls in love with Ganymede (III.v.35–81), although it must be remembered that Phebe too is played by a boy. When Orlando describes Ganymede to his brother Oliver, he says, "The boy is fair, / Of female favour, and bestows himself / Like a ripe sister" (IV.iii.85–87). When Rosalind faints after hearing of Orlando's wound and seeing the bloody handkerchief, Oliver says, "Well then, take a good heart and counterfeit to be a man." She replies, "So I do: but, i'faith, I should have been a woman by right" (IV.iii.172–175). Rosalind's repeated idea "And so I am for no woman" (V.ii.102) is significant, since it is spoken by a boy dressed as a boy.

To an audience at all familiar with the Greek-love tradition, these repeated hints, possibly reinforced by meaningful looks, gestures, or mannerisms of the actors, would have slyly brought to mind the wanton pagan relationship which celebrates the love of beautiful youths. The fact that the setting of the courtship of Orlando and Ganymede is the same pastoral world as found in Barnfield's Greek-love poetry would also not have been missed. The Epilogue simply underscores all these earlier impressions. Rosalind begins by apologizing for her appearance, since "It is not the fashion to see the lady the epilogue." The line has no humor and little meaning unless it's understood as a reference to the real sex of the speaker. And even then it would be out of place in the Epilogue if the idea had not already occurred to the audience previously. The comment is one more reminder of the triple role of boy-actor/Rosalind/Ganymede. The last reminder occurs in the very last sentence of the Epilogue: "If I were a woman I would kiss as many of you as had beards that pleased me, complexions that liked me and breaths that I defied not: and, I am sure, as many as have good beards or good faces or sweet breaths will, for my kind offer, when I make curtsy, bid me farewell" (Ep.17–22). "If I were a woman" is a jest so obvious that even when Rosalind is played by a girl the audience recalls the Elizabethan boy-actor convention. This qualifying clause also suggests something even more significant: that Shakespeare is not *advocating* Greek love. While quite willing to exploit the humorous potential suggested by the Greek-love element, Shakespeare has his Rosalind make it quite clear that the "kind offer" is in spirit only and cannot be fulfilled because of "her" sex. It should be remembered—in spite of Rosalind's protest—that there are many scenes in Shakespeare's plays that *do* involve kissing or embracing between the boy-actor and the older male actor. The very fact that good-natured fun could be poked at Greek love in such a manner is significant evidence in itself that the relationships between the boy-actors and the older actors had not created any public scandals. It is inconceivable that a young actor ever seriously charged with committing a homosexual "abomination" could have acted the role of Rosalind, the parting protestation notwithstanding.

—GORDON LELL, " 'Ganymede' on the Elizabethan Stage: Homosexual Implications
of the Use of Boy-Actors," *Aegis* 1, No. 1 (Fall 1973): 5–6, 12–13

LEO SALINGAR

In contrast ⟨. . .⟩ to Jaques, Rosalind maintains that Time is relative; it 'travels in divers paces with divers persons'. She cannot keep up this position when Orlando is late for an appointment, just as she cannot keep up her 'counterfeit' when she hears he has been injured. But her play-acting enables her to keep Orlando near her, to marry him in pretence, to 'cure' the deadlock between Silvius and Phoebe and to prepare the wedding-masque with pretended magic when (after the fashion of an Italian double plot) her real marriage is hurried forward by Celia's. Her 'cure' has the effect of dispelling the fantasies of courtship in jokes, like the frightening but harmless adventures of the Athenian lovers in the wood. In effect, it is an application of the lesson of the two faces of Silenus in Erasmus's sermon of Folly.

One modern commentator on *As You Like It* ⟨Albert Gilman⟩ thinks Rosalind is merely playful: 'in her scenes with Orlando, [she] is in no danger; thus her original reason for pretending to be a man does not apply. Yet she does pretend, and it is only her disguise that prevents their immediate marriage.' This, surely, is to overlook a cardinal social assumption in the play (which would have been obvious to a dramatist like Marivaux, as well as to Shakespeare's first audiences)—that Rosalind is a princess, while Orlando is no more than a gentleman. But for the misfortune of her father's exile, they might not have met in sympathy as at first; but for the second misfortune of her own exile, as well as his, they could not have met in apparent equality in the Forest. She can hardly marry him 'immediately', after two minutes of stage talk, without appearing a simpleton like Audrey. As in Lodge's story, it is 'the good housewife Fortune' who unexpectedly makes their courtship and marriage possible. But Shakespeare's Rosalind is not merely carried round on the wheel. He shows her acting—in both senses of the word—as well. Her first disguise is imposed by Fortune; but he shows her deciding on a further part after two phases of discussion in the play—the discussion which shows that living in the golden world, as an escape from Fortune, is an unrealisable dream, and the discussion of the consequences of recognising that all the world's a stage. In the background action of the play, 'feigning' corrupts a humane society; Rosalind's 'counterfeiting' restores it. Shakespeare uses the moralists' commonplace of the world as a stage, not to insist on the vanity of life, but to recapture the original, primary purpose of comedy.

—LEO SALINGAR, "The Player in the Play," *Shakespeare and the Traditions of Comedy* (Cambridge: Cambridge University Press, 1974), pp. 297–98

CAROLE McKEWIN

At the court of Duke Frederick, Rosalind and Celia are surrounded by a cankered society in which feminine friendship, like brotherly love, is threatened by envy and a rampant self-regard. The Duke advises Celia concerning Rosalind, "Thou art a fool. She robs thee of thy name, / And thou wilt show more bright and seem more virtuous / When she is gone" (I.iii.76–78). In this context, not only is a woman's identity based on the will of a father, who in this case is *not* virtuous, but also, the counter-universe of feminine friendships is curtailed. It is no wonder, then, that Rosalind and Celia's private conversation at court turns to topics which they can do nothing about—Fortune and Nature.

ROSALIND: What shall be our sport then?
CELIA: Let us sit and mock the good housewife Fortune from her wheel, that her gifts may henceforth be bestowed equally.

ROSALIND: I would we could do so, for her benefits are mightily misplaced, and the bountiful blind woman doth most mistake in her gifts to women. (I.ii.28–34)

Rosalind and Celia express in allegory what is their true condition. Nature has made them women, Fortune has disenfranchised Rosalind, and by extension, Celia and all women. Observing themselves as victims of cosmic forces, their talk, however elegant, is enervated, a flaccid exercise in diversion. This little dialogue, graceful, and yet full of gall, is utterly innocent of the vectors of action, or the issues of conformity and self-assertion. Like the helpless Queen of *Richard II*, these women talk to each other in order to distract themselves.

It is not until they move out of the court, and into the less structured world of Arden, that their energies are renewed. Although the green world is no paradise, it is, by nature, a counter-universe that reverses social codes and hierarchies, and so invites feminine liberty. What had been crucial at court for Celia and Rosalind—the subject of fathers, their literal and metaphoric inheritance—here becomes a matter of casual regard. In Arden, Rosalind merely remarks in passing that she has met her own banished father, but the encounter hardly affects her course of action, and she does not reveal her true identity: "I met the Duke yesterday and had much question with him. He asked me of what parentage I was. I told him, of as good as he; so he laughed and let me go. But what talk we of fathers when there is such a man as Orlando?" (III.iv.31–35). And so Arden fairly bellows out with their talk. In this open air, far from court, where fathers laugh and let daughters go, Ganymede and Aliena shape women's talk into a dynamic art form. They celebrate their bodies, themselves; engage in literary criticism; consider the follies of lovers and love; wonder about the unfaithfulness of men; and laugh at the inanities of women. Thoughtful, irreverent, affectionate, companionable, bawdy, woman's personality resonates and expands, pushing the boundaries of the counter-universe outward to suit herself. Sweet are the conversational uses of letting go in Arden, especially for the queen of feminine conversationalists, Celia, who demonstrates the way a good friend can weave amidst our moods, affirm and qualify them, yet remain herself. More exuberant than Antonio, and as giving; more articulate than Horatio, and as true, Celia is perhaps too good, even for the dazzling Rosalind.

The conversations of Arden show the facets of womanly friendship through verbal exchanges which are, generally, the happiest and most liberated in Shakespeare's canon. Even the shadows have their pleasures. Rosalind's concerns dominate the talk, yet through her insistent regard for Orlando, we have a chance to see the patience, compassion, and astringent humor of Celia. And while the conversations themselves have a giddy freedom that we know cannot last, both women manage to take from Arden a permanent reminder of their spree, when talk was not only a pleasure, but also a means of creating their own worlds. It is Rosalind, after all, who conducts the marriages at the end of the play. Whatever we may think of their choices in husbands, we must admit that Rosalind and Celia have had more than romantic pleasures in a setting where fathers, unwittingly or not, let daughters choose their own mates. In the patriarchal world where most of Shakespeare's women live, that is a step in the right direction.

—CAROLE MCKEWIN, "Counsels of God and Grace: Intimate Conversations between Women in Shakespeare's Plays," *The Woman's Part: Feminist Criticism of Shakespeare*, ed. Carolyn Ruth Swift Lenz, Gayle Greene, and Carol Thomas Neely (Urbana: University of Illinois Press, 1980), pp. 122–24

WOLFGANG ISER

Rosalind and Celia disguise themselves when they cross over from the political world to the pastoral. Celia becomes Aliena, and Rosalind becomes Ganymede. Just as the pastoral world is the counter-image to the political, these two characters assume roles opposite to themselves. The very name Aliena is a clear indication of Celia's self-alienation, and Rosalind alienates herself from her own sex, thus doubling herself in two mutually exclusive ways. There are two basic effects here: first, the radical split between appearance and reality, and secondly the character's own awareness of the split in her person. This in turn is a doubling of the structure of the two different worlds. Consequently, Rosalind will not only speak with two voices, but she will also use both registers of this double-voiced language simultaneously. Whenever this happens, disguise and real character function as reciprocal reflections. However, if the real self is reflected in the disguised character, the original Rosalind cannot remain unchanged, as the mask—being Rosalind's own otherness—adds something to what she has been so far.

Now disguise is a fiction, and in Elizabethan eyes it constituted an illusory concealment of the reality hidden behind it. Therefore the disguise endowed that which was hidden with a higher status of reality than that represented by the disguise. This process is a counter-image of the situation in the political world. Duke Frederick and Oliver were not in disguise, but their conduct *was* a disguise, concealing the reality which motivated their actions and with which they identified themselves. With Rosalind and Celia, the process is turned upside down in that the disguise is seen right from the start as something alienating—either through the name (Aliena) or through the change of sex—so that the character can direct herself as someone split apart from herself, thus enacting a play between the mutually exclusive selves.

When Rosalind speaks as Ganymede, Ganymede must constantly refer back to Rosalind because the disguise cannot be a true representation of herself. And so Rosalind always speaks through Ganymede as if she were someone else, and Ganymede, when he speaks, can only elucidate what Rosalind is. If Rosalind is the hidden reality behind Ganymede, Ganymede is a sort of guinea-pig through whom Rosalind can adapt to reality. Originally Rosalind and Celia assumed their disguises in order to protect themselves on the way to the forest, but the function of the disguise changes once they have entered the pastoral haven. Initially Rosalind became a man to defend her womanhood, but now in the guise of Ganymede she wishes to play the role of the reluctant lady, so that she can test Orlando's love. Thus the character again doubles herself behind the mask by playing the role of the cynic—a role in accordance with the highly elaborate Petrarchan love code.

When Rosalind discovers Orlando's verses on the trees, her reaction is split. At first she speaks ironically of the low standard of this conventional poetry, without thinking of the author. But when she learns that Orlando wrote the verses, and must therefore be in the neighborhood, her attitude changes. She is suddenly shocked by the vast difference between what she is and what she appears to be. She asks Celia: "Good my complexion! Dost thou think though I am caparisoned like a man I have a doublet and hose in my disposition? One inch of delay more is a South Sea of discovery" (III. ii. 191–194). She is afraid that as a woman playing the role of a man she will not have sufficient control over her own emotions: "Do you not know I am a woman? When I think, I must speak. Sweet, say on" (III. ii. 245–246). Here a conflict of language begins to emerge within the conflict of roles, for as a man Rosalind cannot say what she feels, even though it demands immediate expression. How can that be said which must not be said although such a mind must needs say it?

Ganymede begins the conversation with Orlando by making ironic comments on the bad verses which evidently he had placed on the trees. Orlando acknowledges that the verses are his, whereupon Ganymede feigns astonishment at the fact that Orlando has none of the classic symptoms of a lovesick poet:

> A lean cheek, which you have not; a blue eye and sunken, which you have not; an unquestionable spirit, which you have not; a beard neglected, which you have not . . . Then your hose should be ungartered, your bonnet unbanded, your sleeve unbuttoned, your shoe untied, and everything about you demonstrating a careless desolation.   [III. ii. 363–371]

Ganymede criticizes Orlando because his appearance has so little in common with the code of convention that underlies his poetry. But through Ganymede's criticism we can discover Rosalind's own desire to provoke Orlando so that she can hear more about his love. For Ganymede's critique of the Petrarchan clichés in Orlando's verses expresses Rosalind's own dissatisfaction with a love that clearly regards the Petrarchan code as an adequate means of describing itself. The reproach that Orlando does not look like a Petrarchan lover turns into an appeal to make Orlando reveal the true nature of his love, and evidently this can only be done if the conventional code is now abandoned.

The dialogue in this scene is typical of the conversations between the lovers. The silent voice of Rosalind is always speaking through the utterances of Ganymede. This entails a switch from one language function to the other, but frequently they thrust upon them by prevailing social conventions—they deliberately play what they are not or what they do not want to be. And so Orlando, being conscious of the fiction, can hint that Ganymede's acting is no true substitute for the real Rosalind. But while they are both playing their roles, they are also acting themselves. Rosalind is enacting her passion in order to test Orlando, and Orlando is enacting his and thereby leaving the Petrarchan code (as embodied by Ganymede) far behind. While Rosalind and Orlando each act their parts and at the same time play themselves, the game becomes a means of mastering that which is absent. Orlando enacts the fulfillment of his passion—and only the game makes it possible for him to express what is otherwise denied to him—and Rosalind experiences the love of Orlando, which assumes the desired form through the disintegration of the Petrarchan code which Ganymede represents.

Thus it turns out that only the game can be an adequate vehicle for double meaning, for it is understood within the play that whatsoever is enacted must be taken as if it were real. Consequently, the game mirrors the latent which is hidden behind the manifest. By mastering the absent, the game sets in motion a process of change, for it provides a form in which difference is simultaneously present and constantly bridged. Difference emerges as the constitutive matrix of play not least through the basic play movement of back and forth which is a constant effort to overcome difference, but it results only in an endlessly varied patterning of play structures. Obviously the dialogue achieves its ideality when speech loses its finality. But this is possible only in play, which alone can stage that which remains excluded from our everyday reality.

—WOLFGANG ISER, "The Dramatization of Double Meaning in Shakespeare's *As You Like It*," Theatre Journal 35, No. 3 (October 1983): 322–24

MARIANNE L. NOVY

The Petrarchan tradition of love poetry may conceive the role of the lover's partner as beloved rather than as lover in return, and in this emphasis the beloved's feelings, and the lover's need for mutuality, may be not merely shaped by role differentiation but in effect disregarded. Verbally the lover's poems may ask for a response, but they are concerned with his own subjectivity. Petrarchan poetry, Richard Young has suggested, has two basic forms—the blazon or idealizing description of the lady and the introspection of the lover, a description of his sufferings. Both kinds of poetry could be written indefinitely without portraying any interaction between the two parties. Petrarchism is a structure of feeling as well as a poetic tradition; if, as, perhaps, Shakespeare discovered in writing sonnets to his master-mistress, Petrarchan love poetry flourishes in the absence of mutuality, a Petrarchizing imagination, such as Orlando displays in his blazon-like poems about Rosalind, may make mutuality more difficult. *As You Like It* plays on this possibility. But Rosalind plays with Petrarchism, too, and eventually the mutuality that she establishes in her sportive conversations with Orlando again serves as a kind of transition to the mutuality of love; the idealization that begins as a threat to mutuality finally supports it in the celebration of the marriage bond.

Although Orlando and Rosalind clearly fall in love at first sight, the play emphasizes the presence of an obstacle in Orlando to developing his love into a relationship. After their first meeting at the wrestling match, Rosalind gives Orlando a chain. He cannot respond to her verbally; he asks in an aside:

> Can I not say, "I thank you"? My better parts
> Are all thrown down, and that which here stands up
> Is but a quintain, a mere lifeless block.   (1.2.230–32)

Rosalind fruitlessly gives him another chance to speak. After her exit and more of his self-questioning, his last cry in the scene suggests the reason for his silence: "But heavenly Rosalind!" (1.2.270). He acts as if he sees her as far above him, and the poems he writes about her show at greater length the image of love as idealization without hope of mutuality. His role is simply to be the devoted servant who spreads her praise: "Heaven would that she these gifts should have, / And I to live and die her slave" (3.2.147–48).

Silvius, similarly, is content to maintain an idealizing worship with very little mutuality from Phebe:

> So holy and so perfect my love,
> And I in such a poverty of grace,
> That I shall think it a most plenteous crop
> To glean the broken ears after the man
> That the main harvest reaps.   (3.5.98–102)

It is part of Rosalind's role in the play to mock both of the Petrarchan preoccupations that sharply differentiate and isolate the roles of lover and beloved and thus prevent mutuality. In her disguise as Ganymede she teases Orlando for "deifying the name of Rosalind" (3.2.342) and tries to persuade him that his awe of her is unrealistic. When she catalogs the characteristics of the unhappy lover, she makes them sound ridiculous, and she denies Silvius too the dignity of his adoration. But her mockery is not an isolating monologue such as Jaques might fall into; rather it draws her listeners to participate in the mutuality of conversation. In her disguise, after encouraging Orlando to play straight man in her comic routine about time, she leads him to join in the game of "imagining" that Rosalind is present and attainable, and to see that in that game his love can ask for reciprocation.

> ROSALIND: But come, now I will be your Rosalind in a more coming-on dispo-
>   sition; and ask me what you will, I will grant it.
> ORLANDO: Then love me, Rosalind.   (4.1.101–4)

Besides the playful conversations into which Rosalind draws Orlando, there are a number of other examples of mutuality early in *As You Like It*. Involving other bonds than those of romantic love, they are often presented through a verbal ritual in which both partners participate. Orlando and Adam give each other reciprocal praise as ideal master and servant as both of them go off to the Forest of Arden. When the Duke and Orlando recognize each other's "gentleness" (2.7.118) in the forest, Orlando offers a compact that ritualizes their shared ideals and past experiences, and the Duke phrases his courteous acceptance in closely echoing words. When Orlando saves the life of his sleeping brother Oliver, Oliver awakes from his former hostility as well as from his sleep, he tells us later, and reciprocates his brother's love.

With Oliver's quick pursuit of Celia, the play begins its final emphasis on images of mutual love between man and woman. Orlando describes the love of Celia and Oliver in terms that show it as an image of the happiness he wishes. Rosalind's version emphasizes the comical side of their headlong and very physical mutuality:

> your brother and my sister no sooner met but they looked; no sooner looked but they loved; no sooner loved but they sighed; no sooner sighed but they asked one another the reason; no sooner knew the reason but they sought the remedy: and in these degrees have they made a pair of stairs to marriage, which they will climb incontinent, or else be incontinent before marriage: they are in the very wrath of love, and they will together; clubs cannot part them.
> (5.2.31–39)

For all of Rosalind's mockery, the description moves Orlando to more awareness of the inadequacy of a love that is confined to idealization without response: "I can live no longer by thinking" (5.2.48). To his surprise, his companion promises to produce Rosalind, "tomorrow, human as she is" (5.2.64). The adjective is a significant contrast to the celestial words that Orlando used in his earlier praise of her.

In the concluding masque of Hymen, the play finally presents on stage an ideal image of mutual relationship between man and woman. The heavenly imagery reappears in the staged appearance of a god, but the other characters constitute their relationship by their own words—ritual words this time, not the wit of Beatrice and Benedick. The scene's focus is on the mutuality between Rosalind's self-revelation and her father's and Orlando's recognition of her:

> ROSALIND: To you I give myself, for I am yours.
> DUKE: If there be truth in sight, you are my daughter.
> ORLANDO: If there be truth in sight, you are my Rosalind.   (5.4.111–13)

Rosalind's words define her as active giver, as well as passive gift: she does not, as Hymen has implied, wait to be given to Orlando by her father. Now able to respond to her directly, Orlando calls her his, but her next words, while verbally a limitation of her choices, emphasize that the possession is reciprocal: "I'll have no husband, if you be not he" (5.4.117).

The final hymn picks up two of the major kinds of imagery through which characters have pictured their relationships with each other—imagery of food and of religion: "Wedding is great Juno's crown, / O blessed bond of board and bed!" (5.4.135–36). One character speaking of another as food usually reveals a tendency to dominate, as when Touchstone implicitly compares his claim to Audrey to the heathen philosopher's wish to eat a grape. One character speaking of another in religious terms shows some idealization, as when Orlando writes poems about heavenly Rosalind. Rosalind herself characteristically manages to combine the two types of imagery in her humorous praise of Orlando as fruit from Jove's tree and of his kisses as "full of sanctity as the touch of holy bread" (3.4.12–13); perhaps the extreme of either attitude, domination or idealization, makes mutual relationship impossible except in the precarious condition of mutual idealization, presented in *Romeo and Juliet.* The ideal that Hymen describes is one of mutuality; not one partner, but the bond itself, is blessed; neither partner is objectified, but board and bed are mediators in their relationship. Thus, in the way the play has modulated the transition out of Orlando's paralyzing image of love as one-sided idealization, it leaves us again with a kind of mutuality not limited by extreme differentiation of roles but with a fuller sharing.

While in *As You Like It* the initial internal obstacle to mutuality in love appears to be idealization of the beloved, in *Twelfth Night* a more difficult obstacle may be idealization of one's own feelings. The theme of mutuality in its many varieties informs this play even more than the other two we have discussed. To emphasize the development of mutuality in love, the play opens with its lack: several characters who seem particularly content in their apparently static versions of unrequited love. Olivia is ready to mourn seven years out of love for her dead brother. Orsino and Sir Andrew Aguecheek are ineffectually courting her, but neither one confronts her directly. Orsino's words suggest a real enjoyment of dramatizing and glorifying his posture of unrequited lover. As Orsino enjoys reveries of love, Andrew enjoys the revelry with Olivia's uncle, Sir Toby, that his role as her suitor permits him. Both Orsino and Andrew speak of themselves more than of Olivia; their indulgence in unrequited love, the play suggests, coincides with self-love. This coincidence is harshly clearer with Malvolio. As Orsino delights in the verbal prerogatives of courtship and Andrew in its social prerogatives, Malvolio delights in his fantasy of the political prerogatives of marriage. Orsino believes that Olivia must love him in the future, Malvolio believes that she loves him in the present, and Sir Andrew can be led to believe anything; all three of them lack consciousness of her subjectivity.

As Beatrice and Benedick and Orlando and the disguised Rosalind begin their relationships with the verbal mutuality of a game, Viola in her page's disguise easily engages Orsino in a confidential conversation and Olivia in a courting game. Like the plotters in *Much Ado*, she engages them further emotionally by words that lead them to imagine the feelings of others who might love them. Involved in the conversation, they must respond verbally, and that verbal response hints at their response of feeling.

Carrying Orsino's message of love to Olivia, Viola turns conventions to a more urgent and personal description of what it feels like to be denied love; the dialogue has all the energy of her controlled and concealed love for Orsino:

If I did love you in my master's flame,
With such a suff'ring, such a deadly life,
In your denial I would find no sense;
I would not understand it.   (1.5.250–53)

Encouraged by Olivia, she develops an image of herself as wooer demanding response:

O, you should not rest
Between the elements of air and earth
But you should pity me.   (1.5.260–62)

Olivia sees the personal feeling in the speech, feels a response to the imaginary demand the page has presented, and becomes another version of the unrequited lover, a more insistent one.

The love for Orsino that informs Viola's speeches about love to Olivia underlies even more strongly the subsequent dialogue in which she leads him to imagine himself loved by "some lady, as perhaps there is" (2.4.88). Like Rosalind asking Orlando to imagine that he is speaking to Rosalind, Viola is in part asking Orsino to imagine what is real; this process continues when Orsino objects that no woman's feelings could be as strong as his own and Viola presents her second image of the imaginary lover—her father's daughter who never told her love. Rosalind had to disabuse Orlando of some of his idealization of *her* so that he could confront her on a more equal level; Viola, by contrast, must work much more on Orsino's idealization of *himself* by presenting her imaginary sister—and by implication the hypothetical woman who loves him—as equally capable of devotion. In her dialogues with Orsino and Olivia, Viola begins to put them imaginatively in contact with the reality of human feeling as she knows it. But the process brings them all further confusion that she cannot herself resolve.

—MARIANNE L. NOVY, "'As You Smile Not, He's Gagged': Mutuality in
Shakespearean Comedy," *Love's Argument: Gender Relations in Shakespeare*
(Chapel Hill: University of North Carolina Press, 1984), pp. 28–34

KAREN NEWMAN

As You Like It, by its contrasts, illuminates Shakespeare's use of the rhetoric of consciousness. Here we learn about Rosalind and the other characters not through self-revelation in soliloquy, the basic strategy of the New Comic model, but through their interaction with other characters and the contrasting of one attitude with another, of Touchstone's physicality with Silvius' pastoral laments, for example. In fact, the play has only one soliloquy, which closes the first act, in which Oliver expresses his hatred of Orlando. Though Shakespeare has Rosalind use asides to juxtapose her true feelings with her assumed pose as critic of love, these remarks are always addressed to another character, usually Celia. And because Rosalind's disguise is self-consciously assumed, it does not lead to the kind of confusion and suffering experienced by the Antipholi in ⟨The Comedy of⟩ Errors, or by Bottom and the lovers in A Midsummer Night's Dream.

Despite the play's dearth of soliloquies or monologues which manifest a rhetoric of consicousness, we inevitably experience Rosalind as a complex character. Readers of As You Like It generally agree that the play is about testing and education. Rosalind's disguise is intentional; she uses it to expose the conventional postures of love which the other characters assume, to educate Orlando, Silvius and Phebe to less idealized and less self-dramatizing passions. In the process, Rosalind moves back and forth between two identities, as Rosalind and as Ganymede, and in doing so she is educated herself. Sexual disguise brings about this education, but at those moments in the play where self-address and the rhetoric of consciousness might generate in the audience a sense of the inner workings of Rosalind's mind, instead Shakespeare distances us from his characters through scenes of dialogue, through formal, highly stylized language, and through miraculous or supernatural events.

Consider first the scene in which Rosalind is exiled by Duke Frederick. Instead of leaving Rosalind alone on stage to lament her plight in soliloquy, Shakespeare advances the action through a scene of dialogue with Celia. And we should note that Rosalind does not begin as the gallant and powerful impresario of action whom we later encounter in Arden. When Celia insists on following her and suggests they seek refuge in the forest, Rosalind responds in a stereotypically feminine manner:

> Alas, what danger will it be to us,
> Maids as we are, to travel forth so far?
> Beauty provoketh thieves sooner than gold.   (I, iii, 104–6)

Celia, undaunted, suggests disguise, and Rosalind develops Celia's plan by proposing to disguise herself as a man. Celia leads in this scene, not Rosalind, and it is she who speaks the famous lines, 'Now go we in content/To liberty, and not to banishment.' In the forest, Rosalind's language changes, but rather than show us a mind in conflict, Shakespeare has her adopt the linguistic stereotype of a man. Her first words are an oath, a testament to her masculine identity; she assumes the male role of Celia's comforter and exhorts her to courage. Though Shakespeare presents us with a changing Rosalind, we have no insight into how this change comes about other than through her mechanical assumption of masculine disguise and the linguistic stereotypes of male and female.

More important to As You Like It than the inner life are social games which lead the characters not to greater understanding of themselves, but to greater capacities for social interaction and harmonious commitments in love and marriage. Where we might expect to find Rosalind reflecting upon her plight, as at her discovery that Orlando is in the forest writing verses to his beloved Rosalind, Shakespeare reveals her feelings instead through dialogue with Celia and Touchstone. Her many questions are not rhetorical, as we have found so often in characters whose identities are threatened, but literal: 'What did he when thou saw'st him? What said he? How looked he? Wherein went he?' (III, ii, 216–17). At Orlando's appearance, she determines to 'speak to him like a saucy lackey' and proceeds to mock his declared love. Rosalind's love mockery, so different from her extravagant excitement, love sickness, and desperate inquiries to Celia, suggests for us her inner turmoil. What is missing is not a sense of her inner life or personal struggles, her capacity to hold the contrasting views of love she expresses in the play in a poised and balanced equilibrium, but rather self-consciousness about that equipoise expressed through soliloquy. Rosalind's inner debates are externalized in her role as Ganymede/Rosalind, and we are correspondingly distanced from her feelings, however much we may appreciate her character. We share the pleasures of flirtation, of transvestism, of shifting roles and playful irony, all of which testify to Rosalind's fascination by giving her dimensions in excess of her function. We are called upon to hold together, in the study or in performance, the multiple aspects of her character, but we never have the sense that she herself recognizes or struggles with that multiplicity.

Instead of a confessional soliloquy, when confronted with Oliver's highly stylized, almost allegorical tale of Orlando's heroism, Rosalind swoons. In the next scene, when Orlando refuses to continue their game and cries out that he 'can live no longer by thinking' (V, ii, 50), far from fearing the loss of Orlando's company and courtship, Rosalind claims miraculous powers given her by a magician: she promises to materialize Rosalind. Orlando reacts directly: 'Speak'st thou in sober meanings?' (line 69). Her response, however, both answers and evades. She reiterates her promise in language which hints, in its formal balance and repetitions at a magician's spell, ordering Orlando to prepare for the wedding, 'for if you will be married tomorrow, you shall; and to Rosalind if you will' (lines 72–4).

Rosalind's lines have only hinted at the formal and distancing rhetoric which follow. Each character in turn repeats the words of the preceding in response to Silvius' enumeration of 'what 'tis to love'. It is almost as if the characters are under a spell or in a trance, and significantly, after another series of such repetitions, Rosalind breaks the spell, complaining that they all sound 'like the howling of Irish wolves against the moon' (lines 110–11), activity traditionally associated with strange happenings and mysterious, supernatural events.

In the final scene we find Shakespeare using once again the language of spells, vows and the like. It serves to emphasize the ritual festivities of marriage and harmony with which the play ends. The action is no longer directed and ratified by Rosalind, but by Hymen whose miraculous arrival or descent brings about the marital harmony of the play's finale. Whatever sense we might have of the characters' development or maturation is subordinated to a sense of magic and wonder. Only in As You Like It and the late Cymbeline does Shakespeare use the device of the deus ex machina literally. The Abbess of The Comedy of Errors, the Duke of Measure for Measure, Paulina in The Winter's Tale, Prospero in The Tempest, all partake of the supernatural through the roles they play in the final scenes, but only in As You Like It among the early comedies does Shakespeare have a god speak and control the action on stage.

Rosalind's claims of magical powers and the incantatory, stylized and repetitive stichomythia of the two preceding scenes among the lovers prepare for Hymen's arrival and role in the action. The god of marriage's language continues what we have already heard from the other lovers, but with the addition of rhyme:

> You and you no cross shall part.
> You and you are heart in heart.
> You to his love must accord,
> Or have a woman to your lord.
> You and you are sure together,
> As the winter to foul weather.   (V, iv, 130–5)

Having given his blessing to each pair of lovers, Hymen speaks a final quatrain to the assembled company:

> Whiles a wedlock hymn we sing,
> Feed yourselves with questioning,
> That reason wonder may diminish
> How thus we met, and these things finish.   (V, iv, 136–9)

The ensuing action, however, far from explaining away wonder, intensifies it, for before Rosalind can utter a word of explanation, the second and heretofore unintroduced brother of Orlando and Oliver arrives to tell of yet another strange miracle, the conversion of Frederick by 'an old religious man'. We may remember here that Rosalind/Ganymede has told Orlando that she owes her education to 'an old religious uncle'. At III, ii when Rosalind speaks these lines the audience believes them to be false. But at the end of the play, when we hear of the 'old religious man' who converts Duke Frederick, we are reminded of Rosalind's uncle who made a convert of her as well; magic and wonder increase rather than diminish. Even Jaques, whose satiric role has served to offer, along with Ganymede's, a corrective view of life and love, speaks this language of patterned, repetitive rhyming incantation:

> You to your former honour I bequeath,
> Your patience and your virtue well deserve it.
> You to a love that your true faith doth merit:
> You to your land and love and great allies:
> You to a long and well-deserved bed: .
> And you to wrangling, for thy loving voyage
> Is but for two months victuall'd. So to your pleasures.
> I am for other than for dancing measures.   (V, iv, 185–92)

Rosalind's prose epilogue breaks the magical spell which envelops the final action. Her words are designed to call attention to the play as play, to her role as actor, and thereby to dispel the sense of wonder which the finale conveys. This emphasis on magic links *As You Like It* in some ways more closely to *A Midsummer Night's Dream* than to *Twelfth Night* and *Much Ado* with which it is often grouped.

Certainly *Twelfth Night* is a comedy in which wonder plays an important part, but in *Twelfth Night* wonder is associated with fortune, time and human action rather than with magic and the supernatural.

—KAREN NEWMAN, "Magic versus Time: *As You Like It* and *Twelfth Night,*"
Shakespeare's Rhetoric of Comic Character: Dramatic Convention in
Classical and Renaissance Comedy (New York: Methuen, 1985), pp. 94–99

PETER LINDENBAUM

What precisely Jaques is opposed to in the play can be seen from examining Rosalind's (and ultimately Orlando's) very different response to time. Once Rosalind establishes that Orlando is listening to her, the first question she asks of him in the forest is "I pray you, what is't o'clock?" (III.ii.294). The question proves significant, since it is asked by someone very aware of time's passing and of a figure for whom time is not yet consistently important. Orlando earlier expressed considerable dismay over the enforced idleness resulting from his brother's neglect of him (I.i.32–34), and he showed a distaste for wasting time when he first encountered Duke Senior in the forest and observed that the Duke and his followers "Lose and neglect the creeping hours of time" (II.vii.112). But here in III.ii, Orlando answers Rosalind's query with the assertion that "there's no clock in the forest" (295–96). Rosalind's response in turn is that if Orlando were the kind of lover his poems claim he is, he himself would be the forest's clock: "Then there is no true lover in the forest, else sighing every minute and groaning every hour would detect the lazy foot of Time, as well as a clock" (297–99). Were Orlando to become the kind of lover she suggests, he would of course become even more like the ridiculous Silvius than he already is. But Rosalind's humor covers serious concern: despite his claim to be "love-shaked," Orlando does not yet seem to have a committed lover's consciousness of time, or of anything else. He misses his next appointment with his mock-Rosalind, rather casually excusing himself by saying that he has come within an hour of his promise (IV.i.40–41).

Rosalind meanwhile has been very conscious of the time passing when Orlando is away, and while her high spirits consistently temper her concern with a note of mock sentimentality, she reveals a true lover's distress and dedication when she asks Celia, "But why did he swear he would come this morning and comes not?" (III.iv.17–18) or announces, "I'll tell thee Aliena, I cannot be out of the sight of Orlando" (IV.i.205–6). It is largely because she is aware of the true identity of the man she has been speaking to that time trots hard for Rosalind when Orlando is absent. And he is, no doubt, to be excused for his lack of punctuality and for his ability to part for two hours calmly because he does not realize that Ganymede is his real Rosalind. But one of the ways that Shakespeare has of showing that Orlando is worthy of the love of the generally more witty Rosalind is to bring him to her consciousness of time. On the second occasion that he misses an appointment with Ganymede, Orlando has a valid excuse, his fight with the lion which threatened his brother. And despite his wound, he remembers this time to send a messenger to his mock-Rosalind to explain his absence. It is when Orlando finally expresses impatience with the masquerade with Ganymede, when a mock-Rosalind will no longer serve his turn for the real one, that she acknowledges that Orlando has passed his test and is ready to receive her. Rosalind has used a game as a way of showing Orlando that his earlier claim to be a lover was also only a type of game or pose, merely borrowed Petrarchanism. When Orlando now announces that he can "live no longer by thinking" (V.ii.50), Rosalind responds with, "I will weary you then no longer with idle talking," a line which in itself ought to promise fair for Orlando, given his own earlier stated concern over idleness. Mere game playing is now a thing of the past.

Rosalind has been asserting consistently that time is, or should be, important to a lover. But even in the two wooing scenes in the forest when she has been discussing this importance, all movement has in effect stopped while their love is allowed to blossom. It is in these scenes that Shakespeare allows his characters (and us) to relax, to enjoy their pastoral existence more than Sidney's heroes ever could. Orlando may have his obligations to the Duke and he has his fight with the lion, but these are offstage; when onstage the two lovers return over and again to the question whether Orlando is truly in love. Although Rosalind is actually using these encounters to educate Orlando and is not herself idle in them, the two scenes convey a general impression of timelessness, an impression we may in fact not be fully or immediately conscious of as the scenes themselves progress; what points it out forcefully is the abruptness with which the concern for events offstage is reasserted toward the end of IV.i. With no preparation whatsoever, following a speech in which Rosalind discusses the use women make of their wit, Orlando announces: "For these two hours Rosalind, I will leave thee" (168). Orlando's outburst of impatience in V.ii dispels that impression of time-lessness and has the effect of bringing their pastoral sojourn to an end. By his impatience Orlando is expressing a desire that time move on so that he might devote himself to action, action in this context being defined as genuine loving as opposed to a life of pretense or mere thinking about love. Rosalind's own in-terest in a life of such action is to be seen in the complex yet very direct speech which continues from her statement that she will weary Orlando no longer with idle talking:

> Know of me then—for now I speak to some purpose—that I know you are a gentleman of good conceit. I speak not this that you should bear a good opinion of my knowledge, insomuch I say I know you are; neither do I labour for a greater esteem than may in some little measure draw a belief from you to do yourself good, and not to grace me. Believe then, if you please, that I can do strange things. I have since I was three year old conversed with a magician, most profound in his art and yet not damnable. If you do love Rosalind so near the heart as your gesture cries it out, when your brother marries Aliena, shall you marry her.   [V.ii.52–64]

Even though Rosalind is still in disguise as she says this, she shows a desire to get beyond ulterior motives in conversation, to communicate precisely and completely what she means. Language here is stripped bare of any possible ambiguities of expression. In a work with so much play upon and criticism of style, and particularly style in courting, this speech is a breakthrough. In its unambiguous directness it acts out a commitment to action, in this case, to love as opposed to a desire to talk about love as a substitute for the thing itself; such expression stands utterly at odds with both the self-conscious poses of a conventional Petrarchan and pastoral lover like Silvius or the early Orlando and the equally self-conscious detached observations of a Jaques.

Once Orlando and Rosalind have determined that the masquerade should cease, the play's main action is, in effect, completed. Before all the plot complications are resolved and the play's various lovers are paired off in appropriate manner, though, Shakespeare presents us with a picture of yet another pair of pastoral lovers, in a song which itself serves as a reprise for the wooing scenes in the forest. The song helps to enforce a final realistic vision of life in a pastoral world; for it tells of a country lover and his lass who live in a world in which time passes, and in its final two stanzas especially, it insists upon the consequent necessity of seizing the opportunity to love when one can:

> This carol they began that hour,
>   With a hey and a ho and a hey nonino,
> How that a life was but a flower,
>   In spring-time, the only pretty ring-time,
> When birds do sing, hey ding a ding, ding,
> Sweet lovers love the spring.
>
> And therefore take the present time,
>   With a hey and a ho and a hey nonino,
> For love is crowned with the prime,
>   In spring-time, the only pretty ring-time,
> When birds do sing, hey ding a ding, ding,
> Sweet lovers love the spring.   [V.iii.26–37]

Unlike Marvell's appeal to a coy mistress, this song is an uncompromisingly happy one. In that happiness, it reiterates much of the spirit of life in Arden as experienced by Rosalind and Orlando. Like Rosalind herself, the song recognizes time's passing and yet accepts that movement with joy and confidence. Touchstone claims that there is "no great matter in the ditty" and considers that it is "'but time lost to hear such a foolish song" (V.iii.38–39, 43–44). The fool either misses the song's whole point or is merely guilty of indulging in his characteristic contentiousness. In either case, his response serves to remind us that mere criticism, which has been the mode of both Touchstone and Jaques, has not been Shakespeare's full or only purpose in the play. Shakespeare has sought to undermine romanticizing patoralism, and Touchstone and Jaques have helped in that goal, but he has wished to build a fuller vision of life in its place. There has been more going on in *As You Like It* than those who set themselves up as critics within the play's world would have us believe.

All the brief minor debates in *As You Like It* give way finally to a single major debate, one whose opposing sides are expressed in their fullest form in the whole approach toward life of Rosalind and Jaques, respectively. When Jaques decides to stay on in the forest at the end of the play and join the convertite Duke Frederick, he is repeating the act of a former suitor that Ganymede claimed to have "cured" of love: Ganymede drove that lover "'from his mad humour of love to a living humour of madness, which was, to forswear the full stream of the world and live in a nook merely monastic" (III.ii.406–9). Rosalind, for her part, in seeking love and marriage is submitting herself completely to the full stream of the world. The central conflict the two characters embody is at bottom one between an active life and a life of retreat, between a life of love in a world ruled by time and a life of escapist detachment from the world and from other human beings. It is in the particular terms of this conflict that we can perceive Shakespeare's unfairness to the pastoralist position. For that conflict is not the legitimate Renaissance debate between the claims for the active and contemplative life that a work in the pastoral mode might well have prompted, and Shakespeare is no more open to the arguments on behalf of the contemplative life than was Sidney before him. Shakespeare could conceivably have made his extreme pastorlist in the play a Platonic poet or a visionary—after the manner, let us say, of Spenser's Colin Clout of Book VI of *The Faerie Queene*. But in choosing instead to have Jaques betray escapist desires to be free of time's onward movement and of the social world's normal responsibilities, rather than be a true contemplative, the playwright banks his argument so that the pastoralist position is denied full intellectual and moral respectability.

In a debate with terms or sides such as we do have in *As You Like It,* there can be little doubt that Shakespeare's own sympathies lie with Rosalind rather than with the Jaques whose views romantic critics were apt to identify as some version of Shakespeare's own. If we wished, we could easily place not only Shakespeare but all of the play's various characters along a scale between Rosalind's and Jaques's positions. Corin, Celia, and the educated and reformed Orlando, for instance, would in their different ways stand close to Rosalind; Silvius seeks love, but seeks it in a timeless poetic realm and hence would be placed near Jaques. The Duke's position both early and late in the play, though, proves especially important in revealing the play's full stand on conventional pastoralism of, let us say, Lodge's sort. For the Duke (along with his alter ego, Amiens) is, as we have seen, the character most fully identified with Lodge's fictive assumptions; and in a debate with the terms as just defined, a character who indulges in dreams of an Arcadian land free from the usual worldly cares and difficulties would necessarily find himself in Jaques's camp. There are in fact a number of minor details in the play that connect the Duke and Jaques. The metaphor of the world as a stage which Jaques elaborates upon so that it becomes an expression of his own alienation was suggested to him by the Duke (II.vii.137–39); and the Duke confesses early on that it irks him that he and his courtiers are forced to hunt the "native burghers of this desert city" for food (II.i.22–23), a sentiment which the melancholy Jaques elsewhere in the forest carries to his characteristic extreme when he invectively pierces not only the usurping courtiers but even the natural "fat and greasy citizens" of the forest, who in his view have adopted some of mankind's more unattractive qualities (II.i.45–63). Given these metaphoric connections, Jaques takes on the appearance of being, like Amiens, an extension of the Duke himself, and he thereby points up for us the deeper implications of, and dangers in, the Duke's own thinking.

It is to the Duke's credit that he moves at the plays' conclusion from Jaques's camp to that of Rosalind. His pastoral dream proves by the end to have been that of a basically good man on vacation. He was, after all, as Amiens has told us, making the best of bad fortune, his enforced banishment (II.i.18–20), and his essential moral health is affirmed at the play's end by his unhesitating willingness to return to court and take up responsible active life in the political world again. This final act of the Duke's is in turn a direct reflection of the whole play's anti-pastoral argument. For the Duke and the play both, the forest is initially a place of possible ease, idleness, and escape from normal cares and responsibilities, but that initial view provides the stimulus for Shakespeare's eventual insistence upon a more active stance. As Shakespeare proceeds to show that the forest is a realm in which time passes, in which man must make a living, and in which nature can be red in tooth and claw, it becomes increasingly clear that the proper response to this pastoral world is to view it for what it is and assume that life within it is not essentially different from life anywhere else. To a character with the sensibility Shakespeare wishes to endorse, a sensibility like Rosalind's, Arden becomes simply a place like any other where one can commit oneself to a life of responsible action and sympathetic involvement with others in a world constantly in motion.

—PETER LINDENBAUM, "The Forest of Arden," *Changing Landscapes: Anti-Pastoral Sentiment in the English Renaissance* (Athens: University of Georgia Press, 1986), pp. 105–11

ROBERT ORNSTEIN

Rosalind, the only one in the play who can match wits and whimsy with Touchstone, is much less tolerant of poseurs than he. Amused by Jaques, she nevertheless informs him that his melancholy is a tedious affectation. When she laughs at her passion for Orlando she does not make a joke of love; ardent and romantic by nature she is annoyed by Phebe and Silvius, who play at passion without verve or spontaneity because love can thrive on humor but finds no nourishment in arch attitudes and secondhand emotion. She enjoys a bout of wit but she does not, like Portia, take pleasure in matching her cleverness against others. Her wisdom is less practical than Portia's, and it is more likely to be zany in attitude than measured out in witty sentences. She is too wholehearted in her affections to wish to teach Orlando how to be a sensible lover. Her schooling of him is playfully extracurricular; she offers a short course in love and marriage that allows passion its rein but not its pretensions. When Orlando protests that he would have Rosalind as wife "for ever and a day," she advises him to "Say 'a day,' without the 'ever.' " Her ideal of marriage is one that keeps alive the playful excitement of courtship even as it transcends it. She doubts that pangs of love have ever proved fatal and, like Bottom and his colleagues, she exorcises the fear of romantic tragedy:

> The poor world is almost six thousand years old, and in all this time there was not any man died in his own person, *videlicet*, in a love-cause. Troilus had his brains dash'd out with a Grecian club, yet he did what he could to die before, and he is one of the patterns of love. . . . men have died from time to time, and worms have eaten them, but not for love.   (4.1. 94–108)

Skeptical of the tragedy of love, Rosalind believes wholeheartedly in its comedy, and she intends to play her comic role so broadly that Orlando will never be certain of his wife's mood, although he will have no doubt of her devotion. The sensible Theseus patronizes the madness of love; Rosalind only pretends to try to cure it because she knows that the canker in the rose of love is not the exuberance of passion but the routine of marriage, in which the poetry of courtship turns into the dullest of prose.

If Rosalind were as antiromantic as she is sometimes described, she would find Arden absurd; she is able to enjoy the pastoral holiday it affords because she is never arch or self-conscious or clever at someone else's expense. Sunny-natured and resilient, she is not forever on guard against the world. Although wise beyond her years, she can express her feelings with a childlike directness. Orlando's tardiness genuinely upsets her and she can sympathize with Silvius's unrequited love even though his outcries do not evince much suffering. Overcome by passion, he runs off stage, as he knows lovers should, shouting his cruel fair's name. An audience invariably laughs, only to discover that Silvius's anguish is not amusing to Rosalind, who also knows the sorrow of unfulfilled love: "Alas, poor shepherd! Searching of thy wound, I have by hard adventure found mine own."

Rosalind's melancholy is only momentary. Even after she falls in love with Orlando, she is happy enough to be with Celia, whether at court or in Arden, and she is not distressed by his absence or indeed by her separation from her father, to whom she reveals herself only in the last scene of the play. Orlando does not fill her thoughts until she meets him again in the forest and then her delight in the role of Ganymede keeps her from revealing herself to him. Loving in all her relationships, she does not, like Julia or Hermia, live for love, and her destiny is not to lose herself in marriage to Orlando but rather to widen his horizons by making him a proper husband.

At the beginning of the play, Orlando's naiveté does not matter because his sweet nature and chivalric manliness are attractive enough. With a wider experience of life and some schooling by Rosalind, he may develop a sense of humor and a more realistic view of things; but throughout the play he remains a Quixotic innocent, not quite able to cope with a world that does not conform to his heroic expectations. He is described by Adam as a latterday Sir Galahad, not only born centuries too late but destined to pay dearly for his knightly virtues:

> Why are you virtuous? Why do people love you?
> And wherefore are you gentle, strong, and valiant?
> . . . .
>   Your virtues, gentle master,
> Are sanctified and holy traitors to you.   (2.3. 5–13)

Robbed of his inheritance by Oliver, Orlando sets out to redeem his name and make his fortune by chivalric deeds. On the way to challenge the mighty Charles at wrestling, he meets Rosalind, who gives him a token to wear for her sake. She should also send him forth inspired by her confidence; instead she sighs, shakes her head, and hopes that she is mistaken in her estimate of his abilities. As in the old tales, the unknown challenger defeats the mighty champion and need only reveal his identity to receive the reward and recognition he deserves. When he speaks his name to Duke Frederick, however, he is told that he has the wrong father, one who was the Duke's enemy, and only the decency of Le Beau saves him from the usurper's wrath. He tries again to play the knight-errant in Arden by challenging the Duke's party to gain food for Adam, but succeeds only in being invited to dinner. Unable to find savages or dragons to overcome, Orlando turns love poet and proves less successful in this venture than in his knight-errantry. A man like this is a match for any villain and any lion, but he will need a loving wife to appreciate his virtues and to protect him from disillusion in a world that he will never fully understand.

In Lodge's story, the disguised heroine and her lover have one meeting in which they consciously assume the roles of nymph and swain. Shakespeare gives much more space to the masquerade and the role-playing in two lengthy scenes in which Ganymede invites Orlando to imagine that he is courting Rosalind when he speaks to her. Since the Elizabethan stage did not demand realism in disguise, Rosalind remains Rosalind for the audience whether she assumes the guise of Ganymede or plays Ganymede pretending to be Rosalind. Thus her pretenses do not invert or blur her sexual identity, especially when her role was taken by one of the actors in Shakespeare's company who was expert at playing female characters. If there is any risk of unpleasantness in the mock wooing scenes it lies in Orlando's inability to catch any of Ganymede's subtle hinting about her true nature. He is so carried away by Ganymede's impersonation of a woman that he asks her for a kiss. He is also less observant about Ganymede than is Oliver, who brings a bloody napkin from Orlando as a love token. When Ganymede faints, Oliver guesses that "his" passion is in earnest and almost seems to guess that "he" is a woman: "Be of good cheer, youth," he advises, "You a man! You lack a man's heart. . . . Well then, take a good heart and counterfeit to be a man." This is not to say that Orlando should be able to see through Rosalind's disguise any more than Orsino or Olivia should be able to see through Viola's, despite Viola's more urgent hinting about her identity. But Orsino can commune with Cesario and share with this "boy" his most intimate thoughts, while Orlando never progresses beyond a freshman's status in his schooling by Ganymede, who does most of the talking and all of the professing in their scenes together.

Phebe also undertakes the education of her lover Silvius by sneering at his Petrarchan hyperboles while she enjoys all the literary rights and privileges of being the cruel fair of Elizabethan sonnets.

> Thou tell'st me there is murder in mine eye:
> 'Tis pretty, sure, and very probable,
> That eyes, that are the frail'st and softest things,
> Who shut their coward gates on atomies,
> Should be called tyrants, butchers, murtherers!
> Now I do frown on thee with all my heart,
> And if mine eyes can wound, now let them kill thee.
> Now counterfeit to swound; why, now fall down.   (3.5. 10–17)

Silvius and Phebe assume the conventional roles that lovers have in the sonnets: he sighs and pleads and wallows in self-indulgent misery; she postures in deflating his romantic agony, playing the cruel fair while refusing to allow him to be the despairing victim of his mistress's disdain. Rosalind's disguise, which is also a cliché of romantic fabling, never strikes an audience as being a pose because her responses are always truthful even when she deceives and teases Orlando. Her lively interest in his emotional well-being is perfectly genuine, and since she does not love by the book, she can dissect the artificialities of romantic convention at the same time that she ardently affirms the meaning of romantic commitment.

Truth is the burden of Rosalind's message to the pastoral lovers. She advises Silvius to have his eye sight tested because it is myopic fools like him

> That make the world full of ill-favor'd children.
> 'Tis not her glass, but you that flatters her.   (3.5. 53–54)

She would have Phebe appraise her own assets more realistically:

> But, mistress, know yourself, down on your knees,
> And thank heaven, fasting, for a good man's love;
> For I must tell you friendly in your ear,
> Sell when you can, you are not for all markets.
> Cry the man mercy, love him, take his offer.   (3.5. 57–61)

Once Valentine's praises of Silvia made Proteus his rival. Now Rosalind's dispraise of Phebe inspires her passion. As the heroes of the comedies become more gentle—more like Bassanio and Benedick than Demetrius or Petruchio—heroines like Phebe and Olivia become aggressive in pursuing the "men" whose indifference or frankness seems overwhelmingly attractive. Ironically enough the only male character in As You Like It who is an aggressive rivalrous wooer is Touchstone, who is well aware of the ludicrousness of his determined pursuit of Audrey. A master of courtly bravado, Touchstone warns away his rival William in a style that is as precise and as martial as Don Armado's:

> . . . you clown, abandon—which is in the vulgar leave—the society—which in the boorish is company—of this female—which in the common is woman; which together is, abandon the society of this female, or, clown, thou perishest; or to thy better understanding, diest; or (to wit) I kill thee, make thee away, translate thy life into death, thy liberty into bondage. I will deal in poison with thee, or in bastinado, or in steel; I will bandy with thee in faction; I will o'errun thee with [policy]; I will kill thee a hundred and fifty ways.
>
> (5.1. 47–57)

This man could set the murderous Machiavel to school.

Although Touchstone can offer at times a barnyard view of love, his sense of bourgeois propriety is evident in his desire that Audrey have a ladylike bearing at her wedding. He will perforce marry a goatmaid but he has no intention of starting a career in animal husbandry. His natural place is the court, and like most of the exiles he is destined to return to it. Since nothing that happens in Arden can alter the situation at court, however, Shakespeare must take a hand in events. Yet the ending of the play seems neither contrived nor sentimental because the news of Duke Frederick's conversion to a religious life comes after the quadruple wedding ceremony that reunites all the exiles and ensures as much personal happiness as the different lovers of the play are capable of. The news also comes after Touchstone has reminded everyone of the unpleasant realities of court life to which they will soon return. That he is a courtier is beyond doubt because he has all the necessary credentials:

> I have trod a measure; I have flatt'red a lady; I have been politic with my friend, smooth with mine enemy, I have undone three tailors, I have had four quarrels, and like to have fought one. (5.4. 44–47)

By the time Touchstone has finished his explanation of the seven causes of quarrels and degrees of reply (Retort Courteous, Quip Modest, Reply Churlish, Reproof Valiant, and so on), pastoral dreams have given way to fantasies of aristocratic honor, in which courtly cowards may pass muster as heroes, and clever evasions, not cutlasses, are the weapons of choice.

Since there are no clocks in the forest, would-be duellers could not possibly make appointments to run each other through. Yet expectation and desire begin to create an urgent tempo in the pulses of the exiles as the play draws near its close. Touchstone is beset by nibbling desires; Orlando longs for Rosalind, and when he is an hour late for his schooling, it seems an eternity to her. The songs of act 5 also remind us that time passes and seasons change. Where "Under the greenwood tree" was an invitation to waste time in pastoral bliss, "It was a lover and his lass" is a celebration of rural life in farms and villages, where lovers tryst in fields of growing wheat and rye. They will court and marry in the spring, but before long they will be busy with the harvest and preparations for wintry days when icicles hang by the wall and the milk comes frozen home in the pails. Amiens' song anticipates the quadruple wedding celebration of the final scene, in which brides, grooms, friends, and relations gather under the boughs as if in the parish church. Music sounds as Hymen, *"god of every town"* (my emphasis), appears to remind us that if the ceremony took place at court, there would be a wedding masque enacted by mythological gods and goddesses, nymphs and nereids. Hymen does not trail clouds of supernatural glory; he is Rosalind's device for sorting out romantic entanglements, one which allows her to play the blushing bride and say nothing to Orlando of her earlier disguise. This discovery scene does not aim at the sublimity of the final scene of *The Winter's Tale,* but it has mystery enough to awe Orlando, who believes Ganymede's story that "he" was raised in the forest by an uncle who was a great magician.

As in *Much Ado,* the ritual of a wedding ceremony helps to shape the final sense of order and harmony in *As You Like It.* The muddle of unrequited love was ritually expressed by Phebe, Silvius, Orlando, and Rosalind in 5.2. The resolution of romantic muddle also takes a ritual form when Rosalind reveals herself and gives herself in turn to her father and Orlando. As presiding deity, Hymen passes judgment on each pair of lovers in turn, and Jaques pauses to offer his benedictions and add his formulaic predictions about the longevities of the various marriages. Phebe does not get what she thinks she wants, but she probably gets better than she deserves in Silvius. In any event, the sense of compromise in their nuptial as well as in Touchstone's alliance to Audrey keeps the resolution from seeming too pat. The world is not half so bad as satirists like Jaques describe it, nor half so good as sentimentalists like Duke Senior would have us believe. Not all marriages are made in heaven, despite the descent of Hymen, but the bonds of kinship and love, frayed in the opening scenes, are made whole again, and there is reason to hope for happiness in days to come. At this point, Jaques de Boys can materialize to inform everyone of the conversion to holiness of Duke Frederick because it does not matter precisely how the exiles are able to return to town and court, when that return is made to seem inevitable and right.

As You Like It is not more pessimistic about love or life than *Much Ado* or *The Merchant;* it does, however, remind us that not all difficulties can be erased by wit or good will. One can, like Orlando, shun the danger of ambition and still be punished for having the wrong name or the wrong father or the wrong brother. Because the race is not always to the swift, nor the prize to the deserving, men will continue to imagine Ardens and Americas, where innocence can be reborn and the world-weary find a second chance. In the earlier comedies the characters have to cope with the perplexing situations that Shakespeare creates through the presence of identical twins or the interference of a father. In the later comedies the impediments to love and happiness are more than complications of plot. They exist because the world is not "as we like it," because barriers of rank and class exist, and because envy and arrogance exact a price that brings Shakespeare's last romantic fables closer to the edge of tragedy.

—ROBERT ORNSTEIN, *"As You Like It," Shakespeare's Comedies: From Roman Farce to Romantic Mystery* (Newark: University of Delaware Press, 1986), pp. 146–52

JAMES L. CALDERWOOD

In the comedies, on the other hand, the flexible self-awareness of female characters like Julia, Portia, Rosalind, Viola, and Imogen is reflected in their ability to disguise themselves as men. The fact that these disguisings often seem inadequately motivated suggests not just the conventional indifference of comedy to causation and probability but perhaps deeper motives. At one level these disguisings enable the women not only to get their men but also, as if by proxy, to transform them for the better. But the ultimate motive, I suggest, arises from the need to deny death: the women escape life-threatening situations by abandoning their vulnerable femininity and arming themselves with masculine powers.

In *The Merchant of Venice,* for instance, Portia begins as the epitome of the suppressed female, condemned by her father's will to yield her life and fortune to one of a variety of unappealing suitors. "I am," she says later, "locked in one of [the caskets]" like a corpse awaiting burial (3.2), and hence it is not surprising that her first line in the play should be "By my troth, Nerissa, my little body is aweary of this great world" (1.2). Even though she is released from the casket and resuscitated by Bassanio, her plight as a woman in a masculine society has been graphically emblematized as a quasi-death.

Of course it is trickier than that, for Portia's father, though dead, constitutes a patriarchal canopy under which a daughter is culturally compelled to take shelter. From that standpoint it is by adhering to his "will" that Portia is saved from the more predatory financial adventurers who gather around her. In such a world, where wealthy maids are gobbled up in marriage as greedily as Antonio would be gobbled up by Shylock, a woman's only recourse is to transform herself into a man. After all, that is clearly where the power resides. Thus Portia's transformation into the lawyer Balthazar endows her at the trial with the masculine power over life and death—a power she carries back into womanhood and Belmont where as the possessor of secret knowledge she can rescue Bassanio from dishonor and infidelity and can revivify Antonio with news of his ships: "Sweet lady, you have given me life and living."

A similar pattern occurs in *As You Like It* where Rosalind escapes the death-threatening masculinity of Duke Frederick's court (1.3.43–47) and enters a more benign but still masculine world of the forest by transforming herself into Ganymede. "In my heart," she says, "lie there what hidden woman's fear there will, / We'll have a swashing and a martial outside" (1.3). But swashing and martial outsides are unnecessary in the forest, as Orlando discovers when he pulls his sword to demand a hospitality that comes freely with the asking. Arden is by no means a scene of pastoral bliss; the wind blows, the cold nips, and the stomach growls, but here even adversity has sweet uses. The old and near-dying Adam is restored with kindness, and disappears from the play. But if his part and that of Hymen are doubled by one player, then old age is reborn as love. Death, though always a resident of Arcadia (*"Et in Arcadia ego"*), is far more naturally or conventionally a city-dweller. In the forest Death is transformed into love, which is not of the killing variety: "Men have died from time to time and worms have eaten them, but not for love" (4.1).

Rosalind's ability to shift identities to meet occasions, based as it is on her recognition of the mutability of things, enables her not merely to survive in the forest world but also to be worshipped by the doting Orlando. She acquires powers perhaps even more remarkable than Portia's. As a boy actor playing a woman playing a man playing a woman, she marries both sexes within a single identity, and hence becomes qualified to serve as all things to all people, but especially to assume the role of marriage broker:

> [*To Sylvius*] I will help you if I can. [*To Phebe*] I would love you if I could. Tomorrow meet me all together. [*To Phebe*] I will marry you if ever I marry a woman, and I'll be married tomorrow. [*To Orlando*] I will satisfy you if ever I satisfied man, and you shall be married tomorrow. [*To Silvius*] I will content you if what pleases you contents you, and you shall be married tomorrow.
>
> (5.2)

Rosalind's ability to marry everyone, to form sexual unions, is the ability to deny death by giving life.

The tendency in the festive comedies for heroines to die as women by assuming a disguised manhood and then to return with life-enhancing powers is the very stuff of which the romances are made. Imogen is a transition character in this respect because in her the symbolic death-by-male-disguise of Julia, Portia, Rosalind, and Viola is combined with her apparent death as the boy Fidele and her subsequent resurrection in the last scene as Imogen. In the later romances female characters will similarly die, not into masculinity but as a result of masculine repressiveness, and be reborn later. In the tragedies the heroines actually do die— Lavinia in *Titus Andronicus,* Juliet, Portia in *Julius Caesar,* Ophelia, Desdemona, Cordelia, and Cleopatra—confirming the notion that women suffer death while men impose it. Granted, men do in one another at a great rate also. But how, I wonder, should we interpret the fact that in none of the plays does a woman kill a man, not even Goneril, Regan, or Lady Macbeth? Does it stem from a genuine belief in a supposed gentler nature, a feminine inability to do violent evil; and if so, is this a pseudochivalrous myth actually fostered by a masculine fear of and therefore suppression of feminine violence? Or is it simply owing to the fact that women did then, as they do now, fewer deeds of violence than men? In any event the task of the comic heroine is to die and come to life again in such a way as to oblige the men to graduate from death-dealing to life-giving, from killing to begetting.

In this connection we might pause to speculate about Shakespeare's frequent use of women in male roles. The question that arises is whether he is reflecting the male chauvinism of his times or transcending it. Is a woman's assumption of a male disguise construed as a mark of weakness or of strength? More broadly we might regard this as a version of the cultural practice in Elizabethan society, and of course up to very recent times, according to which a wife takes her husband's name at marriage. How to view it? Does the husband give or the wife take the family name?

Considered in the abstract, as a practice endorsed in Shakespeare's time by a patriarchal culture, the giving of a man's name to his wife was surely an act of masculine conquest disguised as protective generosity toward the weaker vessel. But could it not also point up a subtle form of feminine conquest—not an aggressive seizure but a mature acceptance of the male name? That is, feminine submissiveness in such cases might derive from feminine self-assurance, since women are able to subsume themselves nominally without fear of losing their personal identity— something men can never do. This is probably owing to the fact that women define themselves in terms of gender simply by *being* themselves, while men define themselves by proving they are not women. For instance women can accept masculine common nouns (e.g., *guy*) and pronouns (e.g., the much-maligned *he, him, his*) or feminized names of men, like Johanna, Caroline, or Michelle, without feeling psychologically threatened by masculinity, whereas the male ego, or lack of ego, cannot reverse the procedure without a loss of face. The male ego is simply more fragile and vulnerable, based as it is on a culturally endorsed repudiation of the female. Thus transvestism today means a male dressing in female clothing, not the reverse, because the adoption of male dress by women has come to seem perfectly natural; and to other males such transvestism is repellent in a way that suggests a deep fear of loss of identity. It can only be endured when dealt with humorously by Three Stooges or Jerry Lewis types.

Needless to say, the only males in feminine clothing in Shakespeare's plays, if we exclude priests, are the boy actors, although Cleopatra reports that she once adorned a drunken Antony with her "tires and mantles" while she paraded about with his sword. However, even dressing boy actors in women's clothing aroused the ire of Puritans like Stephen Gosson and William Prynne, who attacked this theatrical practice as a violation of the Deuteronomic ban: "The woman shall not wear that which pertaineth unto a man, neither shall a man put on a woman's garment: for all that do so are abomination unto the Lord thy God" (22:5).

As Jonas Barish points out, the real fear of fulminating Puritans was the blurring of sexual boundaries, the typical male phobia about effeminacy. For Shakespeare even to associate with the theater, then, implied at least his willingness to flout the more publicly repressive forms of sexual differentiation in his day.

Whatever the psychological implications of all this, Shakespeare's disguised heroines do reveal a maturity of social understanding and a flexibility of behavior that makes them the controlling influence in their plays. By comparison their male lovers often seem naive, fatuous, and uninterestingly one-dimensional.

Before leaving this subject I should mention two of Shakespeare's female characters who do not explicitly adopt masculine disguises but nevertheless take on male characteristics to deal with death—Lady Macbeth and Volumnia. In *Macbeth* feminine vulnerability of the sort we have seen in the comedies is assigned to Lady Macduff, whose life is forfeited to Macbeth's death-bent agents when her husband abandons her for the safety of England. Her opposite, Lady Macbeth, in order to arm herself for regicide calls on spirits to "unsex me here" and on murdering ministers to "Come to my woman's breasts / And take my milk for gall" (1.5). This is the most graphic instance of the annihilation of femininity through a masculinizing of the heroine, though in this case the motive is not to escape death but to assume its lethal powers. It represents an inversion of the comic heroine's adoption of "a swashing and a martial outside," as Rosalind says, to conceal a "hidden woman's fear." With Lady Macbeth the woman is all on the outside, a veneer of femininity, while the murderous male lurks within; and the toll taken by this willed perversion of nature is registered much later when the lady sleepwalks her way to suicide.

—JAMES L. CALDERWOOD, "Feminine Disguise in Comedy," *Shakespeare and the Denial of Death* (Amherst: University of Massachusetts Press, 1987), pp. 35–39

LEAH S. MARCUS

It is tempting to speculate that the presence of Elizabeth on the throne may have stimulated emulation of her independence on the part of women further down the social scale, as increasing numbers of them in fact separated themselves from the immediate authority of men. But such a contention would be impossible to prove. There are too many other factors that need to be taken into account—shifting economic conditions, changing perceptions of normative family structure. If Elizabeth's rule to some degree encouraged female "misrule," the queen also made it her business to put a firm cap on the phenomenon by insisting on her own male-identified patriarchy and using it to curb court ladies under her direct authority, by fostering the creation of new devices for curbing the waywardness of those who were "mere" women but claimed the prerogatives of men. During the 1590s there was a decided increase in institutionalized devices specifically for the curbing of women. For example, more and more villages invested in "cucking stools" for the punishment of domineering wives and scolds.

What was depicted as a crisis for Tudor society is less threatening in Shakespearean comedy. The "masterless women" of the late comedies are renderings of a contemporary type, but also revisions of the menacing martial women of the early histories. After the Armada, the "woman on top" had been a focus for suppressed rage and fears of powerlessness; in the late 1590s, in Shakespeare at least, it becomes the generative center for more positive fantasies and idealizations. At least some of the comedies were staged at court. What was set up opposite the queen on the occasion of such performances was not a dangerous, demonized virgin like the Norwich icon burned in 1578, but a version of the royal composite in which the deviant and "popish" elements had to a considerable extent been emptied of their menace.

Given the Elizabethan passion for political lock-picking, we can imagine various ways in which Shakespeare's cross-dressed heroines could have registered with contemporary audiences as analogues of Elizabeth. In *The Merchant of Venice*, Portia offers a becoming speech of womanly submission to Bassanio, then heads off in male garb to do justice in a high court of law (to which, incidentally, she brings legal principles like the equity actually practiced in the queen's Court of Chancery). "Man and woman both," Portia enacts over time Queen Elizabeth's standard rhetorical ploy of declaring her weakness as a woman, then successfully asserting her masculine prerogative over a resisting body of men. In *As You Like It*, Rosalind exerts almost complete control over the world of Arden, playing many parts male and female, using her disguise as Ganymede to get what she cannot as a woman, pairing couples off to suit her purposes as Elizabeth was notorious for doing at court. Rosalind's protean, free-form movement in and out of male and female identities is very much like the flirtatious games Elizabeth habitually played with her favorites, to their exasperation or delight. Unlike Portia and Rosalind, Beatrice in *Much Ado About Nothing* does not adopt male disguise, but she can be seen as mimicking some of Elizabeth's strategies with language and royal identity. Like the queen, she makes adamant protests against marriage; she comments that if she is saddled with too young a husband, she will "dresse him in my apparell, and make him my waiting gentlemwoman"—a muted echo of the "Amazon effect." Viola of *Twelfth Night* is less forceful, seemingly less content with her enforced self-sufficiency and only briefly "masterless," but caught up in the same intriguing games of oscillating sexual identities. Any of these possibilities for identification could easily have been intensified during performance through actual imitation of the inflection and mannerisms of Elizabeth. We know that strong-nerved actors were capable of such mimicry at other times, and at least one play from the end of the 1590s actually brought the figure of Elizabeth onto the public stage. But by the same token, through staging, the potential for identification could have been diminished.

Some of the potential resemblances are negative. If Portia seems to carry justice too far against Shylock, for example, does that mean Shakespeare is accusing Queen Elizabeth of a similar deficiency—in the Lopez case of a few years earlier or more generally? Rustlings of the old, threatening "disorderly woman" can be heard on the edges of the comedies' festival inversions. The "horn music" and repeated references to cuckoldry in *As You Like It*, for example, evoke the shaming rituals of the Skimmington, in which the violation of sexual hierarchy was held up to public ridicule. Readings which bring such motifs to the surface can easily be generated, but without much security of interpretation. It is time to move, once again, from the protean referentiality of topical reading to the level of "local" function. To the extent that parallels were (either consciously or subliminally) perceived by a contemporary audience, what might have been their effect, particularly given the sudden concentration of such images just at the end of Elizabeth's reign?

All of the "women's" parts in Shakespeare's plays were, of course, played by men or young boys. But only in certain cases was the sexual multivalence of the "woman" on stage overtly thematized. Joan of Arc is a partial example: when the duke of Burgundy jests, "Pray God she proue not masculine ere long: / If vnderneath the Standard of the French / She carry Armour, as she hath begun," he can be understood on a metadramatic level as gesturing toward the actual sexual identity of the "woman" under the armor. But such a level of theatrical self-consciousness has to be read in from the outside; the play does not constantly gesture toward its own fabricated nature as Shakespearean comedy was to do later on. Indeed, the portrayal of Joan depends on the perception of a fundamental inauthenticity in her self-fashioning as a warrior. She dresses in male armor, but never presents herself as anything other than a woman. She is therefore an incomplete analogue of Queen Elizabeth. When Elizabeth donned elements of male battle dress at Tilbury to incite her troops to valor, she was—and her speech for the occasion made that clear—not merely taking on the dress appropriate to her role as military commander but gesturing toward her sacred identity as monarch. In a secularized epiphany, her masculine accoutrements unfolded her essential "King-like" nature. Or at least such was the intent. We have already considered the possibility that for the disaffected or skeptical among her subjects, the bold gesture may have aroused more uncertainties than it dampened—hence the subversive potential of Joan, a defective analogue of the queen, to suggest flaws in the royal composite itself.

In Shakespeare's comedies, the metadramatic "truth" of the stage woman's male identity is far closer to the surface, if only because the plays repeatedly assault the distinction between their own fictions and an external reality, repeatedly set the actors apart from their roles, male and female, then playfully merge them back into them. At the end of *As You Like It*, the heroine actually steps outside her female identity and confesses her maleness: "If I were a Woman, I would kisse as many of you as had beards that pleas'd me, complexions that lik'd me, and breaths that I defi'de not: And I am sure, as many as haue good beards, or good faces, or sweet breaths, will for my kind offer, when I make curt'sie, bid me farewell." This revelation, surprising, perhaps even shocking, yet "licensed" by the free-form interplay which has preceded it, establishes a layering of sexual identities which is congruent with the queen's anomalous self-presentation rather than subversive of it.

The dramatic construct of a boy clothed as a woman, an altogether credible woman, who then expands her identity through male disguise in such a way as to mirror the activities which would be appropriate to her actual, hidden male identity—that construct precisely replicates visually the composite self-image Queen Elizabeth created over and over again through language. She showed herself a woman on the stage of public life—and she liked to call it that—but with a male identity, her princehood, underlying her obvious femininity and lending her authority, offering the subliminal promise of growth into kingship as a boy actor would grow into a man. She did not, except on highly unusual occasions like Tilbury, dress herself as a man, but performed so effectively the "male" responsibilities of government that in that sphere her subjects were invited to forget—and sometimes did forget—she was female. She called much more attention to her male "immortal body" than Shakespeare's heroines do to their latent maleness, but her emphasis was necessary to achieve the same perception of multivalence. She had to create a new convention which cut across accepted gender distinctions, build a conceptual model which seemed to belie the visual data offered by the "frail" female body that her subjects saw; the sexual identity of those playing female parts on stage was, by contrast, understood from the outset, a familiar theatrical device.

What is distinctive about the four Shakespearean comedies we are considering is not their use of boy actors to play female parts, as all plays before the 1620s in England did, but the fact that they call attention to the convention by acting it out in reverse in the person of the central character through a disguise which replicates the actor's underlying sexual identity. As they watched Shakespeare's heroines move in and out of their manhood, members of the Elizabethan audience witnessed the creation of sexual composites which resembled the "man and woman both" that Queen Elizabeth claimed to be.

—LEAH S. MARCUS, "Elizabeth," *Puzzling Shakespeare: Local Reading and Its Discontents* (Berkeley: University of California Press, 1988), pp. 98–101

ANNE HERRMANN

On 25 January 1620, John Chamberlain wrote in a letter to Dudley Carleton:

Yesterday the bishop of London called together all the Clergie about this towne, and told them he had expressed commaundment from the King to will them to inveigh vehemently and bitterly in theyre sermons, against the insolencie of our women and theyre wearing of *brode brimd hats,* pointed dublets, theyre haire cut short or shorne, and some of them stilettaes or poinards, and such other trinckets of like moment: adding withall that yf pulpit admonitions will not reforme them he would proceed by another course: the truth is the world is very far out of order, but whether this will mende yt God knowes.

Why King James I sought to extinguish a female transvestite movement which began in the 1570s, experienced a revival in 1606–1607 and reached its height in 1620, and which was publicly debated in two anonymous pamphlets, *Hic Mulier: or, The Man-Woman; Being a Medecine to cure the Coltish Disease of the Staggers in thc Masculine-Feminines of our Times* and *Haec-Vir; or The Womanish Man: Being an Answere to a late Book intituled Hic-Mulier,* will never be known. What is known is that the king turned to the authority of the church, a church whose members at the beginning of the movement had argued in anti-theatrical tracts against male cross-dressing. The most cited of these tracts are Stephen Gossen's *The School of Abuse* (1583) which claims that cross-dressing will "adulterate" gender. Men who play the parts of women become like women; and if men become like women, then clothes constitute rather than signify the sex of the subject, suggesting an inherently unstable sexual identity and/or subjectivity.

In the early 1590s John Rainolds, a learned Puritan, William Gager, the leading writer of academic drama at Oxford, and Alberico Gentili, England's most renowned jurist, engaged in a debate (in Latin) over whether Deuteronomy 22:5 applied to actors, specifically university actors who played in private theaters. Rainolds argued that it did, Gentili that it did not, and Gager that it was wrong for men to wear women's clothing unless they did so to save their lives or benefit their country. Sex differences were seen by all as "natural," God-ordained. Transgressing natural distinctions meant transgressing social and moral ones. Both women dressing as men (on the streets) and men dressing as women (on the stage) led to unnatural behavior, particularly behavior that was sexually "unnatural." Women became sexually aggressive and socially undesirable, taking on the identity of "roaring girls," that is, pickpockets or ruffians; men became effeminate and sexually aroused the male members of their theater audience. In the Renaissance, the androgyne was "the erotically irresistible effeminate boy." The object, then, was to contain the contradiction between the essential sex and the lack of an essential gender in order to prevent its proliferation. As soon as female cross-dressers appeared on the streets of London, they ceased to appear on the Shakespearean stage. The first professional English actress made her debut in 1660.

In *As You Like It*, even before Rosalind dresses as Ganymede, two forms of doubling without disguise establish gendered subject positions which distinguish between masculine and feminine without relying on sexual stereotypes. Orlando begins the play by lamenting that the unfair treatment he received from his brother Oliver results in a misleading single self which in fact conceals two: the gentleman by birth and the rustic by education. Afraid that the latter will usurp the former, he invokes the natural bond with his father against the unnatural bond between brothers. To Adam, his surrogate father, he says: "the spirit of my father, which I think is within me, begins to mutiny against this servitude," inflicted by the older brother who has usurped the place of the father. The body of Orlando contains the spirit of the father which begins to rebel against the brother, who insists on containing that spirit in a singularly physical existence: "I, his brother, gain nothing under him but growth, for the which his animals on his dunghills are as much bound to him as I" (1. 1. 13–15). Even though Orlando protests against this purely physical increase, his mutiny takes the form of a wrestling match. His brother then reads Orlando's physical superiority as mental prowess by imagining him as doubly devious, precisely because there is no attempt to disguise his desire to repossess his social position.

In contrast with Orlando, caught between man and beast, Rosalind partakes of an external doubling where two appear as one. Rosalind and Celia, although merely cousins, share a love that (unlike the perverted bond between brothers) is "dearer than the natural bond of sisters" (1. 2. 266). Even though not blood-linked, they have been raised together, creating a bond more "natural" and more permanent than kinship. When Celia's father attempts to separate them by suggesting that the adopted daughter has begun to outshine the "real" one, Celia responds:

> If she be a traitor,
> Why, so am I. We still have slept together,
> Rose at an instant, learned, played, eat together;
> And wheresoe'er we went, like Juno's swans,
> Still we went coupled and inseparable.   [1. 3. 70–74]

While the Duke seeks to turn the two girls into rivals, Celia insists that they are one and the same, and therefore indivisible. Not only has Celia already promised to share her inheritance with Rosalind, but she is willing to relinquish it altogether in order to follow her twice dispossessed "sister" into exile.

Here the difference between the masculine and feminine subject position lies in the difference between the divided and doubled self. The divided self rests on a hierarchy of two terms (like Duke Senior and Duke Frederick, the banished ruler and his usurper) where the disenfranchised term must be restored to its rightful place, the rustic must give way to the gentleman. The doubled self, in contrast, has two parts (or "sisters") which reflect each other and thus become suitable substitutions. In order for the doubled self to enter representation as more than a mimetic repetition, it must divide itself by means of heterosexual difference (thus Ganymede and Aliena). Although both "couples" are banished, the male "couple" requires the restitution of one term, while the female one requires the relinquishment of the bond, figured as the difference between reclaiming and renouncing one's patrimonial inheritance.

For the two women, "falling in love" replaces wrestling as a sport, although, like wrestling, it will divide them since they cannot fall in love with each other. This arrangement is guaranteed by their "naturalized" relationship based on two terms which are not differentiated enough to engage in competition and cannot thus act as complements (except in play or performance in the forest). Instead, Rosalind falls in love with Orlando, prefiguring the verbal match they will have as lovers in Arden. There, the love joust takes place between two men (Orlando and Ganymede as well as two boy players), one of whom plays a woman (Rosalind who dresses as Ganymede in order to play Rosalind). Male homoeroticism, as "unnatural" as the bond between brothers and as "sporty" as the fight between wrestlers, is veiled by the doubled costume of the woman which offers a form of heterosexual legitimation. Rosalind's role as transvestite is likewise prefigured in her dual relationship to "wrestling": she is both wrestler, when Celia encourages her to "wrestle with thy affections" (1. 3. 21) and wrestled, when she says to Orlando:

Sir, you have wrestled well, and overthrown
More than your enemies.   [1. 2. 243–244]

Here the other man is portrayed as antagonist (like the brother) in contrast to the "friend" (or lover) Orlando will find in Ganymede. While men function in terms of contradictions, women function as imitations of each other unless they become men.

When Rosalind does put on her male attire (since a woman alone was a woman to be raped), there is division with the aid of disguise. Disguise is less deceptive than duplicity because it relies on visual rather than linguistic signifiers. Unlike the fictions created by Oliver against Orlando and by Duke Frederick against Rosalind—whereby words are used to fabricate lies enforced as truth by the authority of the speaker—visual disguise presents only one view to the viewer at a time. Without deceit, the signs of masculine and feminine take the form of sexual stereotypes. Even though Rosalind says herself that "a swashing and a martial outside" (1. 3. 118) provides only the deceptive appearance of manly courage, crying and fainting reveal her as a "true" woman. By suggesting that through her disguise "Rosalind becomes 'brother' to herself," Joel Fineman not only privileges the familial bond the play constitutes as perverted (even if finally restored), but also creates a distinction between "feminine" as "natural" and therefore susceptible to mimesis, and "masculine" as deceptive (both politically and dramatically) and therefore suitable for performance. It is this distinction that offers a profounder difference between the sexes than the signifiers of social roles, or sexual stereotypes.

In the forest, Rosalind further "naturalizes" the feminine by mimicking the words of the misogynist. In response to Orlando's suggestion that her way of speaking might be too refined for a place so removed from the court, she says:

> I have been told so by many. But indeed an old religious uncle of mine taught me to speak, who was in his youth an inland man; one that knew courtship too well, for there he fell in love. I have heard him read many lectures against it; and I thank God I am not a woman, to be touched with so many giddy offences as he hath generally taxed their whole sex withal.   [3. 2. 338–345]

Rosalind seeks to emulate the paternal figure, who in this case is not the displaced ruler but the scorned lover, and does so as disciple. Thus she imitates her model by "reading his many lectures," rather than by performing in his place, as son. In the forest the opponent is not another man but woman, made less threatening by the fact that she is played by a man. Rosalind reinforces her disguise through deception—not only is she not a woman but she thanks God she never was one. And in contrast to "man," who appears as contradiction, whether in love or not, corruption contaminates the entire "weaker sex."

If Rosalind breaks her "sisterly" bond with Celia in order to establish an "unnatural" one (both false and homoerotic) with Orlando, what role does Celia play, once one concludes, as Sue-Ellen Case does, that: "The fictional 'Woman' (the character of Rosalind) simply mediates and enhances the homoerotic flirtation between two males." Celia, the one who relinquishes her inheritance but not her sex, is the one who questions Rosalind's identification with and appropriation of masculinist values. This begins even before Rosalind cross-dresses, when she falls in love with Orlando and justifies her feelings by saying: "The Duke my father loved his father dearly." Celia responds: "Doth it therefore ensue that you should love his son dearly? By this kind of chase, I should hate him, for my father hated his father dearly; yet I hate not Orlando" (1. 3. 29–33). Just as Celia breaks with her father in order to follow her "sister," she suggests breaking bonds of kinship in order to pursue the alternative model provided by female friendship (or love). Celia seeks to distinguish between adopting masculine attributes (for survival) and mimicking the misogynist (for play or prowess). Shortly before Rosalind faints, Celia chastizes her for betraying her own sex: "You have simply misused our sex in your loveprate. We must have your doublet and hose plucked over your head, and show the world what the bird hath done to her own nest" (4. 1. 192–195). Becoming a traitor to one's own sex exceeds the treachery perceived by the father—outshining one's sex—which serves as the initial reason for banishment. Celia's defense of her sex, potentially subversive, is contained as conservative because she represents an imitative, same-sex reflection of the cross-dressed heroine who has learned to play with gender distinctions by assuming masculine privilege.

Ultimately it is Touchstone—the fool, not the transvestite—who functions as third term in the form of transgressor, using language to manipulate marriage as that institution which keeps sexual difference in place or at bay. For Wolfgang Iser the fool "is always his own double without ever having to disguise himself" and for Terry Eagleton he "is pure transgression . . . because he appears to lack a body. . . ." It is his "motley coat" (an incongruous mixture of colors and materials) that provides the alternative to male and female dress because the wearer of that coat knows the duplicity of language and can thus manipulate the linguistic performance of the marriage ceremony. He would have it both ways at once, a doubleness based not on disguise, but on the instability of meaning. He knows that every signifier has more than one signified, just as every situation can offer more than one referent. This becomes most apparent when asked whether he likes the life of a shepherd, to which he answers:

> Truly, shepherd, in respect of itself, it is a good life; but in respect that it is a shepherd's life, it is naught. In respect that it is solitary, I like it very well; but in respect that it is private, it is a very vile life. Now in respect it is in the fields, it pleaseth me well; but in respect it is not in the court, it is tedious. As it is a spare life, look you, it fits my humor well; but as there is no more plenty in it, it goes much against my stomach. [3. 2. 13–21]

A single situation is described with a potentially limitless set of oppositions which seem to cancel each other out and thus mean nothing at all. On the one hand, "solitary" and "private" both refer to the separation or isolation of the individual from the community; on the other hand, they are juxtaposed to create a contradiction: is he secluded or is he lonely? What initially appears as nonsense ultimately offers a lesson in linguistics. As long as this word-play remains in the realm of what Touchstone calls "philosophy," it matters little whether meaning is ever stabilized. He nevertheless attempts to transfer this doubleness to the marriage ceremony, the ritual which seeks to arrest sexual indeterminacy by legitimizing the heterosexual couple. Knowing that a whore can become a wife only in name, the fool attempts to arrange an illegal ceremony with Audrey (a country girl) that would pronounce him husband and release him from that pronouncement at the same time. Audrey, no longer a virgin and thus indifferent to whether she is pronounced "wife," sets as little store by the ceremony as Touchstone does. Yet she does so out of a lack of understanding of the figurative: "I do not know what poetical is. Is it honest in deed and word? Is it a true thing?" (3. 3. 16–17). Honesty becomes equated with the "natural" as that which is (hetero)sexually explicit rather than (homosexually) implicit.

Louis Montrose suggests: "Marriage, the social institution at the heart of comedy, serves to ease or eliminate fraternal strife. And fraternity, in turn, serves as a defense against the threat men feel from women." If this is the case, then Rosalind, as "her own 'brother,'" will ease the strife between actors and characters by coordinating the four marriages "to make these doubts all even" (5. 4. 25). Yet the homoeroticism contained by these social roles makes its reappearance in the epilogue, where Rosalind reveals her true sex as masculine: "If I were a woman, I would kiss as many of you as had beards that pleased me, complexions that liked me, and breaths that I defied not; and I am sure, as many as have good beards, or good faces, or sweet breaths, will, for my kind offer, when I make curtsy, bid me farewell" (Epilogue 17–22). The audience knows he is not a woman, that he is a boy actor playing a woman's part. This becomes the most transgressive moment in the play because it suggests that the sport, whether athletic or erotic, takes place, both candidly and confidentially, between men, This is the social contradiction *As You Like It* addresses, placing cross-dressed heroines on the stage at the moment when they ceased to appear on the streets, thereby reinforcing the fact that its point of address was men, not women.

—ANNE HERRMANN, "Travesty and Transgression: Transvestism in Shakespeare, Brecht, and Churchill," *Theatre Journal* 41, No. 2 (May 1989): 135–40

CRITICAL ESSAYS

Harold C. Goddard

AS YOU LIKE IT

I

As You Like It is far from being one of Shakespeare's greatest plays, but it is one of his best-loved ones. "I know nothing better than to be in the forest," says a character in Dostoevsky, "though all things are good." We are in a forest, the Forest of Arden, during four-fifths of As You Like It, but it is a forest that by some magic lets in perpetual sunshine. And not only do we have a sense of constant natural beauty around us; we are in the presence, too, almost continuously, of a number of the other supremely good things of life, song and laughter, simplicity and love; while to guard against surfeit and keep romance within bounds, there is a seasoning of caustic and even cynical wit, plenty of foolishness as a foil for the wisdom, and, for variety, an intermingling of social worlds from courtiers and courtly exiles to shepherds and country bumpkins. In this last respect As You Like It repeats the miracle of A Midsummer-Night's Dream.

As might be expected of a work that is a dramatized version of a pastoral romance (Lodge's *Rosalynde*), the play is the most "natural" and at the same time one of the most artificial of the author's. Yet we so surrender ourselves after a little to its special tone and atmosphere that there is no other work of Shakespeare's in which coincidences, gods from the machine, and what we can only call operatic duets, trios, and quartettes trouble us less or seem less out of place. The snake and lioness that figure in Oliver's sudden conversion might be thought to be enough for one play, but when on top of that in the twinkling of an eye an old religious man turns the cruel usurping Duke, who is on the march with an army against his enemies, into a humble and forgiving hermit, instead of questioning the psychology we accept it meekly and merely observe inwardly that the magic of the Forest of Arden is evidently even more potent than we had supposed.

From *The Meaning of Shakespeare* (Chicago: University of Chicago Press, 1951), pp. 281–88, 291–93.

It is customary to find the main theme of *As You Like It* in the contrast between court and country. "If we present a pastoral," said Thomas Heywood, "we show the harmless love of shepherds, diversely moralized, distinguishing between the craft of the city and the innocency of the sheepcote." The play does indeed involve the question of the relative merits of these types of life, and the conclusion implied seems on the surface to be similar to George Meredith's in "Earth's Secret," namely, that wisdom is to be found in residents neither of the country nor of the city but in those rather who "hither thither fare" between the two,

Close interthreading nature with our kind.

But whoever goes no deeper than this does not get very near the heart of *As You Like It.* Shakespeare was the last person to believe that geography makes the man.

There is generally an Emersonian sentence that comes as close to summing up a Shakespearean play as anything so brief as a sentence can. "A mind might ponder its thought for ages and not gain so much self-knowledge as the passion of love shall teach it in a day." There, compressed, is the essence of *As You Like It,* and, positively or negatively, almost every scene in it is contrived to emphasize that truth. As *Love's Labour's Lost,* to which Emerson's sentence is almost equally pertinent, has to do with the relation of love and learning, *As You Like It* has to do with the relation of love and wisdom. Rosalind is the author's instrument for making clear what that relation is.

II

In no other comedy of Shakespeare's is the heroine so all-important as Rosalind is in this one; she makes the play almost as completely as Hamlet does *Hamlet.* She seems ready to transcend the rather light piece in which she finds herself and, if only the plot would let her, to step straight into tragedy. When Celia, in the second scene of the play, begs her cousin to be more merry, Rosalind, in the first words she utters, replies:

Dear Celia, I show more mirth than I am mistress of; and would you yet I were merrier?

I am not merry; but I do beguile
The thing I am by seeming otherwise,

says Desdemona on the quay at Cyprus and on the edge of her tragedy. The similarity is startling. It clinches, as it were, the impression Rosalind makes on those who admire her most: that she had it in her, in Cordelia's words, to outfrown a false fortune's frown than any she is called on to face in this comedy. In so far as she has, she is a transitional figure.

As You Like It has no lack of interesting characters, but most of them grow pretty thin in Rosalind's presence, like match flames in the sun. However less brilliant, Celia suffers less than she otherwise would because of her loyalty and devotion to her cousin and freedom from jealousy of her. Adam, Corin, and Rosalind's father are characters in their own right, but minor ones. Orlando at his best is thoroughly worthy of the woman he loves, but by and large she sets him in the shade. For the rest, Rosalind exposes, without trying to, their one-sidedness or inferiority, whether by actual contact or in the mind of the reader.

> Heaven Nature charg'd
> That one body should be fill'd
> With all graces. . . .

It is this wholeness of hers by which the others are tried, and in the comparison Touchstone himself (so named possibly for that very reason) fades into a mere manipulator of words, while that other favorite of the commentators, Jaques, is totally eclipsed.

III

One way of taking Jaques is to think of him as a picture, duly attenuated, of what Shakespeare himself might have become if he had let experience sour or embitter him, let his critical powers get the better of his imagination, "philosophy" of poetry. As traveler-libertine Jaques has had his day. Now he would turn spectator-cynic and revenge himself on a world that can no longer afford him pleasure, by proving it foul and infected. The more his vision is darkened the blacker, naturally, what he sees becomes in his eyes. He would withdraw from society entirely if he were not so dependent on it for audience. That is his dilemma. So he alternately retreats and darts forth from his retreat to buttonhole anyone who will listen to his railing. But when he tries to rationalize his misanthropy and pass it off as medicine for a sick world, the Duke Senior administers a deserved rebuke. Your very chiding of sin, he tells him, is "mischievous foul sin" itself.

Jaques prides himself on his wit and wisdom. But he succeeds only in proving how little wit and even "wisdom" amount to when indulged in for their own sakes and at the expense of life. His jests and "philosophy" give the effect of having been long pondered in solitude. But the moment he crosses swords with Orlando and Rosalind, the professional is hopelessly outclassed by the amateurs. Extemporaneously they beat him at his own carefully rehearsed game. Being out of love with life, Jaques thinks of nothing but himself. Being in love with Rosalind, Orlando thinks of himself last and has both the humility and the insight that love bequeaths. When the two men encounter, Jaques' questions and answers sound studied and affected, Orlando's spontaneous and sincere.

JAQ.: Rosalind is your love's name?
ORL.: Yes, just.
JAQ.: I do not like her name.
ORL.: There was no thought of pleasing you when she was christened.
JAQ.: What stature is she of?

> ORL.: Just as high as my heart.
> JAQ.: You are full of pretty answers. Have you not been acquainted with goldsmiths' wives, and conn'd them out of rings?
> ORL.: Not so; but I answer you right painted cloth, from whence you have studied your questions.
> JAQ.: You have a nimble wit: I think 'twas made of Atalanta's heels. Will you sit down with me? and we two will rail against our mistress the world, and all our misery.
> ORL.: I will chide no breather in the world but myself, against whom I know most faults.

There is not a trace of any false note in that answer. It has the ring of the true modesty and true wisdom that only true love imparts. Jaques, of course, misses the point diametrically:

> JAQ.: The worst fault you have is to be in love.
> ORL.: 'Tis a fault I will not change for your best virtue. I am weary of you.

(To tell the truth we are a bit weary of him too.)
And Rosalind outphilosophizes Jaques as utterly as Orlando has outjested him.

> JAQ.: I prithee, pretty youth, let me be better acquainted with thee.
> ROS.: They say you are a melancholy fellow.
> JAQ.: I am so; I do love it better than laughing.
> ROS.: Those that are in extremity of either are abominable fellows, and betray themselves to every modern censure worse than drunkards.
> JAQ.: Why, 'tis good to be sad and say nothing.
> ROS.: Why, then, 'tis good to be a post.
> JAQ.: I have neither the scholar's melancholy, which is emulation; nor the musician's . . .

and after enumerating seven different types of melancholy, he concludes,

> . . . but it is a melancholy of mine own, compounded of many simples, extracted from many objects; and indeed the sundry contemplation of my travels, in which my often rumination wraps me in a most humorous sadness—
> ROS.: A traveller! By my faith, you have great reason to be sad. I fear you have sold your own lands to see other men's; then, to have seen much, and to have nothing, is to have rich eyes and poor hands.
> JAQ.: Yes, I have gained my experience.
> ROS.: And your experience makes you sad. I had rather have a fool to make me merry than experience to make me sad; and to travel for it too!

Love bestows on those who embrace it the experience and wisdom of the race, compared with which the knowledge schools and foreign lands can offer is at the worst a mere counterfeit and at the best a mere beginning. What wonder that

Jaques, after being so thoroughly trounced by the pretty youth whose acquaintance he was seeking a moment before, is glad to sneak away as Orlando enters (what would they have done to him together?), or that Rosalind, after a "Farewell, Monsieur Traveller," turns with relief to her lover.

Even Jaques' most famous speech, his "Seven Ages of Man" as it has come to be called, which he must have rehearsed more times than the modern schoolboy who declaims it, does not deserve its reputation for wisdom. It sometimes seems as if Shakespeare had invented Adam (that grand reconciliation of servant and man) as Jaques' perfect opposite and let him enter this scene, pat, at the exact moment when Jaques is done describing the "last scene of all," as a living refutation of his picture of old age. How Shakespeare loved to let life obliterate language in this way! And he does it here prospectively as well as retrospectively, for the Senior Duke a second later, by his hospitable welcome of Adam and Orlando, obliterates or at least mitigates Amiens' song of man's ingratitude ("Blow, blow, thou winter wind") that immediately follows.

I V

When I read the commentators on Touchstone, I rub my eyes. You would think to hear most of them that he is a genuinely wise and witty man and that Shakespeare so considered him. That Shakespeare knew he could pass him off for that in a theater may be agreed. What he is another matter. A "dull fool" Rosalind calls him on one occasion. "O noble fool! a worthy fool!" says Jaques on another. It is easy to guess with which of the two Shakespeare came nearer to agreeing. The Elizabethan groundlings had to have their clown. At his best, Touchstone is merely one more and one of the most inveterate of the author's word-jugglers, and at his worst (as a wit) precisely what Rosalind called him. What he is at his worst as a man justifies still harsher characterization.

In her first speech after he enters the play in the first act, Rosalind describes him as "the cutter-off of Nature's wit," and his role abundantly justifies her judgment. "Thou speakest wiser than thou art ware of," she says to him on another occasion, and as if expressly to prove the truth of what she says, Touchstone obligingly replies, "Nay, I shall ne'er be ware of mine own wit till I break my shins against it." Which is plainly Shakespeare's conscious and Touchstone's unconscious way of stating that his wit is low. And his manners are even lower, as he shows when he first accosts Corin and Rosalind rebukes him for his rude tone:

TOUCH.:   Holla, you clown!
ROS.: Peace, fool; he's not thy kinsman.
COR.:   Who calls?
TOUCH.: Your betters, sir.
COR.:   Else are they very wretched.
ROS.: Peace, I say. Good even to you, friend.

Nothing could show more succinctly Rosalind's "democracy" in contrast to Touchstone's snobbery. (No wonder the people thought highly of her, as they did of Hamlet.) The superiority in wisdom of this "clown" to the man who condescends to him comes out, as we might predict it would, a little later.

> TOUCH.: Wast ever in court, shepherd?
> COR.: No, truly.
> TOUCH.: Then thou art damned.
> COR.: Nay, I hope.
> TOUCH.: Truly, thou art damned, like an ill-roasted egg, all on one side.

It is an almost invariable rule in Shakespeare, as it is in life, that when one man damns another, even in jest, he unconsciously utters judgment on himself, and the rest of the scene, like Touchstone's whole role, is dedicated to showing that he himself is his own ill-roasted egg, all "wit" and word-play and nothing else.

> COR.: For not being at court? Your reason.
> TOUCH.: Why, if thou never wast at court, thou never sawest good manners [*We have just had, and are now having, a sample of the manners of this "courtier" who greeted Corin as a "clown."*]; if thou never sawest good manners, then thy manners must be wicked; and wickedness is sin, and sin is damnation. Thou art in a parlous state, shepherd.

Corin may be a "silly" shepherd but he is not taken in by this silly verbal legerdemain. He stands up to his "better" stoutly:

> COR.: Not a whit, Touchstone: those that are good manners at the court, are as ridiculous in the country as the behaviour of the country is most mockable at the court,

and he illustrates by pointing out that the habit of kissing hands at court would be uncleanly among shepherds. Whereupon, as we might expect, Touchstone, forgetting his own rule that he who calls himself wise is a fool, cries "Learn of the wise," and descends to an even lower level of sophistry than before. Corin, sensing that it is futile to argue with such a man, refuses to continue, but refuses with a courtesy at the opposite pole from Touchstone's rudeness, and we suddenly realize that Shakespeare has contrived the whole episode as a refutation on the plane of life of the conclusion for which Touchstone is contending: that good manners are impossible for a countryman.

> COR.: You have too courtly a wit for me; I'll rest.

In reply to which we have an example of courtly wit and manners:

> TOUCH.: Wilt thou rest damned? God help thee, shallow man!

Shallow man! the best possible characterization of Touchstone himself at the moment. And as if to show by way of contrast what a deep man is, Shakespeare lets

Corin condense his life into a sentence which, if a sentence ever was, is a perfect blend of modesty and pride:

> COR.: Sir, I am a true labourer: I earn that I eat, get that I wear, owe no man hate, envy no man's happiness, glad of other men's good, content with my harm; and the greatest of my pride is to see my ewes graze and my lambs suck.

It is one of the tersest and one of the finest "creeds" to be found anywhere in Shakespeare, at the farthest possible remove from Touchstone's own which Jaques overheard and quoted. And with all his "wit" the only thing Touchstone can think up by way of retort is the taunt that Corin by his own confession is a "bawd" because, forsooth, he makes his living by the multiplication of his stock. A Hottentot would be ashamed of such reasoning, and as for the jocosity of it, it is close to Touchstone's "low," which is saying a good deal. To the crass animality and ribaldry of this courtier Shakespeare, with another of his sudden switches, instantly opposed the "sanctity" of the man whose very kisses are like "the touch of holy bread": Rosalind, as Ganymede, enters reading snatches of the verses her lover has been hanging or carving on the trees.

> Her worth, being mounted on the wind,
> Through all the world bears Rosalind,

verses which Touchstone, as we would expect, proceeds to parody in such choice lines as:

> If the cat will after kind,
> So be sure will Rosalind.

What wonder that Rosalind rebukes the man as a "dull fool" and tells him that, like a medlar, he will be rotten ere he is ripe. The simile is a manifest double allusion on Shakespeare's part, first, to Touchstone's own "ill-roasted egg" (the same idea under another image), and, second, to Touchstone's summary of human life:

> And so, from hour to hour we ripe and ripe,
> And then from hour to hour we rot and rot.

If we know anything about the man who through the mouth of Edgar in *King Lear* declared that "Ripeness is all," we know what he must have thought of this philosophy of Touchstone's. He must have thought it rotten—rotten not in any modern colloquial sense of the term but rotten in the full implication of the horticultural metaphor.

But even with all this mauling, Shakespeare is not done with Touchstone. Having demonstrated to the hilt that his wit instead of sharpening has dulled his wits, he proceeds to show that his wit has also withered his heart. It is in his interlude with Audrey that we see Touchstone at his moral nadir. It will be said, of course, that this episode is pure farce and that to take it seriously is to show lack of humor. The objection need disturb nobody but the man who makes it. For of all the strange things about this man William Shakespeare one of the most remarkable is the fact that he could contrive no scene so theatrical, no stage effect so comic or dialogue so nonsensical, as to protect himself from the insertion right in the midst of it of touches of nature scientific in their veracity. Such was the grip that truth seems to have had on him. ⟨...⟩

V

And Rosalind is wit with love, which is humor, humor being what wit turns into when it falls in love. But humor is almost a synonym for manysidedness and reconciliation of opposites, and in her versatility, her balance of body, mind, and spirit, Rosalind reminds us of no less a figure than Hamlet himself, the uncontaminated Hamlet. As there is a woman within the Prince of Denmark, so there is a man within this Duke's daughter, but never at the sacrifice of her dominant feminine nature. "Do you not know I am a woman? when I think, I must speak," she says to Celia. She changes color when she first suspects that the verses on the trees are Orlando's, and cries "Alas the day! what shall I do with my doublet and hose?" when the fact that he is in the Forest is confirmed. And she swoons when she hears he is wounded. Yes, Rosalind is a woman in spite of the strength and courage of the man within her. All of which makes her disguise as a boy immeasurably more than a merely theatrical matter.

> That you are fair or wise is vain,
> Or strong, or rich, or generous;
> You must add the untaught strain
> That sheds beauty on the rose.

So says Emerson (in lines enough in themselves to acquit him of being what he is often called, a "puritan"). Rosalind is all of these things: fair and wise and strong and rich (except in a worldly sense) and generous. But not in vain. For she has also, as her name betokens, the untaught strain that sheds beauty on a rose. The Forest of Arden, for all its trees, is, as we remarked, forever flooded with sunshine. There is no mystery about it. Rosalind is in the Forest and she supplies it with an internal light. "Be like the sun," says Dostoevsky. Rosalind is. She attracts everything that comes within her sphere and sheds a radiance over it. She is the pure gold that needs no touchstone.

Rosalind has the world at her feet not just for what she is but because, being what she is, she so conducts her love with Orlando as to make it a pattern for all true love-making. Unimaginative love, whether sentimental or overpassionate, overreaches and defeats itself because it cannot keep its secret. Intentionally or otherwise, it spills over—confesses or gives itself away. (Juliet is no exception: she admitted her love so soon only because Romeo had overheard her in soliloquy by accident.) The love of Silvius for Phebe and of Phebe for Ganymede in this play are examples. Imaginative love is wiser. Taking its cue from the arts, of which it is one and perhaps the highest, it creates a hypothetical case in its own image, a kind of celestial trap under cover of which (only the maddest mixture of metaphors can do it justice) it extorts an unconscious confession from the loved one, all the while keeping a line of retreat fully open in case the confession should be unfavorable, in order that no humiliation may ensue.

In this play Rosalind undertakes to cure Orlando of his love by having him come every day to woo her under the illusion that she is just the boy Ganymede impersonating Rosalind. Thus the love between the two is rehearsed in the kingdom of the imagination, where all true love begins, before any attempt is made to bring it down to the level of everyday life, a situation that permits both lovers to speak now as boldly, now as innocently, as though they were angels or children. (The only conceivable situation that could surpass it as a model of right love-making would be one where each of the lovers was simultaneously luring the other into a confession without that other being aware of what was happening.)

Again we are reminded of the Prince of Denmark. In *Hamlet* a literal play within the play becomes a device (inspired or infernal according to your interpretation of the play) whereby to catch the guilty conscience of a murderer. Here a metaphorical "play" within the play becomes a celestial trap in which to expose the tender heart of a lover. Heaven and hell are at opposite poles, but the one is a model of the other. "Upward, downward," says Heraclitus, "the way is the same." It is not chance that *As You Like It* and *Hamlet* were written not far apart in time.

Love between man and woman having the importance that it does in life, what wonder that a drama that depicts it in perfect action under its happiest aspect should be popular, even though not one in a hundred understands the ground of its fascination. How many a woman who sees or reads *As You Like It* either believes in secret that she does resemble Rosalind or wishes that she did! And how many a man projects on its heroine the image of the woman he loves best, or, if not, the memory of some lost first love who still embodies the purest instincts of his youth, and hears her voice instead of the words printed on the page! Which is why the imaginative man will always prefer to read the play rather than to have some obliterating actress come between the test and his heart. And so Rosalind is a sort of universal image of Woman as Sweetheart, just as Cressida is an image of Woman as Seductress, and Cleopatra of Woman, both good and evil, in a still more universal sense.

In her own way, and on a lower level, Rosalind contributes her mite to our understanding of why Dante chose the Rose as a symbol of the ultimate paradise.

C. L. Barber

SERIOUSNESS AND LEVITY IN *AS YOU LIKE IT*

The Liberty of Arden

The thing that asks for explanation about the Forest of Arden is how this version of pastoral can feel so free when the Duke and his company are so high-minded. Partly the feeling of freedom comes from release from the tension established in the first act at the jealous court:

<blockquote>

Now go we in content
To liberty, and not to banishment.   (I.iii.139–140)
</blockquote>

Several brief court scenes serve to keep this contrast alive. So does Orlando's entrance, sword in hand, to interrupt the Duke's gracious banquet by his threatening demand for food. Such behavior on his part is quite out of character (in Lodge he is most courteous); but his brandishing entrance gives Shakespeare occasion to resolve the attitude of struggle once again, this time by a lyric invocation of "what 'tis to pity and be pitied" (II.vii.117).

But the liberty we enjoy in Arden, though it includes relief from anxiety in brotherliness confirmed "at good men's feasts," is somehow easier than brotherliness usually is. The easiness comes from a witty redefinition of the human situation which makes conflict seem for the moment superfluous. Early in the play, when Celia and Rosalind are talking of ways of being merry by devising sports, Celia's proposal is "Let us sit and mock the good housewife Fortune from her wheel" (I.ii.34–35). The two go on with a "chase" of wit that goes "from Fortune's office to Nature's" (I.ii.43), whirling the two goddesses through many variations; distinctions between them were running in Shakespeare's mind. In Act II, the witty poetry which establishes the greenwood mood of freedom repeatedly mocks Fortune from her wheel by an act of mind which goes from Fortune to Nature:

From *Shakespeare's Festive Comedy: A Study of Dramatic Form and Its Relation to Social Custom* (Princeton: Princeton University Press, 1959), pp. 223–26, 229–39.

A fool, a fool! I met a fool i' th' forest, . . .
Who laid him down and bask'd him in the sun
And rail'd on Lady Fortune in good terms, . . .
"Good morrow, fool," quoth I. "No, sir," quoth he,
"Call me not fool till heaven hath sent me fortune."
And then he drew a dial from his poke,
And looking on it with lack-lustre eye,
Says very wisely, 'It is ten o'clock.
Thus we may see,' quoth he, 'how the world wags.
'Tis but an hour ago since it was nine,
And after one more hour 'twill be eleven;
And so, from hour to hour, we ripe and ripe,
And then, from hour to hour, we rot and rot;
And thereby hangs a tale.'   (II.vii.12–28)

Why does Jaques, in his stylish way, say that his lungs "began to crow like chanti-cleer" to hear the fool "thus moral on the time," when the moral concludes in "rot and rot"? Why do we, who are not "melancholy," feel such large and free delight? Because the fool "finds," with wonderfully bland wit, that nothing whatever happens under the aegis of Fortune. ("Fortune reigns in gifts of the world," said Rosalind at I.ii.44.) The almost tautological inevitability of nine, ten, eleven, says that all we do is ripe and ripe and rot and rot. And so there is no reason not to bask in the sun and "lose and neglect the creeping hours of time" (II.vii.112). As I observed in the introductory chapter, Touchstone's "deep contemplative" moral makes the same statement as the spring song towards the close of the play: "How that a life was but a flower." When they draw the moral, the lover and his lass are only thinking of the "spring time" as they take "the present time" when "love is crowned with the prime." (The refrain mocks them a little for their obliviousness, by its tinkling "the only pretty ring time.") But Touchstone's festive gesture is *not* oblivious.

The extraordinary thing about the poised liberty of the second act is that the reduction of life to the natural and seasonal and physical works all the more convincingly as a festive release by including a recognition that the physical can be unpleasant. The good Duke, in his opening speech, can "translate the stubbornness of fortune" into a benefit: he does it by the witty shift which makes the "icy fang / And churlish chiding of the winter's, wind" into "counsellors / That feelingly per-suade me what I am" (II.i.6–11). The two songs make the same gesture of wel-coming physical pain in place of moral pain:

Come hither, come hither, come hither!
    Here shall he see
    No enemy
But winter and rough weather.   (II.v.5–8)

They are patterned on holiday drinking songs, as we have seen already in consid-ering the Christmas refrain, "Heigh-ho, sing heigh-ho, unto the green holly," and they convey the free solidarity of a group who, since they relax in physical pleasures together, need not fear the fact that "Most friendship is feigning, most loving mere folly."

Jaques' speech on the seven ages of man, which comes at the end of Act II, just before "Blow, Blow, thou winter wind," is another version of the liberating talk about time; it expands Touchstone's "And thereby hangs a tale." The simplification, "All the world's a stage," has such imaginative reach that we are as much astonished as amused, as with Touchstone's summary ripe and rot. But simplification it is, nevertheless; quotations (and recitations) often represent it as though it were dramatist Shakespeare's "philosophy," his last word, or one of them, about what life really comes to. To take it this way is sentimental, puts a part in place of the whole. For it only is *one* aspect of the truth that the roles we play in life are settled by the cycle of growth and decline. To face this part of the truth, to insist on it, brings the kind of relief that goes with accepting folly—indeed this speech is praise of folly, superbly generalized, praise of the folly of living in time (or is it festive abuse? the poise is such that relish and mockery are indistinguishable). Sentimental readings ignore the wit that keeps reducing social roles to caricatures and suggesting that meanings really are only physical relations beyond the control of mind or spirit:

> Then a soldier, . . .
> Seeking the bubble reputation
> Even in the cannon's mouth. And then the justice,
> In fair round belly with good capon lin'd . . . (II.vii.149–154)

Looking back at time and society in this way, we have a detachment and sense of mastery similar to that established by Titania and Oberon's outside view of "the human mortals" and their weather.

"all nature in love mortal in folly"

I have quoted already in the Introduction a riddling comment of Touchstone which moves from acknowledging mortality to accepting the folly of love:

> We that are true lovers run into strange capers; but as all is mortal in nature, so is all nature in love mortal in folly. (II.iv.53–56)

The lovers who in the second half of the play present "nature in love" each exhibit a kind of folly. In each there is a different version of the incongruity between reality and the illusions (in poetry, the hyperboles) which love generates and by which it is expressed. The comic variations are centered around the seriously-felt love of Rosalind and Orlando. The final effect is to enhance the reality of this love by making it independent of illusions, whose incongruity with life is recognized and laughed off. We can see this at closer range by examining each affair in turn.

All-suffering Silvius and his tyrannical little Phebe are a bit of Lodge's version taken over, outwardly intact, and set in a wholly new perspective. A "courting eglogue" between them, in the mode of Lodge, is exhibited almost as a formal spectacle, with Corin for presenter and Rosalind and Celia for audience. It is announced as

> a pageant truly play'd
> Between the pale complexion of true love
> And the red glow of scorn and proud disdain.   (III.iv.55–57)

What we then watch is played "truly"—according to the best current convention: Silvius, employing a familiar gambit, asks for pity; Phebe refuses to believe in love's invisible wound, with exactly the literal-mindedness about hyperbole which the sonneteers imputed to their mistresses. In Lodge's version, the unqualified Petrarchan sentiments of the pair are presented as valid and admirable. Shakespeare lets us feel the charm of the form; but then he has Rosalind break up their pretty pageant. She reminds them that they are nature's creatures, and that love's purposes are contradicted by too absolute a cultivation of romantic liking or loathing: "I must tell you friendly in your ear, / Sell when you can! you are not for all markets" (III.v.59–60). Her exaggerated downrightness humorously underscores the exaggerations of conventional sentiment. And Shakespeare's treatment breaks down Phebe's stereotyped attitudes to a human reality: he lightly suggests an adolescent perversity underlying her resistance to love. The imagery she uses in disputing with Silvius is masterfully squeamish, at once preoccupied with touch and shrinking from it:

> 'Tis pretty, sure, and very probable
> That eyes, which are the frail'st and softest things,
> Who shut their coward gates on atomies,
> Should be call'd tyrants, butchers, murtherers!
> ,,, lean but upon a rush,
> The cicatrice and capable impressure
> Thy palm some moment keeps; but now mine eyes,
> Which I have darted at thee, hurt thee not,...   (III.v.11–25)

Rosalind, before whom this resistance melts, appears in her boy's disguise "like a ripe sister," and the qualities Phebe picks out to praise are feminine. She has, in effect, a girlish crush on the femininity which shows through Rosalind's disguise; the aberrant affection is happily got over when Rosalind reveals her identity and makes it manifest that Phebe has been loving a woman. "Nature to her bias drew in that" is the comment in *Twelfth Night* when Olivia is fortunately extricated from a similar mistaken affection.

Touchstone's affair with Audrey complements the spectacle of exaggerated sentiment by showing love reduced to its lowest common denominator, without any sentiment at all. The fool is detached, objective and resigned when the true-blue lover should be

> All made of passion, and all made of wishes,
> All adoration, duty, and observance.   (V.ii.101–102)

He explains to Jaques his reluctant reasons for getting married:

> JAQUES: Will you be married, motley?
> TOUCHSTONE: As the ox hath his bow, sir, the horse his curb, and the falcon her
>   bells, so man hath his desires; and as pigeons bill, so wedlock would be
>   nibbling.   (III.iii.79–83)

This reverses the relation between desire and its object, as experienced by the other lovers. They are first overwhelmed by the beauty of their mistresses, then impelled by that beauty to desire them. With Touchstone, matters go the other way about: he discovers that man has his troublesome desires, as the horse his curb; then he decides to cope with the situation by marrying Audrey:

> Come, sweet Audrey. We must be married, or we must live in bawdry.
>   (III.iii.98–99)

Like all the motives which Touchstone acknowledges, this priority of desire to attraction is degrading and humiliating. One of the hall-marks of chivalric and Petrarchan idealism is, of course, the high valuation of the lover's mistress, the assumption that his desire springs entirely from her beauty. This attitude of the poets has contributed to that progressively-increasing respect for women so fruitful in modern culture. But to assume that only one girl will do is, after all, an extreme, an ideal attitude: the other half of the truth, which lies in wait to mock sublimity, is instinct—the need of a woman, even if she be an Audrey, because "as pigeons bill, so wedlock would be nibbling." As Touchstone put it on another occasion:

> If the cat will after kind,
> So be sure will Rosalinde.   (III.ii.109–110)

The result of including in Touchstone a representative of what in love is unromantic is not, however, to undercut the play's romance: on the contrary, the fool's cynicism, or one-sided realism, forestalls the cynicism with which the audience might greet a play where his sort of realism had been ignored. We have a sympathy for his downright point of view, not only in connection with love but also in his acknowledgment of the vain and self-gratifying desires excluded by pastoral humility; he embodies the part of ourselves which resists the play's reigning idealism. But he does not do so in a fashion to set himself up in opposition to the play. Romantic commentators construed him as "Hamlet in motley," a devastating critic. They forgot, characteristically, that he is ridiculous: he makes his attitudes preposterous when he values rank and comfort above humility, or follows biology rather than beauty. In laughing at him, we reject the tendency in ourselves which he for the moment represents. The net effect of the fool's part is thus to consolidate the hold of the serious themes by exorcising opposition. The final Shakespearean touch is to make the fool aware that in humiliating himself he is performing a public service. He goes through his part with an irony founded on the fact (and it is a fact) that he is only making manifest the folly which others, including the audience, hide from themselves.

Romantic participation in love and humorous detachment from its follies, the two polar attitudes which are balanced against each other in the action as a whole, meet and are reconciled in Rosalind's personality. Because she remains always aware of love's illusions while she herself is swept along by its deepest currents, she possesses as an attribute of character the power of combining wholehearted feeling and undistorted judgment which gives the play its value. She plays the mocking reveller's role which Berowne played in *Love's Labour's Lost*, with the advantage of disguise. Shakespeare exploits her disguise to permit her to furnish the humorous commentary on her own ardent love affair, thus keeping comic and serious actions going at the same time. In her pretended role of saucy shepherd youth, she can mock at romance and burlesque its gestures while playing the game of putting Orlando through his paces as a suitor, to "cure" him of love. But for the audience, her disguise is transparent, and through it they see the very ardor which she mocks. When, for example, she stages a gayly overdone take-off of the conventional impatience of the lover, her own real impatience comes through the burlesque; yet the fact that she makes fun of exaggerations of the feeling conveys an awareness that it has limits, that there is a difference between romantic hyperbole and human nature:

ORLANDO: For these two hours, Rosalind, I will leave thee.

ROSALIND: Alas, dear love, I cannot lack thee two hours!

ORLANDO: I must attend the Duke at dinner. By two o'clock I will be with thee again.

ROSALIND: Ay, go your ways, go your ways! I knew what you would prove. My friends told me as much, and I thought no less. That flattering tongue of yours won me. 'Tis but one cast away, and so, come death! Two o'clock is your hour?   (IV.i.181–190)

One effect of this indirect, humorous method of conveying feeling is that Rosalind is not committed to the conventional language and attitudes of love, loaded as these inevitably are with sentimentality. Silvius and Phebe are her foils in this: they take their conventional language and their conventional feelings perfectly seriously, with nothing in reserve. As a result they seem naïve and rather trivial. They are no more than what they say, until Rosalind comes forward to realize their personalities for the audience by suggesting what they humanly are beneath what they romantically think themselves. By contrast, the heroine in expressing her own love conveys by her humorous tone a valuation of her sentiments, and so realizes her own personality for herself, without being indebted to another for the favor. She uses the convention where Phebe, being unaware of its exaggerations, abuses it, and Silvius, equally naïve about hyperbole, lets it abuse him. This control of tone is one of the great contributions of Shakespeare's comedy to his dramatic art as a whole. The discipline of comedy in controlling the humorous potentialities of a remark enables the dramatist to express the relation of a speaker to his lines, including the relation of naïveté. The focus of attention is not on the outward action of saying something but on the shifting, uncrystallized life which motivates what is said.

The particular feeling of headlong delight in Rosalind's encounters with Orlando goes with the prose of these scenes, a medium which can put imaginative effects of a very high order to the service of humor and wit. The comic prose of this period is first developed to its full range in Falstaff's part, and steals the show for Benedict and Beatrice in *Much Ado About Nothing*. It combines the extravagant linguistic reach of the early clowns' prose with the sophisticated wit which in the earlier plays was usually cast, less flexibly, in verse. Highly patterned, it is built up of balanced and serial clauses, with everything linked together by alliteration and kicked along by puns. Yet it avoids a stilted, Euphuistic effect because regular patterns are set going only to be broken to underscore humor by asymmetry. The speaker can rock back and forth on antitheses, or climb "a pair of stairs" (V.ii.42) to a climax, then slow down meaningly, or stop dead, and so punctuate a pithy reduction, bizarre exaggeration or broad allusion. T. S. Eliot has observed that we often forget that it was Shakespeare who wrote the greatest prose in the language. Some of it is in *As You Like It*. His control permits him to convey the constant shifting of attitude and point of view which expresses Rosalind's excitement and her poise. Such writing, like the brushwork and line of great painters, is in one sense everything. But the whole design supports each stroke, as each stroke supports the whole design.

The expression of Rosalind's attitude towards being in love, in the great scene of disguised wooing, fulfills the whole movement of the play. The climax comes when Rosalind is able, in the midst of her golden moment, to look beyond it and mock its illusions, including the master illusion that love is an ultimate and final experience, a matter of life and death. Ideally, love should be final, and Orlando is romantically convinced that his is so, that he would die if Rosalind refused him. But Rosalind humorously corrects him, from behind her page's disguise.

> . . . Am not I your Rosalind?
> ORLANDO: I take some joy to say you are, because I would be talking of her.
> ROSALIND: Well, in her person, I say I will not have you.
> ORLANDO: Then in mine own person, I die.
> ROSALIND: No, faith, die by attorney. The poor world is almost six thousand
>   years old, and in all this time there was not any man died in his own
>   person, videlicet, in a love cause. Troilus had his brains dash'd out with a
>   Grecian club; yet he did what he could to die before, and he is one of the
>   patterns of love. Leander, he would have liv'd many a fair year though
>   Hero had turn'd nun, if it had not been for a hot midsummer night; for
>   (good youth) he went but forth to wash him in the Hellespont, and being
>   taken with the cramp, was drown'd; and the foolish chroniclers of that
>   age found it was 'Hero of Sestos.' But these are all lies. Men have died
>   from time to time, and worms have eaten them, but not for love.'

ORLANDO: I would not have my right Rosalind of this mind, for I protest her
    frown might kill me.
ROSALIND: By this hand, it will not kill a fly!   (IV.i.90–108)

A note almost of sadness comes through Rosalind's mockery towards the end. It is
not sorrow that men die from time to time, but that they do not die for love, that
love is not so final as romance would have it. For a moment we experience as
pathos the tension between feeling and judgment which is behind all the laughter.
The same pathos of objectivity is expressed by Chaucer in the sad smile of Pandarus as he contemplates the illusions of Troilus' love. But in *As You Like It* the
mood is dominant only in the moment when the last resistance of feeling to
judgment is being surmounted: the illusions thrown up by feeling are mastered by
laughter and so love is reconciled with judgment. This resolution is complete by the
close of the wooing scene. As Rosalind rides the crest of a wave of happy fulfillment
(for Orlando's behavior to the pretended Rosalind has made it perfectly plain that
he loves the real one) we find her describing with delight, almost in triumph, not
the virtues of marriage, but its fallibility:

> Say 'a day' without the 'ever.' No, no, Orlando! Men are April when they
> woo, December when they wed. Maids are May when they are maids, but the
> sky changes when they are wives.   (IV.i.146–150)

Ordinarily, these would be strange sentiments to proclaim with joy at such a time.
But as Rosalind says them, they clinch the achievement of the humor's purpose.
(The wry, retarding change from the expected cadence at "but the sky changes" is
one of those brush strokes that fulfill the large design.) Love has been made
independent of illusions without becoming any the less intense; it is therefore
inoculated against life's unromantic contradictions. To emphasize by humor the
limitations of the experience has become a way of asserting its reality. The scenes
which follow move rapidly and deftly to complete the consummation of the love
affairs on the level of plot. The treatment becomes more and more frankly artificial,
to end with a masque. But the lack of realism in presentation does not matter,
because a much more important realism in our attitude towards the substance of
romance has been achieved already by the action of the comedy.

In writing of Marvell and the metaphysical poets, T. S. Eliot spoke of an
"alliance of levity and seriousness (by which the seriousness is intensified)." What he
has said about the contribution of wit to this poetry is strikingly applicable to the
function of Shakespeare's comedy in *As You Like It:* that wit conveys "a recognition,
implicit in the expression of every experience, of other kinds of experience which
are possible."[1] The likeness does not consist simply in the fact that the wit of certain
of Shakespeare's characters at times is like the wit of the metaphysicals. The crucial
similarity is in the way the humor functions in the play as a whole to implement a
wider awareness, maintaining proportion where less disciplined and coherent art
falsifies by presenting a part as though it were the whole. The dramatic form is very

different from the lyric: Shakespeare does not have or need the sustained, inclusive poise of metaphysical poetry when, at its rare best, it fulfills Cowley's ideal:

> In a true piece of Wit all things must be
>   Yet all things there agree.

The dramatist tends to show us one thing at a time, and to realize that one thing, in its moment, to the full; his characters go to extremes, comical as well as serious; and no character, not even a Rosalind, is in a position to see all around the play and so be completely poised, for if this were so the play would cease to be dramatic. Shakespeare, moreover, has an Elizabethan delight in extremes for their own sake, beyond the requirements of his form and sometimes damaging to it, an expansiveness which was subordinated later by the seventeenth century's conscious need for coherence. But his extremes, where his art is at its best, are balanced in the whole work. He uses his broad-stroked, wide-swung comedy for the same end that the seventeenth-century poets achieved by their wire-drawn wit. In Silvius and Phebe he exhibits the ridiculous (and perverse) possibilities of that exaggerated romanticism which the metaphysicals so often mocked in their serious love poems. In Touchstone he includes a representative of just those aspects of love which are not romantic, hypostatizing as character what in direct lyric expression would be an irony:

> Love's not so pure and abstract as they use
> To say who have no mistress but their muse.

By Rosalind's mockery a sense of love's limitations is kept alive at the very moments when we most feel its power:

> But at my back I always hear
> Time's winged chariot hurrying near.

The fundamental common characteristic is that the humor is not directed at "some outside sentimentality or stupidity," but is an agency for achieving proportion of judgment and feeling about a seriously felt experience.

As You Like It seems to me the most perfect expression Shakespeare or anyone else achieved of a poise which was possible because a traditional way of living connected different kinds of experience to each other. The play articulates fully the feeling for the rhythms of life which we have seen supporting Nashe's strong but imperfect art in his seasonal pageant. Talboys Dimoke and his friends had a similar sense of times and places when they let holiday lead them to making merry with the Earl of Lincoln; by contrast, the Puritan and/or time-serving partisans of Lincoln could not or would not recognize that holiday gave a license and also set a limit. An inclusive poise such as Shakespeare exhibits in Rosalind was not, doubtless, easy to achieve in any age; no culture was ever so "organic" that it would do men's living for them. What Yeats called Unity of Being became more and more difficult as the Renaissance progressed; indeed, the increasing difficulty of poise must have been a cause of the period's increasing power to express conflict and order it in art. We have seen this from our special standpoint in the fact that the everyday-holiday antithesis was most fully expressed in art when the keeping of holidays was declining.

The humorous recognition, in *As You Like It* and other products of this tradition, of the limits of nature's moment, reflects not only the growing consciousness necessary to enjoy holiday attitudes with poise, but also the fact that in English Christian culture saturnalia was never fully enfranchised. Saturnalian customs existed along with the courtly tradition of romantic love and an ambient disillusion about nature stemming from Christianity. In dramatizing love's intensity as the release of a festive moment, Shakespeare keeps that part of the romantic tradition which makes love an experience of the whole personality, even though he ridicules the wishful absolutes of doctrinaire romantic love. He does not found his comedy on the sort of saturnalian simplification which equates love with sensual gratification. He includes spokesmen for this sort of release in reduction; but they are never given an unqualified predominance, though they contribute to the atmosphere of liberty within which the aristocratic lovers find love. It is the latter who hold the balance near the center. And what gives the predominance to figures like Berowne, Benedict and Beatrice, or Rosalind, is that they enter nature's whirl consciously, with humor that recognizes it as only part of life and places their own extravagance by moving back and forth between holiday and everyday perspectives. Aristophanes provides a revealing contrast here. His comedies present experience entirely polarized by saturnalia; there is little *within* the play to qualify that perspective. Instead, an irony attaches to the whole performance which went with the accepted place of comedy in the Dionysia. Because no such clear-cut role for saturnalia or saturnalian comedy existed within Shakespeare's culture, the play itself had to place that pole of life in relation to life as a whole. Shakespeare had the art to make this necessity into an opportunity for a fuller expression, a more inclusive consciousness.

NOTES

[1] *Selected Essays, 1917–1932* (New York, 1932), pp. 255 and 262.

Walter R. Davis

THE HISTRIONICS OF LODGE'S *ROSALYNDE*

One element in the delicate poise that raises Lodge's *Rosalynde* a cut above the other Elizabethan pastoral romances is the way in which it manages to embody its theme in the net of puzzling disguises so essential to the machinery of a romance plot, instead of allowing them to remain separate (hence making one or the other extraneous) as the usual pastoralist did. Lodge's theme he received from the pastoral tradition; his way of embodying it was quite new.

The Renaissance pastoral romance formed a perfect vehicle for adjusting the actual and the ideal in life because it always placed the real and the ideal side-by-side (with the usual result of implying that the "real" was only apparent, the "ideal" really true). Its setting was always dual: it juxtaposed directly the actual world of human experience—whether stylized or naturalistically represented—to a kind of inner circle, a purified abstraction of that world, or "Arcady," often with a shrine or some supernatural place at its center to indicate its central purity. Thus we have, in Sannazaro's *Arcadia,* Naples against Arcadia, or in Montemayor's *Diana,* a stylized Spain against the pure fields of Ezla, and so forth. The inner pastoral circle represented, more or less concretely, a realization of more than usual possibilities in life, of the natural in accord with the ideal. Descriptive passages stress wonderment at the supernormal or supernatural quality of the natural world assimilated to some ideal of order, of the mutable expressing the permanent, as in this passage from Sidney's *Arcadia:*

> Do you not see how all things conspire to make this countrie a heavenly dwell-ing? Do you not see the grasse, how in colour they excell the Emeralds, every one striving to passe his fellow, and yet they are all kept of an equall height? . . . Certainely, certainely, cousin, it must neede be that some Goddesse inhabiteth this Region, who is the soule of this soyle: for neither is anie lesse then a God-desse, worthie to be shrined in such a heap of pleasures: or anie lesse than a Goddesse could have made it so perfect a plotte of the celestial dwellings,[1]

From *Studies in English Literature 1500–1900* 5, No. 1 (Winter 1965): 151–63.

or this from Lodge's *Rosalynde:*

> Round about in the forme of an Amphitheater were most curiouslie planted
> Pine trees, interseamed with Limons and Citrons, which with the thicknesse of
> their boughes so shadowed the place, that PHOEBUS could not prie into the
> secret of that Arbour; so united were the tops with so thicke a closure, that
> VENUS might there in her jollitie have dallied unseene with her deerest
> paramour.[2]

More generally, the supernatural showed itself in a strange cooperation of art
and nature, as in Sannazaro's cave of Pan, Centorio's fountain, Guarini's or Sidney's
central cave.[3] The plot of pastoral romance usually consisted of the hero's mere
experience of two worlds: his entrance into "Arcady" full of the pain and turmoil
he contracted in the actual world, his experience of calm self-analysis in the inner
pastoral circle, and his return to the outer world in harmony with himself. This
action really amounts to the hero's observation of himself in two contexts—an
actual and an ideal one—or to his living two lives, actual and possible; and this action
is symbolized by a pastoral disguise of the new self he assumes upon entering the
pastoral land. To this pattern correspond Sannazaro's *Arcadia*, Montemayor's *Diana*, Centorio's *L'Aura soave*, Gil Polo's *Diana enamorda*, and even Canto XIX of
Orlando Furioso. The most familiar examples of it in English are Shakespeare's *As
You Like It* and *The Winter's Tale* (along with is non-pastoral romance *The Tempest*), and Ben Jonson's strange oblique romance, *The New Inn*, Sidney's *Arcadia*,
Greene's *Pandosto*, and Book VI of *The Faerie Queene*.

It is important to realize that the English romances exhibit an emphasis new to
the pastoral romance tradition, and that is the explicit intellectualizing or moralizing
of the plot. Sidney is, of course, the first to show this trait; in his *Arcadia*, the setting
becomes openly expressive of values, of ideas; the inner circle becomes the realm
of love and contemplation, the violent world around it, the realm of heroic action.
Therefore his heroes fittingly discuss such matters as the active and contemplative
lives and the nature and operation of love before entering the pastoral retreat. And
in the other English works—even in the most unphilosophical of them—there is at
least an initial lecture about the values of humility or simplicity. Hence the pastoral
disguise signifies not only the discovery of a new aspect of the self, but the conscious acceptance of new values as well. Therefore it is no exaggeration to say that
in Elizabethan romances, the pastoral land is first and foremost a symbol of an
explicit ideal of a desirable state of mind, and that the purpose of the pastoral is to
dramatize a state of mind through correspondence of a man's life to his context.
Greene's Menaphon is able to rise to a sense of this fact:

> Content sitteth in thy minde as *Neptune* in his Sea-throne, who with his
> trident mace appeaseth everie storme. When thou seest the heavens frowne
> thou thinkest on thy faults, and a cleere skie putteth thee in minde of grace;
> the summers glorie tels thee of youths vanitie, the winters parched leaves of

ages declining weaknes. Thus in a myrrour thou measurest thy deedes with equall and considerate motions.[4]

Then the action of the hero in dressing himself as a shepherd and going to live in this land can best be defined as an exploration of his mind, especially touching the relation between what his mind is and the state it might achieve. This is what the action meant to a later pastoral moralist:

> When he went to the pond, Thoreau struck an attitude and did so deliberately, but his posturing was not to draw the attention of others to him, but rather to draw his attention more closely to himself. "I learned this at least by my experiment: that if one advances confidently in the direction of his dreams, and endeavors to live the life which he has imagined, he will meet with a success unexpected in common hours." ... *Walden*, subtitled "Life in the Woods," is not a simple and sincere account of a man's life, either in or out of the woods; it is an account of a man's journey into the mind. . . .[5]

The possibility of striking an attitude in order to clarify one's sense of one's self or position was even more available to the Elizabethans than to Thoreau. Popular prose, for instance, was permeated with histrionics, since the writer usually assumed a fictional situation in which he could confront his audience directly in order to demand their praise, direct asides to them—"Gentle Readers (looke you be gentle now since I have cald you so)"[6]—ask questions of them and give answers, threaten them, and so forth; the pamphleteer, in short, conceived of himself as an actor in a role:

> Hollow there, give me the beard I wore yesterday. O beware of a gray beard and a balde head; for if such a one doo but nod, it is right dudgin and deepe discretion. But soft, I must now make a grave speach.[7]

Then, too, one of the salient characteristics of the poetry of this period is its liberal use of masks, whether the poet is operating solely beneath the mask of pastoral swain or epic bard or Petrarchan lover, or whether within the poem the speaker assumes a mask only to drop it at the end for a fuller realization of his situation, as in *Astrophel and Stella* XLVII or LXXIV or Drayton's "Since there's no help." But more important to our interests here are the situations where the hero of drama or fiction conceives of himself as acting. D. A. Traversi has written that "there is a sense, common in Elizabethan stage heroes and villains, of the speaker playing up to a dramatically acceptable picture of himself";[8] and the Elizabethan stage is filled with characters who take on roles which distort their personalities meaningfully in the sense that they exaggerate or straiten their personalities in order to enable their real powers—Richard III, Othello, Kent and Edgar in *Lear*, Bosola in *The Duchess of Malfi*, Vindice in *The Revengers Tragedy*, for instance. We find this histrionic self-awareness in Euphuistic fiction too, where the extreme dichotomizing pressure frequently forces an act of choice into a decision to embrace one of two opposite dramatic roles, roles which have beneath them contrasting ethical bases. When Euphues decides to court Lucilla, his decision involves not only the betrayal of a friend for love but leaving the whole moral realm of his part as "The Friend" for the uncertain a-moral world of "The Passionate Man"; he must set the roles side-by-side and try to neutralize the dislogistic *exempla* of Tarquin and Paris which point to the role he will embrace. So too must Saladyne, near the beginning of *Rosalynde,* deliberately cast aside his proper role of natural son and protective elder brother for the role of self-loving villain (a role he is just as suddenly released from later) in order to pursue his purposes.

These considerations suggest that conscious artifice, the deliberate playing of a role through a mask, may be of the utmost importance, in Elizabethan literature, to the exploration of human possibilities. And it is Lodge's *Rosalynde* that utilizes histrionics in the interests of ethical clarification more fully than any other work of Elizabethan prose fiction, pastoral or otherwise.

Rosalynde makes nonsense of the usual easy distinctions between "realism" and "stylization" or "natural" and "artificial." Any pastoral work will do this; for while the pastoral land is always assumed to be free from the taints of man's arts, and hence "natural," it is also ideal, completely unreal—because no such natural state has ever existed since the Fall—and hence "artificial." The country will present a natural ideal artificially, the city the vices of artifice in stylization. But in *Rosalynde* the boundary between natural and artificial is blurred more radically and explicitly than in any other Elizabethan romance—so much so, in fact, as to make the blurring thematic. The forest of Arden is a world that never was, pure artifice; in descriptions of the scenery there, the natural is almost completely subordinated to artificial arrangement: "Passing thus on along, about midday they came to a Fountaine, compast with a grove of Cipresse trees, so cunninglie and curiouslie planted, as if some Goddesse had intreated Nature in that place to make her an Arbour...." (36)[9] The keynote here, as in other romances, is the supernormal status of real growing things corresponding to an ideal arrangement. Yet there is a contrary tendency in narrative style, for where country and city meet Lodge seems to have distinguished them by giving the former a more natural and colloquial diction and syntax, the latter higher diction with Euphuistic *similia* and schemes (as in the passage of transition on p. 50).

Furthermore, the expected divisions between "artificial" and "natural" do not apply to the cast of characters. They split, of course, into two groups: the native inhabitants of Arden like Coridon, Montanus, and Phoebe, and the disguised court people Rosalynde, Alinda, Rosader, and Gerismond. Yet to say that the first group acts and speaks "naturally" and the second "artificially" is a gross oversimplification. For one thing, there are degrees of artifice within each group. While the old shepherd Coridon comes as close as anyone in the Elizabethan romances to the actual sixteenth-century rustic, Montanus and Phoebe (whose upbringing is never shown to have been any different from Coridon's) conduct their affairs in the highest courtly style, replete with sonnets, postures, and Euphuistic talk. And while Rosader's conduct as disguised shepherd is totally stylized, Rosalynde's is not at all;

further, Gerismond's pose as a Robin Hood figure allows him to exist in the relaxed greenwood milieu of vigor and plenty.

The presence of degrees of artifice within each group allows some rather surprising crossings between groups; for instance, the disguised king Gerismond playing his role is less stylized in his deeds and speech than the native Montanus and Phoebe. Rosader's and Montanus's approaches to love operate on the same high level, their poetic styles are indistinguishable, and they speak the same Euphuistic prose—this in spite of the fact that one of them is a nobleman playing a part while the other is a shepherd simply being himself. Or, to take a more radical example, Rosalynde is the most fully disguised person in the plot—first as page, then as pastoral swain—yet her actions are the least stylized, the most spontaneous and free from conventional forms. In Arden she shows more wit and common sense than anyone else; beneath her mask she can approach her love for Rosader directly and humorously, reject Phoebe with dispatch and a homely image, and manage a dénouement with delight and tact. Furthermore, her speech approaches the colloquial in diction and syntax more closely than anyone else's in the book; here for example is her way of handling Rosader: "How now Forrester, have I not fitted your turn? Have I not plaide the woman handsomely, and shewed my selfe as coy in graunts, as courteous in desires, and been as full of suspition, as men of flatterie? and yet to salve all, jumpt I not up with the sweete union of love?" In fact, we find that the disguised characters who deliberately swathe themselves in artifice are no more stylized than the undisguised characters, and frequently act with less attention to conventions and codes than the others. It is perhaps less a matter of who you are and where you come from than where you are and what you are doing at present. This consideration leads us to the interesting hypothesis that for Lodge a conscious pose may be a way of being "natural."

Since it is a place—Arden—that determines the pose, we may be better able to discern the function of the pose in *Rosalynde* after inspecting the major differences in values inherent in its two settings, the city of Bordeaux and the countryside of Arden. For though the manners and the styles of the court and country are not clearly distinguished, the significant ideas for which they stand are. For one thing, different kinds of events happen to people in Bordeaux and Arden. Since Bordeaux is in the hands of a usurper, it is fittingly the realm of division and strife, where Torismond has banished Gerismond and later banishes Rosalynde and his own daughter, and then oppresses Saladyne, who likewise has forced his brother into exile; where death rules over Sir John of Bordeaux and the victims of the Norman wrestler; and where constant violence erupts between brothers. The state of Arden under the true kind is, in direct contrast, a place of union and mutual aid: Adam helps Rosader; Rosader saves Adam with the aid of Gerismond, who prevents them both from starving; Rosader saves Saladyne, Saladyne then saves Rosader; Rosalynde helps Montanus, and so forth. The values that cause these events appear clearly in Sir John's legacy at the opening of the book:

> Climbe not my sonnes; aspiring pride is a vapour that ascendeth hie, but soone turneth to a smoake: they which have deep rootes, and poore Cottages great

patience. Forstare at the Starres, stumble upon stones. . . . Low shrubbes tune loks ever upward, and envie aspireth to nestle with dignitie. Take heed my sonnes, the meane is the sweetest melodie; . . . levell your thoughts to be loyall to your Prince. (I I)

As his terms show, the court is ruled by the selfish pride later exhibited by Torismond and Saladyne, while the country exhibits the humility which opens the way to love and giving: Montanus's generosity in giving up Phoebe to Ganimede or Gerismond's largesse proceeding from his content "with a simple Cottage, and a troupe of revelling Woodmen for his traine." One very practical result of the contrasting values is that Bordeaux denies sustenance to the needy while Arden is the inn where homely food is given to all who ask, whether it be at Gerismond's banquet or Alinda's cottage supper. Another is the restriction of natural desires—and hence their complication—in the city as against the peculiar liberty which allows one to act as he feels in the country. The contrast is felt especially in regard to love: in the city Rosader's love for Rosalynde was obscured by his familial misfortunes, while the country allows him free expression and even offers trees to hang sonnets from; Rosalynde's love at court is complicated by her position—"But consider ROSALIND his fortunes, and thy present estate"—while in the freedom of Arden she can even become the wooer. Alinda relates the difference between city and country love to appearance and reality:

> But sir our countrey amours are not like your courtly fancies, nor is our wooing like your suing: for poore shepheards never plaine them til Love paine them, where the Courtiers eyes is full of pasison when his heart is most free from affection; they court to discover their eloquence, we wooe to ease our sorrowes; (108)

and she is right, for pride is the result of man's illusions fostered by dumb fortune, whereas humility represents the actual nature of humankind.

Two recurring terms, each involving both personal and cosmic application, will help us to take the contrast to the general level; they are Fortune, referring both to individual luck and the Goddess Fortuna, and Nature, meaning both one's human nature and the Creation. Bordeaux is the realm of Fortune, Arden the realm of Nature. The forces are not exclusive, but rather interact differently in each place; in the one Fortune suppresses Nature, in the other Nature operates freely to overcome Fortune (just as, in the beginning of the pastoral tradition, Virgil's eclogues demonstrated that human suffering was ameliorated by the influence of the natural world). In the city Fortune tempts Saladyne into villainy with her promises, makes love impossible for Rosalynde, and keeps Rosader's natural nobility obscure, causing him to exclaim:

> Nature hath lent me wit to conceive, but my brother denied me arte to contemplate . . . those good partes that God hath bestowed upon me, the harder is my fortune, and the more his frowardnesse. (17)

Nature can emerge here only in acts of extreme jeopardy—such as Rosader's wrestling or his defense of the manor against law and order—or in flight. In Arden,

Fortune frequently smiles, as when she leads Rosader to Gerismond, Rosalynde to Rosader, or Rosader to Saladyne;[10] when she does not, as when she seeks "to have a bout" with the lovers by the instrumentality of the outlaws, she is so successfully defeated by the brotherly nature of Saladyne and Rosader that she turns "her frowne into a favour" (92).

What Arden "means" is that in the natural world (the world as it was intended to be at the Creation, totally unlike what it has become) one's true human nature emerges. Saladyne's nature is not really villainous (as Torismond's is); therefore, upon awakening from his dangerous dream beneath the lion to find himself confronted by Rosader in Arden, he suddenly asks his brother for forgiveness and reforms. And his subsequent life in Arden, playing the part of a swain and wooing Alinda, is expressive of his true generous nature in a way that his "real-life" status as landowner and elder brother was not. The same is true of Rosader as a forester acting out his loyalty to his outlaw king and giving full vent to his loyalty to his supposedly absent mistress, or of Rosalynde playing the witty downright swain, or of Gerismond or Alinda. Each of the roles, it should be noticed, transforms the merely private state of those who have lost their place in society into a positive ideal of unrestricted action. To return to the hypothesis I proposed a few pages back: it is in this way that, for Lodge, any disguise or conscious role which enables a character to adjust his life to the world of human and cosmic Nature becomes, in effect, a means for expressing his true nature.

A consideration of Lodge's plot-structure will extend our understanding of the relation between the ideal and the disguise. The plot of any pastoral romance is essentially defined by the movement out of the civilized world into the pastoral world; in *Rosalynde* this amounts to leaving the realm of pride, discord, and a human nature distorted by the appearances of Fortune for the land of humility, love, and true nature. As in so many pre-novelistic fictions, the plot is multiple. We have first the "envelope-plot" of Gerismond and Torismond: the selfish brother usurps the good brother's throne and drives him to Arden, where he recovers, reconstructs a government on the natural Robin Hood model, and emerges to reinstate himself. The Saladyne-Rosader plot reinforces this one by parallel on the private level: the avaricious elder brother first oppresses and then exiles the good brother, but then repents in response to his generosity, helps and reinstates him. The main amorous plot of Rosader and Rosalynde shows how love, dampened by the reversals of Fortune under selfish repressors (Saladyne and Torismond) arises whole, fresh, and triumphant in the natural world. The two other love plots expand this one: the Saladyne-Alinda plot parallels it but emphasizes social and economic conditions; the Montanus-Phoebe plot shows the separation of lovers because of Phoebe's pride yielding to union by Montanus's triumphant humility and Rosalynde's charity. All five plots are of course individual variations on the single theme of separation brought about by selfishness yielding to union by means of love, which arises so "naturally" in Arden. Or as Lodge himself puts it:

Heere Gentlemen may you see in EUPHUES GOLDEN LEGACIE, that ... division in Nature as it is a blemish in nurture, so tis a breach of good fortunes; that vertue is not measured by birth but by action; that yonger brethren though inferiour in yeares, yet may be superiour to honours; that concord is the sweetest conclusion, and amitie betwixt brothers more forceable than fortune. (139)

Lodge wove his five variations together in a way most proper to his theme. He divided his book structurally into two parts, separation and reconstruction. The first part, as befits the theme of separation, proceeds by large separate sections of parallel plotting, a series of extrusions from the City to the Forest like that of *King Lear*—first Rosalynde's banishment, then Rosader's escape, then Saladyne's exile (Gerismond's banishment is anterior to the book's opening). The second part, in keeping with the growth of unity, proceeds by much closer interweaving, as Rosader, Saladyne, Alinda, Montanus, Phoebe, and Rosalynde approach their unions in the climactic scene at the end.

Now the hinge on which the plot turns is the *rapprochement* of Rosader and Rosalynde; and that occurs in a delicate interlude at the exact structural center, just after the final extrusion of Saladyne and immediately preceding the first movement toward reconciliation, Rosader's discovery of Saladyne and the lion. The central interlude is the most detached and stylized incident in the whole book; its language is heightened, for it is in verse, in a "wooing eclogue," that they come together; and while Rosader is merely operating out of his woodland pose, though in verse, Rosalynde is stalking behind a whole system of masks—Rosalynde as Ganimede "playing" Rosalynde. Yet it seems that the very masking of identities and feelings is the only condition under which true feelings can come to light; for on this level Rosalynde feels that she can set aside maidenly modesty and act out the truth. Therefore the wooing eclogue begins by Rosader's frank persuasions matched by "Ganimede's" equally frank fears, proceeds to stichomuythia, and ends in a harmony marked by the intimate sharing of a broken stanza:

ROSADER: Oh gaine more great than kingdomes, or a crowne.
ROSALYNDE: Oh trust betraid if *Rosader* abuse me.
ROSADER: First let the heavens conspire to pull me downe,
And heaven and earth as abject quite refuse me.
Let sorrowes streame about my hateful bower,
And restlesse horror hatch within my brest,
Let beauties eye afflict me with a lowre,
Let deepe despaire pursue me without rest;
Ere *Rosalynde* my loyaltie disprove.
Ere *Rosalynde* accuse me for unkinde.
ROSALYNDE: Then *Rosalynde* will grace thee with her love,
Then *Rosalynde* will have thee still in minde.
ROSADER: Then let me triumph more than *Tithons* deere,
Since *Rosalynde* will *Rosader* respect:

Then let my face exile his sorrie cheere,
And frolicke in the comfort of affect:
    And say that *Rosalynde* is onely pitifull,
    Since *Rosalynde* is onely beautifull.   (79–80)

Questions about the relation of fact to fiction come to center on this eclogue. Before entering on it Rosalynde had tested the degrees of conventionality and sincerity in Rosader's love by this pretext:

> I pray thee tell me Forrester, what is this ROSALYNDE, for whom thou pinest away in such passions? Is shee some Nymph that waits upon DIANAES traine, whose chastitie thou hast decyphred in such Epethetes? Or is she some shepheardesse that haunts these plaines, whose beautie hath so bewitched thy fancie, whose name thou shaddowest in covert under the figure of ROSA-LYNDE, as OVID did JULIA under the name of CORINNA? Or say mee for sooth, is it that ROSALYNDE, of whome, we shepheards have heard talke, shee Forrester, that is the Daughter of GERISMOND, that once was King, and now an Outlaw in this Forest of *Arden.* (62–63)

and the issue of the eclogue is, ironically, to turn fiction into fact:

> and thereupon (quoth ALIENA) Ile play the priest, from this day forth GANI-MEDE shall call thee husband, and thou shalt call GANIMEDE wife, and so weele have a marriage. Content (quoth ROSADER) and laught. Content (quoth GANIMEDE) and changed as redde as a rose: and so with a smile and a blush they made up this jesting match, that after proovde to a marriage in earnest; ROSADER ful little thinking he had wooed and wonne his ROSA-LYNDE. (81)

Here in the wooing-eclogue, "fact" and "fiction," the "real" and the "ideal" merge, just as the restricted real-life status of Rosader the youngest son of Sir John and Rosalynde the lost daughter of a deposed king blend into the larger dimensions of themselves which the roles of open rural lover and saucy swain (which may be characterized as the free dream-personalities of the lost) allow. Such is the idealism of Lodge's book, assuming as it does that a more idealistic version of the self is also a truer version of the self, that to raise the situation by masks to a level of supernormal freedom and ingenuousness is also to give its problem more real and lasting solutions than would be otherwise possible. Hence, the wooing eclogue is the symbolic watershed of a plot where the problems of the unnatural "real" world become solved easily by a series of appeals to the true, natural, and "ideal" nature of each character. And the action of the eclogue is synecdochic of the entire plot where one takes up a pose that expresses his real nature (allowing him freedom and loyalty, hence natural love), comes to terms with himself and others in that pose, and eventually drops it by returning to quotidian life. As the lovers use a formal song to test their love, so the whole of *Rosalynde* uses fictional roles as means for testing the availability of an ideal of human conduct.

Lodge, like Sidney, attempted to explore and extend the possibilities of human existence; his thesis, the possibility he explored, was that the world as we know it, with its selfishness and violence, is only the apparent world, whereas the real world is something we never see, an ideal of humility and love. Such a thesis presupposed a Platonic view of reality, and in order to test it Lodge created for each of his major characters and artificial role of ideal generosity or humility or self-sacrifice. W. B. Yeats wrote in his *Autobiography,*

> There is a relation between discipline and the theatrical sense. If we cannot imagine ourselves as different from what we are and assume that second self, we cannot impose a discipline upon ourselves, though we may accept one from others. Active virtue as distinguished from the passive acceptance of a current code is therefore theatrical, consciously dramatic, the wearing of a mask.[11]

I believe that something like this is presented in *Rosalynde:* in order to escape the heartless current codes of Bordeaux, each character enters Arden under a conscious mask, finds his true self and thus achieves meaningful discipline. Each of them therefore finds his proper nature by acting it out dramatically. Saladyne, in acting out the part of a humble and loyal forester, discovers the true nature of an elder brother in protection and self-sacrifice. Rosalynde, in acting out the role of the open and charitable swain, finds for herself the true part of the lover in frank and direct giving. And Gerismond acts out as Robin Hood the true nature of kingship, in giving sustenance to his subjects.

NOTES

[1] *Arcadia,* folio of 1508, pp. 31–32

[2] *Rosalynde,* in the Hunterian Club ed. of Lodge's *Works* by Edmund Gosse, 4 vols. (Glasgow, 1883), Vol. I, part 5, 39.

[3] See Sannazaro, *Arcadia,* ed. Michele Scherillo (Turin, 1888), p. 195; Ascanio Centorio, *L'Aura soave* (Venice, 1556), p. 11; Guarini, *Il pastor fido,* trans. Fanshawe (London, 1647), p. 104; Sidney, *Arcadia,* ed. of 1598, p. 337.

[4] *Menaphon,* ed. Edward Arber (The English Scholar's Library of Old and Modern Works, 12: London, 1880), p. 24. See also the song "O sweet woods" at the end of the Second Eclogues in Sidney's *Arcadia.*

[5] E. B. White, "*Walden*—1954," *The Yale Review,* XLIV (1954), 15, 16.

[6] Nashe, *The Unfortunate Traveller* in *Works,* ed. R. B. McKerrow, 5 vols. (London, 1904–10), II, 217.

[7] Lyly, *Pappe with an Hatchet* in *Works,* ed. R. Warwick Bond, 3 vols. (Oxford, 1902), III, 403.

[8] D. A. Traversi, *Shakespeare: The Last Phase* (London, 1954), p. 7

[9] All quotations from *Rosalynde* are from the Hunterian Club ed. of Lodge's *Works* by Gosse; parenthetical references are to pages in Vol. I, part 5.

[10] See pp. 56, 62, and 83.

[11] Yeats, *Autobiography* (New York, 1938), pp. 400–401.

Edward I. Berry

ROSALYNDE AND ROSALIND

Thomas Lodge's *Rosalynde*, the narrative source of *As You Like It*, provides a particularly instructive guide to Shakespeare's play. As a coherent, engaging, yet thoroughly conventional work, *Rosalynde* enables us to define with unusual precision some of the differences between skill and genius. Critics have drawn upon it to highlight many distinctive features of *As You Like It:* its structural integrity, its thematic and linguistic richness, its moral seriousness, its complex development of romantic and pastoral conventions.[1] A reading of Lodge, I believe, also illuminates Shakespeare's conception of his main character, Rosalind. A comparison of the two heroines allows us to observe the means by which a successful narrative role is transformed into a great dramatic one, to appreciate aspects of Rosalind's characterization that critics have generally ignored, and to discover, in Rosalind's experience, a dynamic that shapes the play as a whole.

In a broad sense Shakespeare seems to have found in Lodge's Rosalynde everything he needed for his own. He alters little in the narrative that directly affects his heroine. In both versions Rosalind falls in love at first sight, is banished into Arden, discovers her beloved in the forest, and engages, while disguised, in a game of courtship with him; in both Rosalind reveals herself to her father and lover in a climactic scene before returning to a renewed court to be married. The characterization of Lodge's Rosalynde is also remarkably similar to Shakespeare's. The vivacity, wit, romantic yearning, and delight in disguise are all present, at least embryonically, in Lodge. Shakespeare's obvious dependence upon Lodge for so many details makes his departures from the source all the more striking and significant. He changes little but with great effect.

I

To begin with the obvious, Shakespeare makes Rosalind the protagonist. She stands so firmly at the enter of the play that the history of its criticism seems in large

From *Shakespeare Quarterly* 31, No. 1 (Spring 1980): 42–52.

part an attempt to explain from different critical perspectives the preeminence of her role. For John Dover Wilson, who tempers somewhat a long tradition of Victorian effusions, she is simply Shakespeare's "ideal woman."[2] For Peter G. Phialas she synthesizes the play's "different and even conflicting attitudes to love" and thereby expresses "Shakespeare's comic approach or attitude to the human situation."[3] For C. L. Barber she maintains an "inclusive poise" of the kind achieved by the whole play.[4] For David Young she "comes to embody the ideals of love and the values of pastoral."[5] For Margaret Boerner Beckman, she "is a seemingly impossible reconciliation of opposites."[6] Whatever the individual merits of these varied perspectives—and we will observe later a collective limitation—they all testify to the centrality of Rosalind's role, and they could not apply to her source. Despite his work's title, Lodge gives his Rosalynde no such importance; she is nearly indistinguishable from Alinda (Celia), whose courtship is given almost equal attention. A comparison with Lodge thus underlines a distinctive feature of the mature comedies and histories—the presence of a central character whose consciousness takes in the central problems of his or her play. Studies of Prince Hal as a character who reconciles oppositions and mediates between extremes often sound like descriptions of Rosalind.

Shakespeare increases not only the stature of Rosalind but her scope. The addition of Touchstone and Jaques to Lodge's story extends the role of the heroine considerably. When Rosalind jests with Touchstone or, better, endures his jests at her and her lover's expense, as in his parody of Orlando's verses, the effect is not only to complicate the comedy of the play but to extend the range of her character. The same is true of her brief encounter with Jaques: "And your experience makes you sad. I had rather have a fool to make me merry than experience to make me sad—and to travel for it too!'" (IV. i. 27–29).[7] Touchstone and Jaques serve as foils to Rosalind, setting off her distinctive qualities. But their presence also adds more subtly to our impression of her psychological richness and poise. In drama as in life, it seems, our appreciation of complexity in character increases with the variety of relationships against which it is defined. The two Rosalinds may share a propensity to playfulness and wit, but the diverse sounding boards provided by Shakespeare create resonances that lie outside Lodge's range.

If Shakespeare enriches Rosalind's character by complicating her social environment, he also enlarges the role symbolically. As the director and "busy actor" (III. iv. 60) in her own "play," and the Epilogue in Shakespeare's, Rosalind becomes in a sense a figure for the playwright himself, a character whose consciousness extends in subtle ways beyond the boundaries of the drama. As a magician, moreover (and Shakespeare alone gives her magical powers),[8] she has a capacity that exceeds even Prospero's: an ability to surprise her audience. When as Ganymed she calls the lovers into her magic circle and promises them fulfillment in love, we rest secure in comic anticipation; all that remains is for her to appear, as she does in Lodge, in her proper attire. When she next enters, however, it is with still music and the god Hymen. Even more mysteriously than Prospero, she can bring down a god to sanction her festivities. Efforts to explain away the appearance of Hymen, as if he were merely Adam or some forester decked out by Rosalind, seem wide of the mark, since the mystery seems integral to the play and adds so effectively to the audience's sense of wonder. At its climax the play becomes a masque-ritual, and Rosalind, the poet-magician, its high priestess. The alias Ganymed, which Lodge includes but only Shakespeare exploits, complements this symbolic extension of the role; for as Rosalind says, Ganymed is "Jove's own page" (I. iii. 124). In the history plays, which develop the mystique of kingship, thee hints of transcendental power in the protagonist seem almost inevitable. In the romantic comedies, as the contrast between the two Rosalinds suggests, the symbolic extension seems to be Shakespeare's distinctive variation on the theme of Petrarchan idealization.

The actresses who have made the role peculiarly their own, however, have attended less to its hints of the supernatural than to its richly human emotional range. Audrey Williamson, who found Edith Evans' Rosalind "the loveliest Shakespearean performance by an actress in approaching twenty years of play going," was most impressed by the variety and volatility of her emotions: "She was wayward and gay, grave and loving, in an instant; as changing in moods as an April day, yet with a glow at the heart as bright as Juliet's own."[9] We can recognize in much of this description not only Shakespeare's Rosalind but Lodge's; the essential difference lies in the phrase "in an instant." For what impresses us about Shakespeare's heroine, and differentiates her from Lodge's, is a compression of thought and feeling that makes her every exchange a rich psychological event. The distinction is a subtle one, but perhaps a close look at a single episode, that in which Rosalind falls in love (I. ii.), will help to make it clear.

II

In both versions Rosalind falls in love at the Duke's wrestling match. In Lodge's narrative Rosalynde and Rosader (Orlando) fall in love without even exchanging words; Rosalynde's armorous glances alone give Rosader enough strength to defeat the Norman wrestler. As a token of her love, Rosalynde takes a jewel from her neck and sends it after Rosader, who replies in kind with a sonnet. In *As You Like It* the characters converse, however haltingly, and the jewel becomes a chain given in person. The differences are significant in several ways. Shakespeare's version is obviously more dramatic, but is also more symbolic, since the golden chain becomes by the end of the play a bond of love that unites not only Rosalind and Orlando but, in Hymen's song, earth and heaven. More important from the point of view of psychology is the fact that in giving the chain Shakespeare's Rosalind has far more on her mind than Lodge's. Shakespeare creates this psychological density not so much by what the character says, though that is part of it, but by complicating the situation to which she must respond and thus generating pressures beneath the words.

In Lodge's account there is little preparation for Rosalynde's declaration of love. When she sends her jewel to Rosader, we know only that she is remarkably beautiful (Lodge describes her in a set piece), that her father has been banished, and that she had been trading amorous glances with Rosader at the wrestling match. The state of mind in which she sends the jewel typifies Lodge's conventionality: "she accounted love a toye, and fancie a momentarie passion, that as it was taken in with a gaze, might bee shaken off with a winck; and therefore feared not to dallie in the flame" (p. 172). Although Rosalind is genuinely "touched" by Rosader's "beautie and valour" (p. 172), her gift expresses only a naive flirtatiousness. The psychology is conventional, but not unnatural.

In *As You Like It* Shakespeare prepares for the meeting of the lovers by introducing Rosalind and Celia briefly prior to the wrestling match. The episode serves the usual expository purposes, but it also sets in motion psychological currents that complicate and intensify Rosalind's eventual response to Orlando. Rosalind enters the play melancholy for her banished father. "I pray thee Rosalind, sweet my coz, be merry" (I. ii. 1–2) are Celia's opening words. Shakespeare's first gesture, then, is to open up areas of feeling that Lodge never explores."[10] When Celia tries to snap her out of her melancholy, the game Rosalind proposes is that of "falling in love" (1. 25). That she considers love a sport reminds us of Lodge's Rosalynde, who "dallies" with its flame, but that the sport serves as a psychological defense against melancholy shows how far Shakespeare goes beyond the conventional psychology of Lodge.

When Rosalind actually falls in love, moreover, the reality, like the game, is intertwined with her love for her father. The bond between Duke Senior and the dead Sir Rowland ties Rosalind immediately to Orlando:

> My father lov'd Sir Rowland as his soul,
> And all the world was of my father's mind.
> Had I before known this young man his son,
> I should have given him tears unto entreaties,
> Ere he should thus have ventur'd.   (II. 235–39)

What we witness in this episode, then, is not a sudden, inexplicable passion, but a subtle psychological modulation from one kind of love, one kind of yearning, to another. And Rosalind's love for Orlando, like that for her father, is complicated by melancholy. For because Duke Frederick and Sir Rowland are enemies—as they are not in Lodge—Rosalind gives her chain to Orlando with little hope of fulfillment: "Wear this for me: one out of suits with Fortune, / That could give more but that her hand lacks means" (II. 246–47). In Lodge, by contrast, nothing stands between the lovers until Rosalind's banishment.

By altering a few details, then, Shakespeare creates in Rosalind's falling in love a dramatic moment of considerable psychological and emotional complexity. Though not without playfulness, Shakespeare's Rosalind is hardly "dallying" with love. With a subtle emotional logic, her yearning for a banished father is transformed into a passion for the son of her father's friend, who is himself beyond her reach. The modulation not only intensifies and enriches the emotion of the scene, providing several kinds of feeling in an instant, but helps to make it psychologically

credible. If Shakespeare is conventional in giving us love at first sight, he is exceptional in providing a convincing psychology behind the convention.

Having introduced the motif of parental love, Shakespeare does not let it
drop. In the brief exchange between Rosalind and Celia immediately after Rosalind
has fallen in love—a scene that has no counterpart in Lodge—Celia's opening brings
us back to Rosalind's melancholy: "Why, cousin, why, Rosalind! Cupid have mercy,
not a word?" (I. iii. 1–2). This time, as Celia's needling makes clear, Rosalind's
melancholy derives from a different source: "But is all this for your father?" (I. 10).
Rosalind's witty reply—"No, some of it is for my child's father" (I. 11)—casts her
relationship to fatherhood in an entirely new light. That she goes on, half-
humorously, to rationalize her new love in terms of the old—"The Duke my father
lov'd his father dearly" (ll.29–30)—is hardly logical, as Celia warily demonstrates:
"By this kind of chase, I should hate him, for my father hated his father dearly . . ."
(ll. 32–33). But behind the specious logic lies an emotional truth. What Rosalind's
love forces upon her—and what love demands from all of Shakespeare's comic
heroines—is a reorientation of feelings toward those for whom she already has
strong emotional ties. We are reminded of Hermia and Egeus, or Viola and Sebastian, or Portia and her father's "will." As we shall see, the experience in Arden
resolves the apparent tension between two loves and enables Rosalind to give
herself fully to both. Though unmotivated once she is in Arden, the period of
separation from her father seems as necessary to Rosalind's development as her
role-playing with Orlando.

III

Much of the psychological complexity that Shakespeare achieves in Rosalind's
role hinges upon his ability to transform Lodge's mannered prose into an expressive instrument. It is difficult to find in the two works passages close enough for
meaningful comparison, but perhaps a few lines that Shakespeare steals from
Lodge's Alinda (Celia) will serve to illustrate differences that are pervasive. The
passages occur on different occasions, but both refer to Rosalind's witty slander
against her own sex:

> And I pray you (quoth *Aliena*) if your roabes were off, what metall are you
> made of that you are so satyricall against women? Is it not a foule bird defiles
> the owne nest?   (Lodge, p. 181)

> You have simply misus'd our sex in your love-prate. We must have your
> doublet and hose pluck'd over your head, and show the world what the bird
> hath done to her own nest.   (Shakespeare, IV. i. 201–4)

Although Lodge's version is by no means excessively artificial—Lodge is far more
euphuistic elsewhere—Shakespeare's is both more natural and more vital. He
avoids Lodge's alliteration and balanced questions, adds raciness to the diction (in
"love-prate" and "pluck'd," in particular), compresses the ideas, and transforms an

illustrative proverb into an expressive metaphor. Through these changes Shakespeare achieves an impression of rapid, vivid, and spontaneous thought. His Celia actually perceives the doublet and hose being plucked over the head—so graphically and immediately, in fact, that the proverb that leaps into her mind becomes concretely visual and humorously obscene. Conversation in *Rosalynde* is little more than relaxed oratory; in *As You Like It*, though often based on euphuistic patterns, a conversation is thought in action. Celia discovers the full reach of her jest only a step before the audience does.

Rosalind's jesting reaches even farther than Celia's and plays a more complicated role in her personality. Rosalind's wit is, of course, a mark of that "inclusive poise" that holds her at the center of the play, but it also fulfills a subtle psychological function. Like the disguise of Ganymed that she takes on in Arden, her wit offers a protective shield behind which Rosalind can explore and test her identity. A simple phrase like "No, some of it is for my child's father" not only expresses her emotional entanglement in her potential roles—as daughter, wife, mother, sexual partner—but enables her to detach from herself from them momentarily and turn them around in the freedom of imaginative play. To see her wit as merely a static attribute of character, as is implied in most discussions of the role, is to ignore its creative function. Shakespeare's fondness for witty heroes and heroines in the mature histories and comedies, one suspects, owes something to the fact that they tend to be engaged in defining their identities in play before assuming adult roles—as married women, or, in Hal's case, as king.

IV

The fact that Rosalind links her new melancholy for Orlando with that for her father, as we have seen, suggests another dimension that Shakespeare adds to the role, that of psychological development. If we sometimes respond to Shakespearean characters as if they inhabited the real world, wondering how many children lady Macbeth might have had, we do so in part because the roles develop with an internal consistency that we associate with living people. The point may seem obvious, but Lodge, like many Elizabethan writers—Marlowe, say—seems relatively unconcerned with this aspect of character. Perhaps because his interest lies more in convention than in characterization, Lodge tends to think in individual scenes alone. His Rosalynde, though consistent, is not developed with the continuity that seems central to our conception of "personality." On the other hand, despite his dependence upon the scenic unit and his fascination with the interplay of conventions (nowhere more evident than in *As You Like It*) Shakespeare portrays in his heroine a continuous psychological development.

Rosalind's relations with Silvius and Phebe provide a case in point. Lodge treats the Silvius-Phebe plot more seriously than Shakespeare—plays it "straight," as it were, as a paradigm of unrequited love—and develops it with the same conventionality he lavishes upon the other pairs of lovers. By heightening the artificiality of the Silvius-Phebe episodes, Shakespeare indirectly increases our acceptance of the love between Rosalind and Orlando; the conventionality of the Silvius-Phebe affair serves as a lightning rod to draw off the laughter of disbelief. The most important difference for our purposes, however, is that only Shakespeare integrates the Silvius-Phebe plot into Rosalind's psychological development.

The scene in which Phebe falls in love with Rosalind disguised as Ganymed (III. v) appears in both Lodge and Shakespeare and exploits similar comic effects. In both versions Rosalind reproaches Phebe for her cruelty and pride, only to pre-cipitate her love. The most significant difference between the two episodes is that Shakespeare's Rosalind interrupts the wooing, as Ralph Berry puts it, with "quite astonishing warmth—and rudeness."[11] Amazed at the effect of her words, Rosalind admits to being out of temper: "she'll fall in love with my anger" (l. 67). Berry's question—"Why so much heat?" (p. 183)—is perceptive, for it directs us to the psychological dynamics of the scene, which is generally viewed merely as comic commentary on Silvius and Phebe's allegiance to the artifical conventions of pastoral love.[12] Rosalind plays the role of satirist here, of course; but she is neither detached nor objective. Her satire, like that of Jaques, is fueled by private motives. Berry suggests that Rosalind's harshness springs from a nature "motivated above all by a will to dominate" (p. 184). But this explanation strikes me as unnecessarily cynical. More to the point, it is based upon the mistaken assumption that Rosalind's char-acter is static.

To explain Rosalind's passion, we need only return to the conversation with Celia that immediately precedes the scene in question. This exchange, which occurs only in Shakespeare, focuses on Rosalind's anxiety at Orlando's failure to keep his appointment: "But why did he swear he would come this morning and comes not?" (III. iv. 18–19). Celia's wry humor does little to put Rosalind at ease: "Yes, I think he is not a pick-purse nor a horse-stealer, but for his verity in love, I do think him as concave as a cover'd goblet or a worm-eaten nut" (ll. 22–25). In his wooing of Phebe, then, Silvius becomes a reflector for Rosalind's own predicament, as he was, indeed, at their first encounter: "Jove, Jove! this shepherd's passion / Is much upon my fashion" (ll. iv. 60–61). Rosalind sees in Phebe's indifference to love a counter-part to Orlando's, and in Silvius' frustration a mirror of her own. Her ire is thus directed more at the absent Orlando than at poor Phebe. As if to accentuate her comic anxiety, Shakespeare splices between Orlando's earlier promise to return and this episode the scene in which Touchstone betrays his doubtful motives in wooing Audrey, calling into question the truth of all lovers' verses: "the truest poetry is the most feigning, and lovers are given to poetry; and what they swear in poetry may be said as lovers they do feign" (III. iii. 19–22).

When Silvius presents Rosalind with Phebe's letter, he himself bears the burden of her frustration. Rosalind is again on edge from waiting: "How say you now? Is it not past two a'clock? And here much Orlando!" (IV. iii. 1–2). She therefore plays a brutal game with Silvius as he reads the letter, leading him on only to reveal its devastating contents, and prompting even Celia to sympathy: "Alas, poor shepherd!" (l. 65). The phrase echoes Rosalind's sentiment upon her first meeting with Silvius: "Alas, poor shepherd, searching of [thy wound], / I have by hard adventure found mine own" (II. iv. 44–45). Now, however, Rosalind is utterly without compassion: "Do you pity him? No, he deserves no pity. Wilt thou love such a woman? What, to make thee an instrument, and play false strains upon thee? not to be endur'd!" (IV. iii. 66–69). Read "man" for "woman" in this outburst and its motive becomes clear. Rosalind sees herself reflected yet again in Silvius' lamentable mirror; she sees herself as an instrument played upon by a lover so indifferent that he will not even keep time. And this time her anger turns inward, against her own folly at loving such a man.

To see Rosalind as merely a detached satirist in these episodes is to over-simplify the emotions they evoke and to ignore their significance in the development of her love. Rosalind certainly makes sport of Silvius and Phebe, but the game she plays is psychologically significant.

V

Rosalind's comic anxiety about Orlando's love also underlies the scenes of their mock-courtship. Lodge's version serves as the basis for Shakespeare's, for in Lodge Rosalynde's disguise enables her to test her lover, pitting her suspicions of man's inconstancy against his protestations of faithful love. In *Rosalynde*, however, the game is played in verse, not in prose. After listening to one of Rosader's sonnets, Rosalynde proposes that he pretend she is indeed Rosalynde and woo her in an amorous eclogue. He does so, only to be answered by a skeptical sonnet of her own, which he then parries with a romantic reply. So it goes until Rosalynde, convinced of his love, finally yields, completing his rhyme, and Alinda plays the priest for their mock-marriage. As Lodge observes, it is a "jesting match, that after proovde to a marriage in earnest" (p. 214).

Aside from the shift from verse to prose, Shakespeare makes two other changes that are important for the characterization of his Rosalind: he complicates her skepticism by injecting a strong dose of antifeminism—Lodge's Rosalynde is concerned only with man's inconstancy, not woman's[13]—and, as we have seen, he adds Rosalind's obsession with keeping time. Both of these elements are crucial to Rosalind's plan to "cure" Orlando of his love-sickness (and the medical motif is itself Shakespeare's invention). In Shakespeare, however, the scheme is motivated, not by a conventional feminine skepticism, as is the testing in Lodge, but by specific insights into Orlando's behavior as a lover. For Shakespeare invents two episodes in Act III, scene ii that afford Rosalind some disconcerting discoveries: the episode in which Orlando's verses are found and mocked by Celia, Touchstone, and Rosalind herself, and the episode in which Orlando and Jaques, as Signior Love and Monsieur Melancholy, exchange barbed compliments. Rosalind's impulsive decision to speak to Orlando "like a saucy lackey, and under that habit play the knave with him" (ll. 295–97) is playful, of course, but again the sport is psychologically significant: the conventional behavior that threatens to turn Orlando into an allegory

(Signior Love) must be made to yield its true meaning. If merely a role, it may be false; if truly felt, it may be dangerously naive. The "cure" that Rosalind proposes thus enables her to play out two kinds of doubts. Is his love true?—"men are April when they woo, December when they wed" (IV. i. 147–48). Is his idealism, his "deifying" of Rosalind, strong enough to sustain contact with her human fallibility?—"maids are May when they are maids, but the sky changes when they are wives" (IV. i. 148–49).

In attacking women, then, Rosalind works toward (but hopes against) Orlando's disillusionment. By being exposed to woman's "real" nature—her capriciousness, her shrewishness, her faithlessness—Orlando will be driven, like Ganymed's earlier "patient," to "forswear the full stream of the world, and to live in a nook merely monastic" (III. ii. 419–21).[14] To such a "nook" the play's true cynic, Jaques, finally retires. Ganymed's "physic" is thus of the kind that Don John administers in a heavier dose to Claudio in *Much Ado About Nothing*. When Claudio "discovers" Hero playing the role of Ganymed's portrait of Rosalind, he betrays the emptiness of his conventional romanticism by losing faith and turning cynic:

> For thee I'll lock up all the gates of love,
> And on my eyelids shall conjecture hang,
> To turn all beauty into thoughts of harm,
> And never shall it more be gracious.   (IV. i. 105–8)

Unlike Claudio, whose test is admittedly more severe, Orlando refuses to be shaken. He perseveres despite Ganymed's many variations upon the theme of woman's frailty: "Virtue is no horn-maker; and my Rosalind is virtuous" (IV. i. 63–64). In a forest with horns behind every tree and a Touchstone behind every verse, Orlando remains true to his own image of Rosalind. His idealism is not shattered by his exposure to what Touchstone would call, if he traded in clichés, "real life."

Rosalind asks more from Orlando than resistance to Ganymed's anti-feminism, however; she demands that he prove his own faith. And since a lover's words are ambiguous, as Touchstone's example confirms, she demands proof in action: Orlando must keep time. While Lodge's version of the mock-wooing culminates in Rosalynde's yielding in reality, Shakespeare's end with her demanding, despite her passionate impatience, another interview, to be kept on time. As she herself observes at the end of the scene, "Time is the old justice that examines all such offenders, and let Time try" (IV. i. 199–200). This insistence upon deeds as well as words serves in many ways as a paradigm of the difference between Lodge's art and Shakespeare's. Lodge's Rosalynde is wooed and won in verse; she voices her skepticism in poetry and yields in poetry. Her agreement to participate in the wooing eclogue seems symbolic of Lodge's attitude toward his art: she moves into the realm of fiction and accepts it as truth. By contrast, the attitude of Shakespeare's heroine mirrors his double allegiance, to both art and life. Rosalind's acceptance of Orlando depends ultimately upon deeds rather than words; she will yield only if he can treat their fiction as if it were reality, keeping time for Ganymed as if he were

Orlando's "very" Rosalind. Orlando's faith is true only if he lives by it. Rosalind's delightful obsession with punctuality therefore expresses much more than her conventional impatience as a lover.

Because of this concern with time, the wooing in *As You Like It* is not resolved until Rosalind, hearing Oliver's explanation for Orlando's second instance of tardiness, swoons. Fainting at the sight of blood betrays Rosalind's femininity, of course, and much of the comedy of the scene hinges upon her inability to keep her masculine disguise under control. But in a way that even Celia does not quite see, "There is more in it" (IV. iii. 159). It is not merely the sight of Orlando's blood that makes Rosalind swoon, but what it signifies. For in listening to Oliver's story Rosalind makes two crucial discoveries: that Orlando has kept time to the best of his ability (the bloody napkin is an emblem of his faith), and that he has saved his "unnatural" brother. Rosalind's anxious question underlines the importance of her of this latter act: "But to Orlando: did he leave him there, / Food to the suck'd and hungry lioness?" (II. 125–26). For Orlando's deed, which is described emblematically and invested with Herculean overtones,[15] brings both Rosalind and the audience to the recognition of a paradox: by breaking his oath, Orlando has kept his faith. By proving himself his brother's keeper, by acting out of charity rather than revenge, Orlando has proven his love for Rosalind. A similar paradox is employed, although sophistically, by Berowne in *Love's Labour's Lost:*

> It is religion to be thus forsworn:
> For charity itself fulfills the law,
> And who can sever love from charity?   (IV. iii. 360–62)[16]

In a way that Berowne is too immature to take seriously, Orlando has "forsworn" himself religiously and joined romantic love with religious charity. The religious vocabulary that Orlando repeatedly employs as lover—he vows to keep time, for example, "With no less religion than if thou wert indeed my Rosalind" (IV. i. 197–98)—thus proves to be no mere Petrarchan convention. Orlando keeps time, not according to the dictates of the court or of conventional courtship, but according to the forest of Arden, in which there are no clocks, and in which to "fleet the time carelessly" (I. i. 118) may be a way of redeeming it.[17]

The relationship between faith and charity developed in Orlando's action places his love against a familiar theological background. As the official homily "Of Faith" makes abundantly clear, the Anglican church stressed that the proof of faith is always charity: "true fayth doeth euer bring foorth good works, as S. *James* sayth: Shew me thy fayth by thy deeds."[18] Religious faith is not at issue in *As You Like It*, of course, but romantic faith is at the center of the play. Orlando swears "by the faith of my love" (III. ii. 428) to woo Ganymed as if he were Rosalind and earns, finally, even Jaques' blessing: "You to a love, that your true faith doth merit..." (V. iv. 188). In the case of Silvius, romantic faith is played out in terms of Petrarchan convention; his truth to Phebe, despite her cruelty, is rewarded in marriage. In the case of Orlando, the ultimate test of romantic faith is brotherly love.

The play climaxes, then, not merely in a celebration of romantic love. The act that breaks through Rosalind's disguise and allows her finally to abandon it is an act that joins love and charity. This redefinition of love is dramatized in the masque with which the play concludes, for Hymen presents marriage as a force that binds not only individuals but the universe as a whole:

> Then is there mirth in heaven,
> When earthly things made even
>   Atone together.   (V. iv. 108–10)

It is this expansion of love's meaning that enables Rosalind to give herself equally to her father and her husband, and in precisely the same words: "To you [*Duke Senior*] I give myself, for I am yours. / To you [*Orlando*] I give myself, for I am yours" (ll. 116–17).

VI

In his article "Thematic Unity and the Homogenization of Character," Richard Levin has objected to a tendency in modern criticism to subordinate character to theme, as if a play owed its life to the dramatization of an idea rather than "a particular moving human experience."[19] While the best criticism of *As You Like It* has managed to explore the play's themes and conventions without losing touch with its "human experience," it has not entirely avoided oversimplifying Rosalind's role, even when most insisting upon its complexity. To see Rosalind as an "ideal woman," or as a synthesis of "conflicting attitudes towards love," or as a representative of "the ideals of love and the values of the pastoral" is to conceive of this engaging character as the static embodiment of an idea.[20] To counter this tendency, a reading of Lodge proves particularly helpful. For a comparison of the two central roles enables us not only to appreciate the depth, subtlety, and complexity of Shakespeare's character but, above all, to appreciate its dynamic quality. If Shakespeare inherited from Lyly a comic drama of dialectics, in which characters define themselves along a spectrum of ideas, he welded to it a developmental conception of character. Rosalind is not merely reconciler of oppositions, but a figure who, through the experience of "playing" at love, discovers more fully who she is.

NOTES

[1] Among the many source studies are Geoffrey Bullough, ed., *Narrative and Dramatic Sources of Shakespeare*, II (London: Routledge & Kegan Paul, 1958), 143–57; Agnes Latham, ed., *As You Like It*, The Arden Shakespeare (London: Methuen, 1975), pp. xxxv–xlvi; Marco Mincoff, "What Shakespeare Did to *Rosalynde*," *Shakespeare Jahrbuch*, 98 (1960), 78–89 (rpt. in Jay L. Halio, ed., *Twentieth Century Interpretations of* As You Like It [Englewood Cliffs, N. J.: Prentice-Hall, 1968], pp. 98–106); Kenneth Muir, *Shakespeare's Sources*, I (London: Methuen, 1957), 55–66; Robert B. Pierce, "The Moral Languages of *Rosalynde* and *As You Like It*," *Studies in Philology*, 68 (1971), 167–76; Albert H. Tolman, "Shakespeare's Manipulation of His Sources in *As You Like It*," *Modern Language Notes*, 37 (1922), 65–76. As will become apparent, I disagree with Mincoff's assertion that Shakespeare's Rosalind "is less complex and less true to nature than Lodge's" (Halio, p. 106).

[2] Shakespeare's *Happy Comedies* (London: Faber and Faber, 1962), p. 162

[3] *Shakespeare's Romantic Comedies: The Development of Their Form and Meaning* (Chapel Hill: Univ. of North Carolina Press, 1966), pp. 243, 242.

[4] *Shakespeare's Festive Comedy: A Study of Dramatic Form and Its Relation to Social Custom* (1959; rpt. Cleveland: World Publishing, 1963), p. 238.

[5] *The Heart's Forest: A Study of Rosalind's Pastoral Plays* (New Haven and London: Yale Univ. Press, 1972), p. 68.

[6] "The Figure of Rosalind in *As You Like It*," *Shakespeare Quarterly*, 29 (1978), 44.

[7] *The Riverside Shakespeare*, gen. ed. G. Blakemore Evans (Boston: Houghton Mifflin, 1974). All Shakespeare quotations are from this edition.

[8] In Lodge's version Rosalynde tells Rosader that she has a friend experienced in magic who can bring Rosalynde to him; see Bullough, II, 246. All further references to Lodge's *Rosalynde. Euphues golden legacie* (London, 1590) will be taken from Bullough, II, 158–256.

[9] *Old Vic Drama* (London: Rockliff, 1948), p. 63.

[10] Lodge refers to Rosalynde's sorrow for her father's plight only once, briefly, when she discovers him in the forest (pp. 247–48).

[11] *Shakespeare's Comedies: Explorations in Form* (Princeton: Princeton Univ. Press, 1972), p. 183.

[12] See, for example, Phialas, pp. 250–52.

[13] The passage in which Alinda accuses Rosalynde of slandering women, quoted above, is the only one that touches upon this theme, and it is unconnected with the mock-courtship.

[14] It may be worth noting that in his *Anatomy of Melancholy* (London, 1621), Robert Burton proposes a remarkably similar remedy for love-melancholy; see Floyd Dell and Paul Jordan-Smith, eds., *The Anatomy of Melancholy* (New York: Tudor, 1938), pp. 777–96.

[15] For an illuminating study of the symbolic dimensions of Orlando's role, see Richard Knowles, "Myth and Type in *As You Like It*," *ELH*, 33 (1966), 1–22.

[16] In "Love versus Charity in *Love's Labor's Lost*" (*Shakespeare Studies*, 10 [1977], 17–41), R. Chris Hassel, Jr., develops the theological controversies that may lie behind these lines.

[17] I draw here upon two studies of the theme of time in the play which, although insightful in many regards, have little to say about Rosalind's insistence upon punctuality: Jay L. Halio, "'No Clock in the Forest': Time in *As You Like It*," *Studies in English Literature*, 2 (1962), 197–207 (rpt. in Halio, pp. 88–97); Rawdon Wilson, "The Way to Arden: Attitudes toward Time in *As You Like It*," *Shakespeare Quarterly*, 26 (1975), 16–24.

[18] Mary Ellen Rickey and Thomas B. Stroup, eds., *Certaine Sermons or Homilies: A Facsimile Reproduction of the Edition of 1623* (Gainesville, Fla.: Scholar's Facsimiles & Reprints, 1968), p. 29.

[19] *Modern Language Quarterly*, 33 (1972), 29.

[20] A rare exception to this tendency is William J. Martz's treatment of Rosalind in *Shakespeare's Universe of Comedy* (New York: David Lewis, 1971), pp. 84–99. Although we define Rosalind's development in different terms, our interpretations are generally complementary. There are also some illuminating remarks on Rosalind's mock-courtship as a lesson in awareness preparatory to marriage in D. J. Palmer, "*As You Like It* and the Idea of Play," *Critical Quarterly*, 13 (1971), 240–43, and Helen Gardner, "*As You Like It*" (Halio, pp. 55–69). Gardner's essay originally appeared in *More Talking of Shakespeare*, ed. John Garrett (New York: Theatre Arts Books, 1959), pp. 17–32.

Charles R. Forker

MULTIPLE PERSPECTIVES
IN ARDEN

The make-believe action and perfunctory exposition of *As You Like It* notoriously attenuated,[1] are obviously designed to throw the emphasis of the comedy on the rural setting and on the variety of characters and attitudes that can meet, converse, and interact in the forest of Arden. The haste with which Shakespeare maneuvers his figures into the woods may suggest the escapist impulse that underlies much pastoral literature, but Shakespeare's play, as has often been observed, is anything but an evasion of reality. What the dramatist gives us in addition to the contrivances of fairy tale and the richly varied characters, ranging from dukes to country bumpkins, is a subtle web of contrasting attitudes and values that comprise the real interest and substance of the play. The apparent simplifications of pastoral become devices for isolating certain kinds of complexity and focusing them with the precision of a finely ground lens. Arden, then, is a carefully prepared context in which multiple perspectives or points of view may compete for our interest and attention and can modify each other through contact, intersection, and reciprocating patterns of stimulus and response. Like most pastoral settings, it is conceived mainly as a place of temporary rather than permanent residence, the literal geography being less important than the emotions, stances, or verities for which it becomes the symbolic backdrop. Shakespeare makes his green world a place of growth—ethical, psychological, and spiritual as well as merely vegetative—but he is more interested in how the human heart may internalize this landscape than in the landscape for its own sake.

The assured yet delicate equipoise of *As You Like It* may be illustrated with reference to four sets of contrasting, complementary, but sometimes overlapping perspectives that emerge from an overview of the comedy. These may be expressed under the headings Nature versus Grace, Life versus Art (or naturalness versus artificiality), Time versus Timelessness, and Subjectivity versus Objectivity. In combination all are symptoms of the thematic fullness and intricacy of the play, and

From *Fancy's Images: Contexts, Settings, and Perspectives in Shakespeare and His Contemporaries* (Carbondale: Southern Illinois University Press, 1990), pp. 71–78. First published in *Iowa State Journal of Research* 54 (1980): 421–30.

they point to a comprehensiveness of vision characteristic of Shakespeare's mature art, a comprehensiveness to which Norman Rabkin has applied the term "complementarity."[2] Indeed inclusiveness appears to be one of the several significances embedded in the play's rather casual title—a signal, so to say, of the recognition that there are many ways to look at experience and that no single attitude can contain the whole truth.

In a well-known essay on Spenser, A. S. P. Woodhouse pointed out some years ago that Elizabethans were accustomed to thinking about reality in terms of the double order of nature and grace, distinguishing the human from the divine, the corrupt from the perfect, the finite from the infinite, and the fallen world of creation from the unfallen world of the Creator. Some thinkers such as Calvin stressed the divergence of the two orders, exalting grace as nearly beyond man's ken and depreciating nature on account of original sin and innate human depravity. Others such as Hooker, emphasizing the unity of all creation, tended to see the two orders as the poles of a continuum. Thus conceived, "the order of grace was the superstructure whose foundations were securely laid in nature," and nature might therefore be understood as "an ascending scale, at whose successive levels are added, first, life, then consciousness, then rationality and a moral sense, and finally religious feeling, which last marks the transition to the order of grace."[3] Certainly As You Like It, especially in the first act, acknowledges the fallen condition of the world, and even the forest, however idyllically or invitingly presented, is not wholly free from selfishness, inconvenience, or danger. Nevertheless, Shakespeare's concept of physical nature in the comedies is much closer to Hooker's than to Calvin's. It is a conception that allows us to see the green world as a mirror of grace while yet retaining some consciousness of the barriers that separate us from it.

This duality, of course, is one of the traditional advantages of pastoral settings, and it might be said that the playwright in this instance simply exploits its possibilities. In any case, it is clear that in Shakespeare's hands, Arden becomes a highly idealized place, a *locus amoenus* defined in large measure by an ethos of relaxation, art, romantic love, and pastoral *otium*. The banished duke lives there with his followers in a state of contentment, abundance, good fellowship, and loving generosity to strangers. He enjoys peace; he has beautiful music and the pleasures of the hunt for entertainment, and the harmonies of God's handiwork to contemplate in earth, in water, and in sky. Compared with the hateful and envious court from which he has been exiled, the woods are reasonably "free from peril" (II. i. 4), and he can discover "tongues in trees, books in the running brooks, / Sermons in stones, and good in everything" (II. i. 16–17).

Arden is both self-contained and self-sufficient, it knows no malice or politics, and it is a setting "exempt from public haunt" that can "feelingly persuade" (II. i. 11–15) the dispossessed duke to cultivate a profounder knowledge of himself. The Robin Hood style of his sylvan court is such that "many young gentlemen flock to him every day" to live "carelessly, as they did in the golden world" (I. i. 112–114). Not surprisingly, the errant princesses think of the forest as "liberty" rather than "banishment" (I. iii. 136). It is a place where starving travelers like Orlando's old servant are "providently cater[ed] for" (II. iii. 44) by the same God who feeds the ravens and the sparrows, where men, remembering the "holy bell" of the church, share their feasts "in gentleness" and wipe from their eyes the tears "that sacred pity hath engend'red" (II. vii. 120–123). The forest, then, is partly a reflection of divinity, a second Book of Revelation (as the Elizabethans liked to conceive of nature), and when characters enter it, they seem to change for the better. Orlando's wicked brother is converted from hate to love almost instantly, as if by magic, as soon as he crosses the border. And with like speed, the worldly Frederick abandons both his usurped throne and his fratricidal hostility for the monastic cell of a "convertite" (V. iv. 183) upon reaching "the skirts of this wild wood" (V. iv. 158). One thinks of Marvell's equally unspoiled landscape, "Where willing Nature does to all dispence / A wild and fragrant Innocence."[4] Hymen's lyrics at the quadruple marriage suggest the numinous possiblities of the forest glade, the pervasiveness of Deity, and the sense in which nature may become the fictive coordinate or physical prefigurement of paradise itself: "Then is there mirth in heaven, / When earthly things made even / Atone together" (V. iv. 107–109).

But if Shakespeare associates the greenwood both with Eden and with the golden world of classical tradition, he does not equate it with them. Arden is far from being prelapsarian. As such, it represents not only the world as one could wish it—as we like it—but also the world in its more negative aspect. The deer are slaughtered there so that the exiles may banquet on venison, and the duke worries about usurping the rights of the animals even as his own rights have been usurped. The winter winds blow bitterly under a freezing sky; a lioness, a snake, and the "venomous" toad (II. i. 13) may threaten life; and Orlando at first speaks of the place as "this uncouth forest" (II. vi. 6) and "this desert inaccessible" (II. vii. 109). To some the forest may be merry; to others its boughs are "melancholy" (II. vii. 110). Arden does not eliminate weariness, old age, or the possibility of sudden death. Adam nearly expires from hunger; Oliver and Orlando have brushes with a nature red in tooth and claw. Even the virtuous duke must capitalize on "the uses of adversity" (II. i. 12), must "*translate* the stubbornness of fortune" by means of inner adjustment to the quietness and sweetness of his Arden "style" (II. i. 19–20; emphasis added). Some of the natives are self-seeking—Corin's churlish master, for instance, and the cruelly proud Phebe. An ignorant priest, Sir Oliver Martext, wanders about only too willing to marry and persons of 'opposite gender "as they join wainscot" (III. iii. 79–80), and sluttishness and stupidity appear in the persons of Audrey and William.

The forest symbolizes both the fallen world, where seasonal change—"the penalty of Adam" (II. i. 5)—still reminds men of their imperfection, and the Edenic world of innocence and charity that we half remember from the prehistory of myth and look forward to as the reward of our salvation. The biblical name and character of Orlando's faithful servant—a role Shakespeare is said to have played himself— crystallize the bifocal attitude toward nature that the play encourages. In his age and physical weakness, old Adam may be an archetype of human limitation and transience, but his saintly virtues also identify him with the lost innocence for which man is perennially nostalgic: "O good old man, how well in thee appears / The constant service of the antique world" (II. iii. 56–57).

Although *As You Like It* has religious overtones without being explicitly doctrinal, it is also a very literary and style-conscious play. Conversational spontaneity jostles set speeches or "arias" of studied rhetorical artifice. As Jaques carefully divides man's advance from infancy to decrepitude into "seven ages" (II. vii. 142), so Touchstone distinguishes the seven steps of quarreling from "the Quip Modest" to "the Lie Direct" (V. iv. 75–81). Anaphora, chiasmus, antithesis, parison, and other euphuistic embellishments are deliberately imported into the dialogue to suggest the civilizing—and sometimes overcivilizing—effects of nurture upon nature. Prose and verse encroach upon each other. The woods reverberate with rhymes, classical allusions, aphorisms, and witty juxtapositions. Such effects exploit the delightful interplay between the artificiality of familiar pastoral conventions and the gentle mockery of these same conventions. Some features of Arden can exist only by poetic license—a climate that accommodates both the tropical palm and the English holly, a weeping deer whose tears augment the water level of the stream by which he stands, a lover who festoons every tree in sight with amorous verses to a supposedly absent lady, a shepherd and shepherdess whose sole reason for being is too woo and be wooed in highly patterned iambic pentameter. Silvius undergoes a thousand humiliations and emotional deaths for a cold nymph whom he compares with Petrarchan exuberance to an executioner, a tyrant, a butcher, and a murderer, because she stubbornly refuses to return his affection. A classical god appears out of nowhere to join four couples in the ceremonial dancing of a court masque, the most elaborately contrived of all Elizabethan art forms, in the middle of the forest.

Of course Shakespeare continually undercuts the literary and artificial postures with satirical deflation of the romantic clichés and a sense of life's actuality. Touchstone, who at one point insists that "the truest poetry is the most feigning" (III. iii. 17–18), is forever parodying the Platonic love poems by reducing the high-flown rhetoric of romance to mere animal sexuality and bawdry:

> If a hart do lack a hind,
> Let him seek out Rosalind.
> If the cat will after kind,
> So be sure will Rosalind.
> Winter'd garments must be lin'd,
> So must slender Rosalind.
> They that reap must sheaf and bind;
> Then to cart with Rosalind.
> Sweetest nut hath sourest rind,
> Such a nut is Rosalind.
> He that sweetest rose will find
> Must find love's prick and Rosalind.   (III. ii. 99–110)

The sacramental unity of marriage can be compared irreverently to the sudden "fight of two rams" whose locked horns "clubs cannot part" (V. ii. 29–40). Irrefutably Touchstone points out that at one level, at least, mating is primarily a matter of mere instinct: "As the ox hath his bow, sir, the horse his curb, and the falcon her bells, so man hath his desires; and as pigeons bill, so wedlock would be nibbling" (III. iii. 73–75). Rosalind, though she is in love herself, understands the difference between romantic literature and life. The tragic love stories of Troilus and Leander are mere "lies," constructs of pure fiction: "Men have died from time to time, and worms have eaten them, but not for love" (IV. i. 101–102). Thus, by taking a lofty view of amorous dedication and by voicing the Platonic doctrine that poets are liars, Rosalind can function both as idealist and realist at once. The comedy celebrates romance, but it also makes us aware of how ridiculously lovers behave when they adopt literary poses.

Jaques thinks it asinine for a man to leave "wealth and ease" (II. v. 48) for rustic playacting, enabling us to smile at the duke in Lincoln green rather as we smile at Marie Antoinette at the *Petit Trianon* for affecting the exquisite ruralities of a Fragonard shepherdess. Corin and Touchstone debate the age-old question of sophistication versus simplicity, and the clown, making nonsense of the subject by reducing it to a medley of logical contradiction and tautology, travesties a dialectic on the precise value of pastoral retreat that informs the comedy as a whole:

> Truly, shepherd, in respect of itself, it is a good life; but in respect that it is a shepherd's life, it is naught. In respect that it is solitary, I like it very well; but in respect that it is private, it is a very vile life. Now, in respect it is in the fields, it pleaseth me well; but in respect it is not in the court it is tedious. As it is a spare life, look you, it fits my humor well; but as there is no more plenty in it, it goes much against my stomach. Hast any philosophy in thee, shepherd?
> (III. ii. 13–21)

Audrey keeps smelly goats, not the freshly laundered sheep of literary convention, and the word "poetical" (III. iii. 15) is not in her vocabulary. Corin knows about real sheep, how greasy they are and how they actually reproduce themselves. Still, his emphasis on the biology of the shepherd's trade and Touchstone's witty censure of a calling that subsists on "the copulation of cattle," on "be[ing] bawd to a bell-wether" (III. ii. 78–79), in no way wrecks the pastoral idealization of Arden. Much of the sophisticated pleasure in *As You Like It* derives from appreciating the many ways in which art and life cut athwart, without annihilating, each other.

When Rosalind asks at one point, "I pray you, what is 't o'clock?" and Orlando replies that "there's no clock in the forest" (III. ii. 295–297), Shakespeare calls attention to another set of contrary perspectives in the play. Logically, the opposition of time to timelessness is one aspect of the polarity between the temporal and the eternal, between nature and grace, but by virtue of its prominence, the play elevates this concern almost to the status of a separate theme.[5] Rosalind rebukes Orlando for being an hour late for his appointment with her and then retires to "sigh till he come" (IV. i. 209) again. Defining a lover (partly on the basis of her own feelings) as someone who "sigh[s] every minute and groan[s] every hour" (III. ii.

299), she goes on wittily to anatomize the "divers paces" (ambling, trotting, gal-
loping, etc.) in which Time may travel, depending upon a person's state of mind
(iii. ii. 303–327). She herself has been forced to quit the court within "ten days"
(I. iii. 41) and, as prime mover of the comic action, is necessarily aware of time
and its importunities. Touchstone, the literal timekeeper in the forest, looks at his
dial "with lack-luster eye" to note how "from hour to hour, we ripe and ripe, /
And then, from hour to hour, we rot and rot; / And thereby hangs a tale" (II.
vii. 21–28). Jaques too is very conscious of transience, seeing all life as a de-
pressing progress from "the infant, / Mewling and puking in the nurse's arms" to
"second childishness and mere oblivion, / Sans teeth, sans eyes, sans taste, sans
everything" (II. vii. 142–165).

The forest may echo with the *carpe diem* lyricism of a song like "It was a lover
and his lass" (V. iii. 15); it may contain Rosalind's urgency of love, Audrey's impatience to be wed, or Jaques' and Touchstone's pessimistic comments on death and
dissolution. But Arden also represents a state of contentment and holiday freedom
emancipated from the constraints of the clock and the calendar. The banished duke
"fleet[s] the time carelessly" (I. i. 113–114); he "lose[s] and neglect[s] the creeping
hours of time" (II. vii. 111), not worrying about when he will be able to retrieve his
usurped throne. Orlando, having complained of enforced idleness at home, wanders dreamily through the greenwood with no thought of obtaining justice from his
wicked brother. Rosalind does not trouble to seek out her exiled father even
though he is in the immediate vicinity, and Celia announces after arriving in Arden,
"I like this place, / And willingly could waste my time in it" (II. iv. 90–91). Life in the
forest is untrammeled by chores or routines, and even eating and sleeping are
apparently casual and unregulated. One of the lessons of the forest is that the
holiness of the heart's affections, the world of selflessness and joy truly experienced, may liberate us from thinking in terms of yesterday or tomorrow and put
us in touch with what is timeless. It is not always necessary or desirable to conceive
of time chronometrically; one may regard it with Walton or Thoreau as simply a
"stream" to "go a-fishing in."[6]

The paradoxical view of time that pastoral and antipastoral attitudes in combination may promulgate is symbolized by both the songs of the play and its
numerous references to seasonal change. Although by definition music is sequential
and performed in obedience to time, it may nevertheless evoke a sense of the
timeless by transporting the listener or performer to a higher emotional state, thus
freeing him from merely quotidian preoccupations. Moreover, its recurrences suggest changelessness through the very processes of change. A chorus such as "Then
heigh-ho, the holly! / This life is most jolly" (II. vii. 181–182) must produce some
such effect. Similarly the regularity of seasonal rhythms, the inevitability by which
"winter and rough weather" (II. v. 8) yield to "spring time, the only pretty ring time"
(V. iii. 18), can give rise to a concept of transcendent permanence. In Spenser's
"Mutabilitie Cantos," Nature articulates a Christain Neoplatonic philosophy of time
that, while not explicitly stated in *As You Like It,* is nevertheless consistent with the
strain of pastoral idealism in the play:

I well consider all that ye haue sayd,
>   And find that all things stedfastnes doe hate
>   And changed be: yet being rightly wayd
>   They are not changed from their first estate;
>   But by their change their being doe dilate:
>   And turning to themselues at length againe,
>   Do worke their owne perfection so by fate:
>   Then ouer them Change doth not rule and raigne;
> But they raigne ouer change, and doe their states maintaine.

(The Faerie Queene, VII. vii. 58)[7]

The final pair of opposites—objectivity and subjectivity—is as much a part of Shakespeare's theme in *As You Like It* as the others I have mentioned, chiefly because romance is one thing for those whose emotions are deeply engaged in it and something quite different to those who merely look on from a position of detachment.[8] It has been wisely said that there is only one thing sillier than being in love, and that is thinking that love itself is silly. Shakespeare allows us as his audience to take both positions at once—to see love through the eyes of both the lover and the skeptic. Therefore we have the double privilege of laughing *with* the characters at the same time that we laugh *at* them. To the lovesick Silvius, Phebe is a goddess of love, a paragon of celestial beauty, but we know that he re-creates her in the image of his own ideal because of the emotion he feels. Phebe in turn thinks that she loves Rosalind in the same way that Silvius loves her because she cannot penetrate the male disguise of the person to whom she is superficially attracted. But Rosalind can be brutally objective about Phebe's distinctly limited charms:

>   mistress, know yourself. Down on your knees,
> And thank heaven, fasting, for a good man's love;
> For I must tell you friendly in your ear,
> Sell when you can, you are not for all markets.

(III. v. 57–60)

We can see that Audrey is taking a fool (and probably a libertine as well) for her husband when she accepts Touchstone so uncritically, but love does not see with the eyes of reason or practicality, nor do we desire that it should.

Touchstone, the professional fool, rudely hails Corin as "you clown!" (II. iv. 62) because he can see on first meeting that the old rustic prefers the country to the court; but we soon learn that the pot is calling the kettle black, or rather that a shallow kind of wit is rebuking the wisdom born of age and experience. To the fool, wisdom may look like folly, and yet we are permitted to enjoy the fun of Touchstone's mistake without being solemnly judicial or moralistic about it. Some men, like the duke and his companion foresters, are inclined to see a deer as the natural source of sport and food, while more earnest observers, like Jaques, may be moved to look upon the same animal as an emblem of human suffering. *As You Like It* not only shows up the limitation of both points of view but also enables us to recognize how dreary the world would be if it were composed exclusively of archery enthusiasts, connoisseurs of venison, solicitors for the SPCA, or fanatic vegetarians. One of the important lessons of Arden is that to a great extent truth is relative, and that beauty, especially in the case of lovers, resides in the eye of the beholder.

Amidst this welter of attitudes and perspectives, how, we might ask, does Shakespeare unify his play? One way, I would suggest, is to make us more or less continuously aware of his own medium—the theatre—during the progress of the comedy. Of course we enter Arden with the hero and heroine, participating imaginatively and sympathetically in their experience. But at the same time, we keep our distance from the stage because Shakespeare is forever calling our attention to the conventions and artificialities that make the theatrical illusion distinct from life. One of the more amusing instances of this *Verfremdungseffekt* is Jaques' hasty departure from the stage when Orlando greets Rosalind decasyllabically in the midst of a prose scene: "nay, then, God buy you, an you talk in blank verse!" (IV. i. 29). The discrepant awareness keeps us responding to the experience of the play on two separate planes of reality. It is one of the techniques Shakespeare uses to habituate us to holding contrary perspectives or attitudes in equilibrium. Jaques' famous speech, "all the world's a stage, / And all the men and women merely players" (II. vii. 138–139), is the most obvious example of this self-consciousness, but other characters also use the same ancient metaphor. The duke speaks of life as "this wide and universal theatre" (II. vii. 136), Corin refers to the wooing of Phebe as "a pageant truly play'd / Between the pale complexion of true love / And the red glow of scorn and proud disdain" (III. iv. 50–52), and Rosalind "prove[s] a busy actor in their play" (III. iv. 57). "All the world's a stage" was, after all, an idea very close to Shakespeare's heart, for (as already noted in chapter 1) his own playhouse, newly constructed in 1599, was called the Globe, and the words of Jaques just quoted are a translation of the theatre's motto: *Totus mundus agit histrionem* ("All the world practices stage-playing").

The world of theatre is both like life and different from it at the same time. Not only do human actors play the roles of Touchstone and Jaques and the exiled duke; inside the play proper these characters all play roles to each other, showing different sides of themselves, striking different postures in different situations and relationships. Touchstone, for instance, plays the critic of courtly values while he is still at court, but when he is talking to a country swain in Arden, he pretends to be the spokesman for courtly elegance and sophistication. Jaques adopts melancholia as a conscious stance to impress others, claiming that he rails satirically against the world to cure it of its pride and folly. But he himself is the most prideful and egotistical of all the characters, and his steadfast refusal to participate in the happiness of others is a kind of foolishness that makes all his vaunted travel and experience nearly worthless. It may be true that babies vomit, that lovers sigh like furnaces, that some old men turn into senile vegetables, but to pretend that these images define infancy, adolescence, or old age is an absurd falsification of what everyone knows. Shakespeare makes the hollowness of Jaques' melancholic role obvious by bringing the dignified and lovable old man Adam onstage immediately after the facile generalizations on the toothless senility of the aged. The banished duke may take on the role of Robin Hood for a time, but he abandons it quickly enough when the opportunity comes to regain his dukedom.

The character of Rosalind, a beautiful girl who is disguised as a boy for most of the play (and who of course was acted by a boy in Shakespeare's theatre), focuses the tension between the play world and the real world most creatively and variously for us. She is a role-player of the richest humor and complexity, for she pretends to give disinterested lessons in wooing to the very man she wants to woo her. Her first words at the beginning of the comedy set the characteristic tone of her utterance: "Dear Celia. I show more mirth than I am mistress of" (I. ii. 2–3). We watch her playing a theatrical game that combines pretense with sincerity, that involves both detachment and engagement at the same time, that mediates between an acerbic, intelligent wittiness and the pathos of longing. She sets up, and acts in, a joyous and theatrically contrived comedy-within-a-comedy that merges with what we accept as a deeply felt reality. When Rosalind (in her disguise as Ganymede) faints at the sight of the bloody napkin, the evidence of Orlando's injury, and then pretends that she only "counterfeited" (IV. iii. 167) shock as part of the wooing game, Shakespeare gives us a wonderfully effective example of humor and pathos fusing. and Rosalind's serious yet playful role-playing is intimately related to that deepening self-awareness that seems always to be concomitant with Shakespeare's celebration of romantic love.[9]

George Bernard Shaw remarked that the role of Rosalind "is to the actress what Hamlet is to the actor"—a part so intrinsically varied and fascinating that, with any competence at all, the performer who undertakes it can scarcely fail.[10] Much of this fascination and variety lies in the multiple perspectives of the play that converge so charmingly in her. She is both natural and gracious, strong and frail, virtuous and full of mischief, divinely beautiful and humanly earthy all at once. She is conscious of time at the very moment that she seems to occupy and irradiate a world of timeless contentment. She is an activist without being too crudely or obviously aggressive. She is both a lover and a mocker of love, by turns both a subjectivist and an objectivist. As soulful and sensitive princess, as clever teacher and manipulator, as actor-actress, as stage manager, and finally as epilogue to her own play (a function that gives fresh meaning to Jaques' proverb on life's exits and entrances), she makes it possible for us to share more fully than do any of the more limited characters the unique matrix of perspectives that is Shakespeare's comic art. Rosalind is the very symbol of theatre as they liked it at the Globe in 1599, and as we continue still to like it.

NOTES

[1] Harold Jenkins in "As You Like It", Shakespeare Survey, 8 (1955), calls the foundation of the story "flimsy" and its disguisings "inconsequential" (p. 14); Anne Barton in "As You Like It" and Twelfth Night: Shakespeare's Sense of an Ending," Shakespearian Comedy, ed. David Palmer and Malcolm Bradbury, Stratford-upon-Avon Studies, 14 (London: Edward Arnold, 1972), refers to the "plotlessness" of the play (p. 163); Agnes Latham in her introduction to the new Arden edition (London: Methuen, 1975) echoes these judgments: "at a superficial level, very little seems to happen" (p. lxxx).

[2] Norman Rabkin, *Shakespeare and the Common Understanding* (New York: Free Press, 1967); see especially pp. 1–19.

[3] A. S. P. Woodhouse, "Nature and Grace in *The Faerie Queene*," *ELH*, 16 (1949), 196, 218.

[4] Marvell, "The Mower against Gardens" (11. 33–34), in H. M. Margoliouth, ed., *The Poems and Letters of Andrew Marvell*, 3d ed. (Oxford: Clarendon Press, 1971), I, 44.

[5] Jay L. Halio devotes an entire essay to the topic: " 'No Clock in the Forest': Time in *As You Like It*," *Studies in English Literature*, 2 (1962), 197–207; rpt. in *Twentieth Century Interpretations of* As You Like It, ed. Jay L. Halio (Englewood Cliffs, N. J.: Prentice-Hall, 1968), pp. 88–97.

[6] Henry David Thoreau, *Walden*, ed. J. Lyndon Shanley (Princeton: Princeton University Press, 1971), p. 98.

[7] Edwin Greenlaw, Charles Grosvenor Osgood, Frederick Morgan Padelford, et al., eds., *The Works of Edmund Spenser: A Variorum Edition*, 10 vols. (Baltimore: Johns Hopkins Press, 1932–57), VI, 180.

[8] John Russell Brown in a chapter to which I am heavily indebted develops this point; see "Love's Order and the Judgement of *As You Like It*," in *Shakespeare and His Comedies* (London: Methuen, 1957), pp. 141–159.

[9] Walter R. Davis perceptively analyzes the relation of disguise to self-discovery in Shakespeare's major source, Lodge's *Rosalynde;* see "Masking in Arden," *Studies in English Literature*, 5 (1965), 151–163. Since in the prose romance Arden represents the adjustment of the actual to the ideal, masking or deliberate role-playing serves "the interests of ethical clarification" (p. 155).

[10] Edwin Wilson, ed., *Shaw on Shakespeare* (New York: E. P. Dutton, 1961), p. 32.

R. Chris Hassel, Jr.

THE FOLLY OF THE LOVERS

Touchstone's blundering philosophizing and Rosalind's epilogue leave little doubt that *As You Like It* is intensely interested in the realities that transcend the greatest feignings of fools, lovers, and artists. Man requires conventional rituals and roles to embody otherwise inexpressible feelings and truths, and to convey them to others.[1] But absurdity can result from an inadequate understanding of this conventionality. Touchstone is one extreme exemplar of such folly. He tries on as many roles as he has observed—lover, traveller, courtier, scholar, literary critic, philosopher, duellist, husband—but he can only be an insensitive parodist, a fool, a stone, in each of them. On the other extreme is the contemplative Jaques, who anatomizes but resists all roles. As a result he remains a mere observer of life, uninvolved in most of the follies and the joys of its earnest if foolish conventionality. He is even more a fool, as Rosalind tries to tell him, for this uninvolvement. But he recognizes his folly even less than Touchstone, and he would not change it.

Unlike Touchstone, the other characters, according to their capacities, reveal even while they experience it the complex truth which underlies their conventional feignings. The vision of *As You Like It* is not the satiric *Narrenschiff* Jaques might have presented but an affirmative celebration of man's follies and his potentialities. The widespread role-playing that goes on among most of them heightens the positive, creative connections between psychologial and aesthetic conventions. And these connections, paradoxically, are highlighted by the character, Jaques, who seems to understand them least, during his cynical anatomy of the world as a stage. The others discover what he may never know, that all of the roles people (or artists) play can be creative as well as static, profound as well as foolish, and are often both at once. But when they work, these aesthetic or romantic conventions, these rituals and roles of artists and lovers, can lead to expressions and under-standings of otherwise inaccessible truths. Their mutual feignings thus emerge from the comic vision of *As You Like It* as legitimate and essential ways to understand and cope with the humbling reality of man's finitude.

From *Faith and Folly in Shakespeare* (Athens: University of Georgia Press, 1980), pp. 131–44.

Orlando and Rosalind are the most realistic pair of characters in the play, but they engage us also as the most feigning. That their elaborately conventional behavior both edifies them and enriches their characterization illustrates how central the concept of "most faining" is to the play's vision of the wisdom of folly. It is precisely because the emotions and impulses of love are so erratic, so powerful, and so confusing that love's seemingly foolish rituals and conventions, like those of art and religion, can serve such vital functions. Each of these feignings channels chaotic impulses into creative, acceptable, and comprehensible patterns, patterns which do not have to be rediscovered by each new lover, but which rather are the common legacy of all. Their gamelike, ritualized behavior in Arden thus frees Orlando and Rosalind from the stumbling, tongue-tied attempts at communication that they undergo at their first meeting. It simultaneously frees them from embarrassing frankness, from the "base truth" of their physical impulses, and from the threat of its direct, nonfigurative, sexual gratification. Orlando is given a voice by these formal and prescribed rituals and games, even if for a while it is a foolish voice. Rosalind as Ganymede is given a protective if foolish disguise against her lover and herself. Their feignings, their romantic rituals, are therefore true in many ways. They control their love, making it more formal than it really is—more orderly—giving it a prescribed, repeatable, and socially acceptable form of expression. They direct their intensely personal, even idiosyncratic emotion into a universalized form, which grants it dignity and importance. And they remind the lovers of their continuing folly while allowing them to express and refine their enduring love.

That they can embrace the folly of this feigning as well as its exhilarating joy attests to their unusual comic wisdom. It also points to their role in the play's analogous aesthetic vision. Like the play, and unlike Jaques, both Rosalind and Orlando are fully aware of their own folly and of the inescapable folly of love. Also like the play, as Mark Van Doren notices, both of them delight in that folly without ever becoming cynical about it.[2] D. J. Palmer has recently suggested that the lovers' unusual awareness of their own folly is connected to the play's theme of universal feigning: "There is a general agreement in the play that, as the song puts it, 'most loving is folly,' and accordingly Rosalind's counterfeit wooing is intended not merely to ridicule the foolishness of lovers, herself included, but to make it fully aware of itself in terms of a charade, a pretense, in which it is foolish to be wise."[3] Orlando "will chide no breather in the world but myself, against whom I know most faults" (III. ii. 267–68). Rosalind knows that if "love is merely a madness . . . the lunacy is so ordinary that the whippers are in love too" (III. ii. 376–80). They obviously share a joyous understanding that love, like faith, is a manner of madness. That understanding is surely related to Erasmian and Pauline paradoxes.

Orlando loves Rosalind at first sight, and he continues to love her throughout the whole play. The "heavenly Rosalind" of their first meeting is a faith from which he never substantially wavers, through all of the tests his love must encounter. But that first faith is strengthened by the conventional postures, the feignings, that both Orlando and Rosalind go on to assume. On their first meeting he can say nothing:

> Can I not say 'I thank you'? My better parts
> Are all thrown down, and that which here stands up
> Is but a quintain, a mere lifeless block.   (I. ii. 230–32)

By the time he has reached Arden, he says far too much, in bad verses pasted upon every tree:

> O Rosalind! these trees shall be my books,
> And in their barks my thoughts I'll character.   (III. ii. 5–6)

But this howling, love-struck, tree-carving Petrarchan lover, like the earlier speechless one, will be laughed out of his excessive conventionality by the criticism of Touchstone and Jaques as well as Celia and Rosalind, so that by the beginning of Act IV he will have only a single line of blank verse: "Good day and happiness, dear Rosalind" (IV. i. 27). This is still too much for Jaques, but it represents a considerable moderation in Orlando's excessively conventional and foolish behavior.

Orlando's sudden change into the humor of a Petrarchan lover continues to parody the play's literary heritage and its own conventionality. But it also reveals a momentary narcissism and a reluctance to grow up that Orlando must overcome. Like the antics of the gentlemen of *Love's Labour's Lost*, Orlando's false pose is too much surface and too little substance, therefore an impediment to both growth and self-expression. Orlando must learn that he can "live no longer by thinking" (V. ii. 48), at least like this, too conventionally, in ways that obscure emotions and spirit rather than expressing them. Certainly the courtly pose is far less deeply ingrained in Orlando than it is in Berowne, and therefore more easily cured by Rosalind. But Orlando's immaculate dress, like his belief that a perfect woman loves him, must bother Rosalind; both excesses betray too much self-love, not just a conventional posture. Paradoxically, Rosalind's disguise, her feigning as Ganymede, functions to erode the false surface of Orlando's courtly humor and his narcissism at once, and thus frees him to love her more truly. This contrast between productive and unproductive folly, like the change finally effected in Orlando, is nicely opposed to Jaques's static anatomy of the seven ages of man. Man is not doomed to be the lover, though he may have to learn just how much of the lover to avoid and how much to keep by trying on the whole role briefly. Folly like Orlando's can free as well as enslave, especially if a Rosalind is around.

Much like his satiric counterpart, Silvius, Orlando is also something less than a man in his courtly pose. As Rosalind justly asks Celia of his versifying, "Is it a man?" Celia's answer, "And a chain that you once wore, about his neck" (III. ii. 172), reminds us that Orlando is, indeed, a man, victorious over both Charles and Rosalind. But it also suggests distressing if amusing changes since then. Even before his effeminate and immature courtliness, Orlando's love of Rosalind seems to have cost him some manliness. If he has overthrown more than his enemies, he is also left somewhat impotent in Rosalind's presence after the wrestling:

> My better parts
> Are all thrown down, and that which here stands up
> Is but a quintain, a mere lifeless block. (I. ii. 230–32)

Silvius is similarly emasculated by Phebe's scorn. As Rosalind admonishes him, "Well, go your way to her, for I see love hath made thee a tame snake" (IV. iii. 70–71). That both of them finally become better men through Rosalind's feigning intervention as a man, and that Rosalind and Phebe also become less masculine through the same contrivance suggest that Shakespeare is having a bit of fun with their androgynous relationships. A similar interest in shifting sexual roles in Rosalind's epilogue suggests its relationship to the whole play. Like the other roles and elements the play depicts and satirizes—fools, philosophers, the artistic form—so even the most basic human roles of male and female are never absolute. On the most basic physiological level of Touchstone's relationship to Audrey, the man needs the woman, the woman the man, for sexual satisfaction. In another sense, there is some yin and yang, some *res extensa* and some *res cogitans,* some dominance and some submissiveness, in all of us. Especially is this ambivalence true during adolescence, "as a squash is before 'tis a peascod, or a codling when 'tis almost an apple" (*Twelfth Night,* I. v. 151–52). Having to court another man—an effeminate one at that, appropriately called "Ganymede"—is the perfect purgative to drive out Orlando's excessive courtliness and his immaturity, along with his sexual ambivalence. But neither Orlando nor Rosalind can reject all such ambivalence, or they would both become as simplistic as a Charles or an Audrey, a virtuous Adam or a villainous Frederick. The sorting out, the juggling, never completely end. One can never be completely male, or mature, or natural, without becoming as static as the frozen portraits of Jaques's ages. If such ambivalence, social or sexual, is embarrassing, it is also an inevitable folly of the maturing personality. Shakespeare has ingeniously woven these ideas into the roles and disguises in As You Like It.

Orlando's related conventional assumptions about "the beloved" are also moderated by the edification of Rosalind-Ganymede, who has more than academic reasons for wanting to dispel his extremest expectations of his lover. Even Rosalind could never live up to his image of her perfection, and she would reject it if she could. For such a static posture of Platonic perfection is really no role at all for her; it is rather a non-role, another meaningless convention. Nor could Rosalind ever live with a rhapsodic sap who thinks that people die for love. So she tells Orlando, "Men have died from time to time, and worms have eaten them, but not for love" (IV. i. 96–98). The stories to the contrary are "all lies," most feignings. Still, it must be pleasant and flattering for Rosalind to have a lover who momentarily believes in them, or one who would not be cured of his love except to prove his faith (III. ii. 449). It is likewise both silly and exciting for her to find those verses everywhere. Orlando is proving himself a good Petrarchan lover and a good man even as he is being cured of the worst excesses of his tribe. And Rosalind, in spite of her own good taste, rather likes it.

Another important lesson for them both is the lesson of the horns that Benedick and Beatrice also grapple with in *Much Ado About Nothing*. No woman is perfect; many are quite imperfect. Orlando must at least acknowledge the possibility of imperfection in Rosalind before his edification is complete. Their love-game will dispel his excessively conventional faith in all women; but at the same time it will intensify his faith in one woman, Rosalind. We never seriously think, despite her warnings, that he will have any reason to repent this faith.

She begins her lesson during their first meeting in the forest. Women are "touched with so many giddy offenses" (III. ii. 330) that they can hardly be re-counted. Among them are many of the roles Rosalind-Ganymede will play in the courting game:

> changeable, longing and liking, proud, fantastical, apish, shallow, inconstant, full
> of tears, full of smiles; for every passion something and for no passion truly
> anything, as boys and women are for the most part cattle of this color; would
> now like him, now loathe him; then entertain him, then forswear him; now
> weep for him, then spit at him.   (III. ii. 385–91)

Of Rosalind's actual relationship to these roles we shall have more to say later, but we can see that their catalogue here is designed to disillusion the excessively trustful Petrarchan lover of his naive image of the beloved. She is likely to prove less than perfect, if better than this.

Specifically, she is likely to cuckold him. This threatening imperfection is the focus of Ganymede's assault on Orlando's continued faith in their next meeting. The destiny of any husband is "horns; which such as you are fain to be beholding to your wives for" (IV. i. 54–55). Orlando is sure to meet "your wife's wit going to your neighbor's bed" (IV. i. 155). And he will find her ever changeable:

> Maids are May when they are maids, but the sky changes when they are wives.
> I will be more jealous of thee than a Barbary cock-pigeon over his hen, more
> clamorous than a parrot against rain, more new-fangled than an ape, more
> giddy in my desires than a monkey. I will weep for nothing ... when you are
> disposed to be merry; I will laugh like a hyen, ... when thou art inclined to
> sleep.   (IV. i. 135–42)

In short, she might be jealous, henpecking, fashion-conscious, lecherous, opposite in all things—the perfect shrew. Of course she will not, but she could be any or all of these things at one time or another, and Orlando no less than Benedick must at least be aware of the possibilities to appreciate what he actually gets, and to be forewarned of what could be his. If Benedick fears too much of this, Orlando fears it too little, and Rosalind's game is an important corrective for his naïveté. The song of the foresters about horns (Act IV, Scene ii), the constant, blessed state of cuckoldry, is a conventional statement of the same truth about human imperfection.[4] Without that awareness, Orlando will never be ready to wed, for he will be unable to expect, let alone cherish, the imperfection that is his, hers, and everyone's.

Rosalind also becomes more worthy of love and more aware of herself as a result of the games that she plays with Orlando and the Petrarchan masks that she tries on. In fact, there is an extremely complex character behind the feignings of her role. Her disguise as Ganymede results from expediency, to be sure. It also betrays to a degree her own reluctance to mature and a decided enjoyment of controlling the action, of dominating events and people. She looks forward, for example, to playing a man:

> Were it not better,
> Because that I am more than common tall,
> That I did suit me all points like a man?
> A gallant curtal-axe upon my thigh,
> A boar-spear in my hand.   (I. iii. 111–15)

She has also promised Orlando that she will try to dominate him once they are wed. There is some truth in her role and her promise, and Orlando had better heed it.

The ritualized courting of Rosalind and Orlando, while certainly a game they both enjoy, grants her the proper courting she deserves as the daughter of the Duke. It also provides a civilized context she can control even though she is in Arden. For while they go through those conventional, even silly paces of boy courting boy, she is truly well-courted and Orlando well-trained in courting. Both are also thus protected from the potential folly of their unchecked passion. Further, as Rosalind enacts the conventions and rituals of the disdainful maiden—scorn, indifference, impatience, haughtiness, jealousy, spite, sarcasm, cynicism, and most of the others—she is doing more than parodying the conventional Petrarchan woman, though she is certainly doing that. She is also trying those postures on in a context in which she cannot be held accountable, much as the lovers in A *Midsummer Night's Dream* can behave madly, violently, and cruelly without personal blame because of Puck's magic potion. Rosalind is evaluating, like Orlando, the excessive postures of the courted woman, and approaching womanhood and the *via media* as a result of their game.

A good example of the complexity of her feigning occurs during her response to Orlando's verses. Though she can lament the lame feet and the tedious homily of his words as she plays the traditionally disdainful maid, she can also be secretly delighted that they are written to her. Thus Touchstone's assault on their "false gallop" and their "bad fruit" is aimed more at Rosalind's edification than at Orlando's: "If the cat will after kind, / So be sure will Rosalinde." Her kind, Touchstone is saying, is the nutty fool of love: "Sweetest nut hath sourest rind, / Such a nut is Rosalinde" (III. ii. 98–99, 104–5). Her folly in loving the verses while she pretends to criticize them is especially clear when she tries lamely to defend them and herself against Touchstone's criticisms: "Out, fool! . . . Peace, you dull fool! I found them on a tree" (III. ii. 94, 110). As the fool says of these attempts to avoid embarrassment, "You have said; but whether wisely or no, let the forest judge" (III. ii. 116–17). This is one of his few chances to expose unacknowledged folly in the play, and he does it brilliantly. For the nuts who read and secretly love such bad verses are of the same kind as the nuts who write them. And "truly, the tree yields bad fruit" (III. ii. 111). Though that is momentarily an embarrassing folly for Rosalind to bear, it is also a joyous one.

Its joy becomes obvious in her later exchange with Celia, which she begins by feigning indifference and scorn towards the poet. But after Rosalind's criticism of the tedious and lame verses ("I was never so berhymed since Pythagoras' time that I was an Irish rat, which I can hardly remember" [III. ii. 168–69]), she is soon beside herself to find out who wrote them, and to confirm her hope that it is Orlando:

> I prithee tell me who is it quickly, and speak apace. I would thou couldst stammer, that thou mightst pour this concealed man out of thy mouth. . . . Is he of God's making? What manner of man? Is his head worth a hat? or his chin worth a beard?   (III. ii. 188–96 passim)

And then when it is confirmed, this recently and soon-again-to-be disdainful maiden sputters out her joy and her love in a foolish and delightful explosion of questions too many for Gargantua's mouth to answer:

> Alas the day! what shall I do with my doublet and hose? What did he when thou saw'st him? What said he? How looked he? Wherein went he? What makes he here? Did he ask for me? Where remains he? How parted he with thee? and when shalt thou see him again? Answer me in one word.
>   (III. ii. 208–13)

Because this delicious exuberance, this high folly, this near madness of her womanly love bursts quite through her feignings both as Ganymede and as the haughty mistress, we are never in any doubt that Rosalind is truer than Ganymede: "Good my complexion! Dost thou think, though I am caparisoned like a man, I have a doublet and hose in my disposition?" (III. ii. 185–87). Fortunately for us and for Orlando, even her most feigning is never that true. Here, and when she faints at the sight of the handkerchief, the true folly of her great love is most manifest. The folly and the joy are both conveyed again just after this exchange by the continued images of nuts and fruits. Celia answers Rosalind, "I found him under a tree, like a dropped acorn." And though·Rosalind can hardly have forgotten Touchstone's recent chiding, she has little doubt about the quality of the fruit this oak tree bears: "It may well be called Jove's tree when it drops such fruit" (III. ii. 225–26). When she later says in the most horribly conventional Petrarchan style, "he comes to kill my heart," we see that Rosalind and Orlando are nuts of the same tree, and we smile and are delighted.

There are other brilliant glimpses of the true Rosalind through her feigning with Orlando, and we consistently see her womanhood better because she is playing the man. When, for example, she questions Orlando's lack of the proper symptoms of love, "lean cheek," sunken eye, "beard neglected," "shoe untied" and the rest (III. ii. 352ff.), she is reciting romantic conventions that don't always represent reality. But she is also a bit distressed that Orlando does not conform more exactly with the textbook lover, and voices that distress through her feigning. She is still a little unsure of him; do those neat clothes suggest vestiges of narcissism? In a similar way her test of his faith is a real test as well as a game. She enjoys the excuse to be around Orlando, but she would also like to be as sure of his love as possible. Of course absolute surety is not vouchsafed to the true lovers in Shakespearean comedy. Hazard is a major ingredient of love's folly and its faith. And Rosalind always has some sense of hazard, though Orlando is as sure a bet as Shakespeare will depict.

Rosalind's distrust, her fear of imperfection, surfaces more clearly when we see Rosalind-Ganymede again. She "will weep," even if "tears do not become a man," because Orlando is late. "His very hair is of the dissembling color" she says, and yet, "I'faith, his hair is of a good color." Celia chides her with more of the nut joke: "An excellent color. Your chestnut was ever the only color.... But why did he swear he would come this morning, and comes not?" A question to be asked. For Rosalind, no less than Orlando, must learn of her mate's possible imperfections as she tests his faith in her. Perhaps he is a "worm-eaten nut," without "verity in love" (III. iv. 1–23 passim). As Celia says, you are a fool to believe in a brave young man, especially in Arden:

> O, that's a brave man; he writes brave verses, speaks brave words, swears brave oaths, and breaks them bravely, quite traverse, athwart the heart of his lover, as a puisny tilter, that spurs his horse but on one side, breaks his staff like a noble goose. But all's brave that youth mounts and folly guides.
>
> (III. iv. 36–41)

But Rosalind chooses to be that fool, despite her doubts; so later does Celia with the tarnished but redeemed Oliver. Their choice of such folly represents a faith in more than feigning, and it is destined to end happily for both of them.

C. L. Barber comments best on this paradoxical lesson on their mutual fallibility that Orlando and Rosalind must both undergo:

> As Rosalind rides the crest of a wave of happy fulfillment... we find her describing with delight, almost in triumph, not the virtues of marriage, but its fallibility.... Ordinarily, these would be strange sentiments to proclaim with joy at such a time. But as Rosalind says them, they clinch the achievement of the humor's purpose. Love has been made independent of illusions without becoming any the less intense; it is therefore inoculated against life's unromantic contradictions.[5]

That they can both learn so much of their folly and simultaneously strengthen their faith in one another through the charade Rosalind-Ganymede conjures for them in the forest is one of the great achievements of Shakespeare's art. It continues to draw strength from the Erasmian and Pauline paradoxes about faith and folly that lie behind it, even though those paradoxes are more deeply submergd than they were in Love's Labour's Lost, A Midsummer Night's Dream, or Much Ado About Nothing.

Rosalind's upbraiding of Orlando for being an hour late is also more than a mere feigning, though she quickly enough forgives him for his snail's pace. After all, he has only stood up a stand-in, and so he can hardly be blamed for making light of the transgression. Though we know better, this whole relationship seems to him a feigning pure and simple, and it is one that he will increasingly tire of. In the sequence that follows, Rosalind directs her own courting, and edifies Orlando as well as she can concerning the Petrarchan excesses he still exhibits, especially his naïveté about perfect women. Her playful feigning ends with another promise to meet in the forest. After Orlando's departure, she reminds us again of the true love that lies behind her feigned cynicism: "O coz, coz, coz, my pretty little coz, that thou didst know how many fathom deep I am in love!" (IV. i. 189–90).

Then she almost destroys her cover by swooning over the bloody napkin (IV. iii. 157). And Orlando finally does tire of the feigning: "I can live no longer by thinking" (V. ii. 48). The conventions of lovers are supposed to free as well as restrict. Their rituals are supposed to allow the lovers to express inexpressible feelings, to perceive imperceivable truth, and to sense their communion with all past and future lovers. Like the conventions of religion or of art, the lovers' observances can make them larger than themselves, at least momentarily. But they are also feignings that are less than life, and finally their celebrants must return to the world of the body as well as the mind. For none of us can live forever by thinking, and least of all can lovers, unless they are of the hopelessly ethereal kind (like Orsino through most of *Twelfth Night*). Even he must finally see Viola in her woman's weeds, as must Orlando now in *As You Like It*. His feignings, like Rosalind's, were "most true"; but because of that they must finally be superseded by that elusive experience we like to call "real life." That return to the literal is also the thrust of Rosalind's epilogue. The fools have paradoxically deprived themselves of this joy by remaining oblivious to their own folly. The play has revelled in its absurd conventionality, and found there its "greatest poetry." The lovers, by embracing the follies of their feignings with an analogous joy, have evidenced the spiritual health they share with the play's attitude toward itself. They have also equipped themselves for the vicissitudes, as well as the joys, of life ever after. Their delicious balancing of play and seriousness, artifice and realism, folly and profundity, defines and emphasizes the atmosphere of humility in which the whole play must be understood.

Again, this strenuous comic vision demands an unusual degree of assent from the audience. Shakespeare and his audience must share a healthy sense of their mutual inabilities to express or understand the inexpressible and the inconceivable for the play to work fully. D. J. Palmer has already suggested that the self-conscious role-playing of the lovers and Shakespeare's playfulness with his art both involve the audience in "the equivocal relations between fiction and reality, game and earnest, folly and wisdom."[6] The blundering foolery of Touchstone and Jaques also contributes to this vision, especially when Touchstone discusses the "most faining" of artists and lovers. So, we will recall, did Bottom's Pauline allusions and the lovers' Erasmian ones as they awoke to a new wisdom in *A Midsummer Night's Dream*.

Both plays, because they display an interest in the limits of human understanding and expression, would naturally have drawn upon and suggested such familiar and analogous Erasmian and Pauline paradoxes about foolish wits and wise fools.

NOTES

[1] Although many critics mention role-playing as a motif in *As You Like It*, few consider it as central as I do. See especially D. J. Palmer, *"As You Like It and the Idea of Play," Critical Quarterly* 13 (1971): 237–38. For other prominent statements see Muriel C. Bradbrook, *Shakespeare and Elizabethan Poetry* (New York: Oxford University Press, 1952), p. 220; P. V. Kreider, "Genial Literary Satire in the Forest of Arden," *Shakespeare Association Bulletin* 10 (1935): 212.
[2] Mark Van Doren, *Shakespeare* (Garden City: Doubleday, 1953), pp. 127–35.
[3] D. J. Palmer, "Art and Nature in *As You Like It,*" *Philological Quarterly* 49 (1970): 38.
[4] Peter J. Seng, "The Forester's Song in *As You Like It,*" *Shakespeare Quarterly* 10 (1959): 249.
[5] C. L. Barber, *Shakespeare's Festive Comedy* (Princeton: Princeton University Press, 1959), p. 236.
[6] Palmer, "Idea of Play," p. 235.

William C. Carroll
''FORGET TO BE A WOMAN''

The actor's knowledge of metamorphosis is necessarily first-hand, for each working moment on the stage requires an act of self-transformation; and that act must be accompanied (*pace* Bottom) by a self-immolating transgression of apparent boundaries. Yet neither act can ever be complete. It is one thing, moreover, for an Elizabethan actor to become a Bottom or a Iago, and something else again to switch sexes and become a Rosalind; and when Rosalind asks us to pretend that she is not a woman, and she isn't, vertigo sets in. Shakespeare was aware of the inherent thematic possibilities of his own craft from the very beginning of his career, but he seems to have grown increasingly self-conscious, in the comedies, of women disguising and therefore transforming themselves; as actors and as "women," they become two (or more) things in one.

The women in Shakespeare's comedies often assume conventional disguises for various practical or symbolic reasons. The four ladies in *Love's Labour's Lost* assume masks and exchange "favours" so as to confuse the men. A similar exchange and confusion occurs in *Much Ado About Nothing*, with the further complication that Hero's face remains veiled during her second marriage to Claudio. In *Measure for Measure* and *All's Well That Ends Well* certain signs are exchanged between Diana-Helena and Mariana-Isabella so that the bed tricks will work with the exchanged bodies. But in many of the comedies, Shakespeare pushes the dramatic possibilities even further, to their mimetic limit, making the central women undergo metamorphosis to become someone else. In several cases, the woman must temporarily become her psychological and sexual antithesis, a man, and so we find a shadow-cast of "male" players: "Sebastian" (Julia in *The Two Gentlemen of Verona*), "Balthasar" (Portia in *The Merchant of Venice*), "Ganymede" (Rosalind in *As You Like It*), "Cesario" (Viola in *Twelfth Night*), and "Fidele" (Imogen in *Cymbeline*). Each of them, as Pisanio tells Imogen, "must forget to be a woman" (*Cym.* III.iv.155). Only by passing through this forgetting can each woman truly be a woman.

From *The Metamorphoses of Shakespearean Comedy* (Princeton: Princeton University Press, 1985), pp. 103–7, 127–37.

Recent critical studies of role-playing in Shakespeare have provided useful commentary on this female- to male-phenomenon.[1] Yet Shakespeare's recurring interest in women's becoming men, and its confinement to the comedies and romances, is perhaps better illuminated through the larger and even more obsessive question of metamorphosis in general, and the power of love to generate change in particular. Only when a woman is trying to get a man must she become a man. Julia, Portia, Rosalind, and Viola achieve marriage only after the necessary detour through transformation; like all lovers in Shakespearean comedy, they will become something other, and *then* return to themselves and their men. The details vary in the different cases, but Shakespeare takes the usual lover-into-loved-one transformation even further, turning the women into images of their men, so that two become one in a rather literal sense. This cross-dressing produces effects similar to those of doubling (both are available in *Twelfth Night*), but with greater paradoxical moments of illusion and belief. Shakespeare will not hesitate to invoke the metadramatic possibilities either, for the woman-to-man transformation mirrors the man-to-woman illusion the actor has already generated. All the paradoxes of cross-dressing, like those of doubling, represent the constant resurrection and transgression of specifically *theatrical* boundaries—self-willed change in its most protean mode—but these paradoxes also represent an investigation of sexual boundaries, of androgyny *as* metamorphosis.

Mircea Eliade has offered one useful way of thinking about this obligatory Shakespearean androgyny through transvestism. The ritual significance of such initiatory androgyny, he argues, is clear (he is speaking here of a male's experience): "One cannot become a sexually adult male before knowing the coexistence of the sexes, androgyny; in other words, one cannot attain a particular and well-defined mode without first knowing the total mode of being." Shakespearean comedy, it seems, enacts a similar ritual for certain of its female characters, and, vicariously, for its audience; the end result, in Eliade's terms, is

> a coming out of one's self, a transcending of one's own historically controlled situation, and a recovering of an original situation, no longer human or historical since it precedes the foundation of human society; a paradoxical situation impossible to maintain in profane time, in a historical epoch, but which it is important to reconstitute periodically in order to restore, if only for a brief moment, the initial completeness, the intact source of holiness and power.[2]

We need not subscribe to all Eliade's points to recognize immediately that the transcendence of one's self, the contact with some source of holiness and power, flows naturally from Shakespearean sexual disguise, and that these sexual disguises seem to stand mysteriously at the heart of each play's experience.

Although female sexual disguise may be traced back to Greek and Roman comedy, through the miracle play, and to such romantic plays as *Clyomon and Clamydes* (c. 1570), Lyly's *Gallathea* (c. 1584), and Greene's *James the Fourth* (c. 1591),[3] in none of these instances does the play's central vision come to be so embodied in the heroine and her disguise as in Shakespeare, nor does anyone return to the motif as frequently as Shakespeare does. The mere fact of a sexual disguise was savaged by the theater's Puritan critics, who denounced the players' very existence, and they surely would have extended their net to include Rosalind and Viola; as one critic argued, "Player's practices can hardly be warranted in religion: for a man to put on woman's apparel, and a woman a man's, is plain prohibition."[4] As Jonson's Zeal-of-the-Land Busy echoes to the puppets: "my main argument against you is that you are an abomination, for the male among you putteth on the apparel of the female, and the female of the male" (*Bartholomew Fair*, V.v.101–4). Phillip Stubbes fulminated, in a familiar allusion, against what he implies was an everyday occurrence on the streets: "*Proteus*, that Monster, could never chaunge him self into so many fourmes & shapes as these women doo ... these Women may not improperly be called *Hermaphroditi*, that is, Monsters of bothe kindes, half women, half men."[5] To find so many boys playing women, and so many "women" disguised as men in Shakespeare, in comparison with his dramatic predecessors and in opposition to the moral policemen of the day, suggests that Shakespeare quite deliberately came to employ such moments as preeminent instances of metamorphosis, as literal embodiments of two-in-one.

In four of his romantic comedies, Shakespeare requires his heroine to cross-dress and change sex temporarily, while her man remains essentially the same. In some instances, the woman in fact doubles the appearance or behavior of her love—Portia becomes harsh and judging, as Bassanio was of Shylock; Rosalind feigns being foolish and "romantic," like Orlando—though in other cases she becomes the opposite of her man, an emblem of loving constancy and devotion—like Julia and Viola. In every case, though, it is the woman who must change. The reasons for this are complex. In one sense, only the women are *capable* of such self-transformation. Moreover, the men have already changed, by falling in love, though they usually must be "cured" of it, as Orlando is by Rosalind, and transformed to some further state where they can see more clearly and are fully worthy of their women.

It seems, finally, that the woman becomes the man not only to get the man but also more importantly for the sake of the man: her embodied changes run parallel with some process of change within him. At the same time, though the woman changes name, sex, and costume, her disposition and personality are altered to a much lesser degree. In these transformations through disguise, the salient features of character come out more sharply: there was always something reserved, cool, orderly, and dispassionate about Portia in the first place; there was always something playful, clever, and quickwitted about Rosalind before she ever climbed into trunkhose; and something sad, silvery, and elegiac about Viola even though she didn't lose her brother and has to fence with Toby. The women go *through* the changes but without essentially changing, whereas the men, always and ever themselves, come out the other end looking different, altered in shape and point of view by what the women have done in their stead. The women are doing for the men what the men can't do for themselves.

Every lover must be, and inescapably is, transformed by love; as we have seen, this transformative process must be fully worked through before the completion of marriage can occur. In *The Taming of the Shrew*, Kate must be kated and de-shrewed; in *A Midsummer Night's Dream*, the human lovers must confront the otherness of their own desires, embodied in comic monsters, before repairing to the best bride-bed. In *Twelfth Night*, we saw, Viola must become Cesario in order to survive her own disappointments, and to transform Orsino and Olivia from their self-imprisonments. Viola's method was to become male *and* female, lover and beloved; her close cousins—Julia, Portia, and Rosalind—employ similar guises, as we will now see. It is the lesser blot, as Julia tells us, for "Women to change their shapes than men their minds." ⟨. . .⟩

"Do you not know I am a woman?" (III.ii.250) Rosalind asks Celia. It is a difficult question to answer, given the complex levels of her disguise and role-playing, not to mention the negative phrasing of the question, by which either yes or no may mean the same thing. In no other play by Shakespeare does a woman stand so centrally as Rosalind does in *As You Like It;* and her sexual disguise as Ganymede, "Jove's own page" (I.iii.123; cf. *Met*, X.161 7) represents the transformed otherness of the lover even as it liberates her to be more truly herself.[6]

Shakespeare creates a circle of real and apparent transformations around Rosalind, from Celia's comic oath, "when I break that oath, let me turn monster" (I.ii.20–1), through Duke Senior's complaint about the absent Jaques, "I think he be transformed into a beast, / For I can nowhere find him like a man" (II.vii.1–2), to Rosalind's mockery of Silvius, "Well, go your way to her, for I see love hath made thee a tame snake" (IV.iii.68–9). The pastoral forest of Shakespeare's romance sources was just such a place where one might turn monster, be transformed into a beast, or be made a tame snake. It was the natural locus of transformation, the place, like the woods in *A Midsummer Night's Dream*, where the boundary be-tween man and beast might disappear. But in *As You Like It* the forest of Arden is something else again, more "reflecting mirror" (in David Young's phrase) than anything else, a *selva oscura* with the accent on the last term. The beastly trans-formations in Arden are figurative or hypothetical, yet more instances of the virtue of "if."

Shakespeare seems both skeptical and credulous about transformation in *As You Like It,* making it by turns "real" and "feigned." The miraculous conversions of Duke Frederick and Oliver at the end of the play seem deliberately contrived and unconvincing; other transformations, through the power of love for example, are enacted quite seriously. One mythological model for the action is that of Jove's adventures in Arcady in Book II of the *Metamorphoses*, and the story of Baucis and Philemon in Book VIII. But this background is clearly viewed in the play as extrava-gant and comical. Phebe's letter to Rosalind invokes transformation simply as a poetic cliché: "Art thou god, to shepherd turned, / That a maiden's heart hath burned?" (IV.iii.41–2). In the play's famous passage about "feigning," Ovid (in exile) appears once again:

> TOUCHSTONE: I am here with thee and thy goats, as the most capricious poet, honest Ovid, was among the Goths.

JAQUES: [*Aside*] O knowledge ill-inhabited, worse than Jove in a thatched house!

TOUCHSTONE: When a man's verses cannot be understood, nor a man's good wit seconded with the forward child, understanding, it strikes a man more dead than a great reckoning in a little room. Truly, I would the gods had made thee poetical.

AUDREY: I do not know what poetical is. Is it honest in deed and word? Is it a true thing?

TOUCHSTONE: No, truly; for the truest poetry is the most feigning, and lovers are given to poetry, and what they swear in poetry may be said as lovers they do feign.   (III.iii.6–21)

From the thatched house through the little room to the great stage, from Ovid through Marlowe to Shakespeare, we can trace the history of an attitude toward feigning as something by turns magical and preposterous, true and false. The ability to "feign," as we will see, allows Rosalind freely to transform herself as she likes it.

Like Jove and Mercury among the rustics, or Ovid among the goats, Celia and Rosalind ("Aliena" and "Ganymede") walk transformed in Arcadia. But even before they depart for Arden, they have undergone the psychological transformation of fusion, as Celia testifies:

> We still have slept together,
> Rose at an instant, learned, played, eat together;
> And wheresoe'er we went, like Juno's swans,
> Still we went coupled and inseparable.
> . . . .
>   . . . thou and I am one.
> Shall we be sund'red, shall we part, sweet girl?   (I.iii.72–5, 96–7)

This friendship will reach even to a joint wedding with brothers, when they will be made two in one, coupled and inseparable, in quite another way. There is a hint of this further change to come in the allusion to Juno's swans; the Arden editor believes that this is a transposition of the legend of Venus' swans, which traditionally drew her chariot (as in *Met*, X 831, the story of Venus and Adonis), though they might also be the men whom Venus angrily transformed into swans (*Met*, XIV.564ff.). In either case, Venus, or love, engineers the transformation. Yet Rosalind and Celia will discover that even the love which makes them one will dissolve and reform in another direction.

Just as the forest of Arden is a real mirage—a bare stage but also a verbal and imaginative forest—so Touchstone shows us how to see it both ways, offering us a "natural perspective" of the shepherd's life that wholly depends on the viewer's transforming eye:

Truly, shepherd, in respect of itself, it is a good life; but in respect that it is a shepherd's life, it is naught. In respect that it is solitary, I like it very well; but in respect that it is private, it is a very vile life. Now in respect it is in the fields, it pleaseth me well; but in respect it is not in the court, it is tedious. As it is a spare life, look you, it fits my humor well; but as there is no more plenty in it, it goes much against my stomach. (III.ii.13–21)

But the fact is that everyone from the court, not just Touchstone, sees things double, with "parted eye." The Duke has been able to "translate the stubbornness of fortune / Into so quiet and so sweet a style" (II.i.19–20), Jaques can be counted on to "moralize this spectacle" (l. 44), and Jaques admires Touchstone precisely because he can "moral on the time" (II.vii.29).[7]

We find that only Rosalind, whose way is to conjure us, can "translate," "moralize," or transform herself without deception, however; she best exemplifies the pleasures of transformation in the forest. She is not only Celia's double but, as one of Orlando's poems asserts, always seems more than one person.

> Therefore heaven Nature charged
> That one body should be filled
> With all graces wide-enlarged.
> Nature presently distilled
> Helen's cheek, but not her heart,
> Cleopatra's majesty,
> Atalanta's better part,
> Sad Lucretia's modesty.
> Thus Rosalind of many parts
> By heavenly synod was devised,
> Of many faces, eyes, and hearts,
> To have the touches dearest prized. (III.ii.141–52)

For us as well as for Orlando, she is a quintessence, an epitome of many qualities squeezed into one body, a kind of metaphysical conceit. The several layers of her actual physical disguising repeat the effect.

Rosalind's transformation into Ganymede is considerably more complex, and developed further, than similar sex-changes in the earlier comedies. All possible permutations of cross-dressing are at work now, and it is more important than ever before that Rosalind be changed into a male. The change begins like all the others, with the obliteration of the boundaries of the feminine:

> Were it not better,
> Because that I am more than common tall,
> That I did suit me all points like a man?
> A gallant curtle-ax upon my thigh,
> A boar-spear in my hand; and, in my heart
> Lie there what hidden woman's fear there will,
> We'll have a swashing and a martial outside,
> As many other mannish cowards have
> That do outface it with their semblances. (I.iii.113–21)

Again manliness is just a matter of props, and once again the woman assumes the most stereotypically masculine qualities. The urge to forget she is a woman drives Rosalind to adopt the kind of clichés she will mock elsewhere, as in Orlando's marks (or lack of them) as a lover (III.ii.371–81). Yet her transformation will not be so complete as to annihilate all trace of her former self; Ganymede is still both Rosalind and not Rosalind. At the end of the play Orlando tells Rosalind's father, "the first time that I ever saw him / Methought he was a brother to your daughter" (V.iv. 28–9), and the description of her given to Oliver declares that "the boy is fair, / Of female favor, and bestows himself / Like a ripe sister" (IV.iii.84–6). Rosalind is thus both her own brother and her brother's sister. Shakespeare does not develop Ganymede's androgynous nature as he will Cesario's in *Twelfth Night,* where both male and female fall in love with the pliant hermaphrodite, but Ganymede's am-bivalent nature—"I thank God I am not a woman, to be so touched with so many giddy offenses as he hath generally taxed their whole sex withal" (III.ii.346–9)—forms the heart of the wooing scenes.

It is in the forest scenes with Orlando that Rosalind/Ganymede best reveals her ability to transform herself suitably for a ripe occasion. Within six lines of one scene, she says both "And I am your Rosalind" and "What would you say to me now, and I were your very very Rosalind?" (Iv.i.62, 66–8). The space between asserting and feigning, in which the assertion is (doubly) feigned and the feigning is actually true, is once again the natural locus of transformation. The play's well-known "if" clauses serve as a rough index to the amount of transformation required of Rosalind, reaching a crescendo in the fifth act when she begins to promise everyone a fulfillment as he likes it. This ability to feign all takes on an emergency quality when Ganymede faints upon hearing Oliver's story of the lion, and Rosalind employs one of Falstaff's favorite words, "counterfeit," to explain how she had only feigned. In her relief at recovering her presence of mind, she responds to Oliver's "take a good heart and counterfeit to be a man" with a duplicitous self-assertion, "So I do; but, i'faith, I should have been a woman by right" (IV.iii.171–4).

Rosalind's role frequently requires her to remind Orlando of the essential natural mutability of things, which we cannot evade or prevent, even as she ex-emplifies willed and redemptive change for us in her role-playing. Against Orlando's absurdly rigid lover's vows ("for ever and a day"), somewhat reminiscent of Pro-teus's, Rosalind opposes a quite different image of change in life:

> Say "a day," without the "ever." No, no, Orlando. Men are April when they woo, December when they wed. Maids are May when they are maids, but the sky changes when they are wives.

And she describes her future actions, half-seriously, as a series of antithetical re-actions:

> I will be more jealous of thee than a Barbary cock-pigeon over his hen, more clamorous than a parrot against rain, more newfangled than an ape, more giddy in my desires than a monkey. I will weep for nothing, like Diana in the

fountain, and I will do that when you are disposed to be merry; I will laugh like a hyen, and that when thou art inclined to sleep.   (IV.I.142–52)

Although each emblematic simile depicts her in a constant attitude, always weeping or always laughing, the sum total of the images implies a constant inconstancy, "more giddy" than all of them put together in fact. Earlier, she had told Orlando how she had been able to cure one other lover, who had imagined Ganymede his mistress:

> I set him every day to woo me. At which time would I, being but a moonish youth, grieve, be effeminate, changeable, longing and liking, proud, fantastical, apish, shallow, inconstant, full of tears, full of smiles; for every passion something and for no passion truly anything, as boys and women are for the most part cattle of this color; would now like him, now loathe him; then entertain him, then forswear him; now weep for him, then spit at him; that I drave my suitor from his mad humor of love to a living humor of madness.
>
>   (III.ii.403–13)

Here is totally protean life. Having described masculine stereotypes when taking on her disguise, Rosalind now, as a putative male, invokes feminine clichés of fickleness and unpredictability. Shakespeare is making comically explicit what has been implicit in most of these comedies, that transformation and mutability are powers somehow linked to feminine energies, and that these powers are finally healthier and more realistic than the masculine rigidities of, say, Shylock or the *senex* fathers, or even the harmless but sterile melancholy of Jaques. Spenser had identified Mutability as a goddess, to be sure, but Shakespeare goes beyond the allegory to locate this power of self-transformation in individualized, mysterious, believable young women.[8]

As You Like It concludes in a flood of transformations, with the tide of "if" clauses demonstrating the complete virtuosity of Rosalind's powers: "Believe then, if you please, that I can do strange things. I have, since I was three years old, conversed with a magician, most profound in his art and yet not damnable" (V.ii. 58–61). In a *commedia* pastoral, this would be literally true, and Rosalind would herself have actual magical powers. But Shakespeare has redefined and transformed transformation, so that here it is an expression of the fictive self, the virtue of "if," and it requires a complicity of imaginative belief on the audience's part. The audience within the play must approach our own faith in Ganymede:

> [To Silvius] I will help you if I can. [To Phebe] I would love you if I could. Tomorrow meet me all together. [To Phebe] I will marry you if ever I marry woman, and I'll be married tomorrow. [To Orlando] I will satisfy you if ever I satisfied man, and you shall be married tomorrow. [To Silvius] I will content you if what pleases you contents you, and you shall be married tomorrow.
>
>   (V.ii.110–17)

Rosalind's round of hypothetical promises, and the play's deepest movement, runs towards the transformations of marriage. The earlier comedies have moved under the same impulse, but none has had so many and such appropriate marriages, as Jaques notes: "There is, sure, another flood toward, and these couples are coming to the ark" (V.iv.35–6). *Twelfth Night* reveals most spectacularly how marriage becomes the deepest transformation of two into one, in which the energies of desire, the very origins of transformation, are harnessed but not suppressed by this ritualized institution. In *As You Like It,* Rosalind and Celia will undergo division of their "coupled and inseparable" state to form new and more lasting (though not for "ever") relations with Orlando and Oliver, and become if not sisters then sisters-in-law.

The appropriate but unexpected figure presiding over these ceremonies—and it should be noted that he enters just after Touchstone's virtuoso rendition of the degrees of lying (more feigning) and "much virtue in if"—is Hymen, god of marriage. His presence is almost inevitable here because his function is to preside over, to embody, the metamorphic process of marriage:

> Then is there mirth in heaven
> When earthly things made even
>   Atone together.   (V.iv.108–10)

The verb "atone" has a New Testament echo in it, and also bears its literal meaning, "to set at one"—to make two into one. Marriage is a strange thing, a "blessed bond" (l. 142) which both binds and liberates.

Like Julia, Portia, and Viola, Rosalind has been destined for this encounter with marriage, but only after her love has transformed her into someone else, only after she has become the embodiment of masculine *and* feminine love. She disguises herself initially for reasons of safety, but she soon realizes the potential of play-acting. Before Hymen has even made an appearance, Rosalind/Ganymede engineers a feigned, "if" marriage with Orlando as the natural culmination of their wooing scenes:

> ROSALIND: Come, sister, you shall be the priest and marry us. Give me your
>   hand, Orlando. What do you say, sister?
> ORLANDO: Pray thee marry us.
> CELIA: I cannot say the words.
> ROSALIND: You must begin, "Will you, Orlando"—
> CELIA: Go to. Will you, Orlando, have to wife this Rosalind?
> ORLANDO: I will.
> ROSALIND: Ay, but when?
> ORLANDO: Why now, as fast as she can marry us.
> ROSALIND: Then you must say, "I take thee, Rosalind, for wife."
> ORLANDO: I take thee, Rosalind, for wife.
> ROSALIND: I might ask you for your commission; but I do take thee, Orlando, for
>   my husband. There's a girl goes before the priest, and certainly a wom-
>   an's thought runs before her actions.   (IV.i.120–37)

Rosalind plays all the parts here, bride, bridegroom, priest; *she* is Hymen. This scene seems even more tantalizing when we realize that this mock marriage has the legal authority of a valid marriage, as marriage *per verba de praesenti;*[9] thus Rosalind's insistence on Orlando's precise present-tense acceptance of her. This is her true marriage as Ganymede, presided over by herself as Hymen; as the play ends, and Rosalind (unlike Viola) has returned to her own shape, she will be married as herself, her own magical powers now embodied in Hymen. Among the couples "coming to the ark" in the final scene are Touchstone and Audrey, whose mock marriage in III.iii, under the auspices of Sir Oliver Mar-text, had failed of completion. For Touchstone, "wedlock would be nibbling" (III.iii.80–1), and Rosalind would certainly agree (in the first act, Orlando, she says, is already "my child's father"—I.iii.11). Yet marriage is also something more mysterious and transcending than mere nibbling. Even Touchstone, "amongst the rest of the country copulatives," presses in "to swear and to forswear, according as marriage binds and blood breaks" (V.iv.57–9). These "rites" will end, like all true marriages, "in true delights" (l. 198).

Shakespeare's disguised women have been hermaphroditic, the boundaries of their femininity and masculinity increasingly an issue in the plays, culminating in Viola's Cesario, who attracts both male and female devotion. These young women have always been at least two beings by the sheer fact of their disguises, and frequently more, as they have learned to control their transformative powers. Shakespeare seems to have seen yet more potential in each succeeding play, ending in the specially triumphant mysteries of Rosalind and Viola. The disease is catching, for even the melodramatically bad brother Oliver is reformed at the end of *As You Like It:*

> 'Twas I. But 'tis not. I do not shame
> To tell you what I was, since my conversion
> So sweetly tastes, being the thing I am.   (IV.iii.134–6)

He doesn't yet realize that his "conversion" hasn't ended, that only the end of the play will place limits on it. And in fact the experience of conversion may leap across the boundary of the stage to engulf the audience. The most fundamental transformation, the most important taking on of disguise, occurs among the actors, before the audience sits down. But in *As You Like It,* Shakespeare is confident enough to disenchant us, as he had once before with the fairies in *A Midsummer Night's Dream,* to undo the one mimetic transformation we never saw begin but placed a complicit belief in. The epilogue begins with Rosalind speaking but ends with the actor's words: another case of " 'Twas I. But 'tis not I." The speaker's initial difficulty is to overcome the limitations of disguise:

> What a case am I in then, that am neither a good epilogue, nor cannot insinuate with you in the behalf of a good play! I am not furnished like a beggar; therefore to beg will not become me.

But the solution is by now a familiar one: "My way is to conjure you" (ll. 7–11). She has been a combination of entreatment and magic (as the pun has it) all along, and the final demystification occurs when *she* metamorphoses into *he*, as a kind of theatrical Iphis or Gallathea, with the play's final hypothetical:

> If I were a woman, I would kiss as many of you as had beards that pleased me, complexions that liked me, and breaths that I defied not; and I am sure, as many as have good beards, or good faces, or sweet breaths, will, for my kind offer, when I make curtsy, bid me farewell.   (ll. 16–22)

Rosalind's last transformation thus occurs before our eyes, though as usual we don't know it has happened until its cessation is asserted. We had forgotten she was not a woman.

NOTES

[1] For a recent general discussion of role-playing, see Thomas Van Laan, *Role-Playing in Shakespeare* (Toronto: Univ. of Toronto Press, 1978), especially pp. 102–16. Still useful studies of disguise include Victor O. Freeburg, *Disguise Plots in Elizabethan Drama* (1915; rpt. New York: Benjamin Blom, 1965), and M. C. Bradbrook, "Shakespeare and the Use of Disguise in Elizabethan Drama," *Essays in Criticism* 2 (1952), 159–68. Recent commentaries on sexual disguise in particular include F. H. Mares, "Viola and Other Transvestist Heroines in Shakespeare's Comedies," *Stratford Papers, 1965–1967*, ed. B. A. W. Jackson (McMaster Univ. Library Press, 1969); Juliet Dusinberre, *Shakespeare and the Nature of Women* (London: Macmillan, 1975), 231–71; Paula S. Berggren, "The Woman's Part: Female Sexuality as Power in Shakespeare's Plays," *The Woman's Part: Feminist Criticism of Shakespeare*, ed. Carolyn Ruth Swift Lenz, Gayle Greene, and Carol Thomas Neely (Urbana, Ill.: Univ. of Illinois Press, 1980); Nancy K. Hayles, "Sexual Disguise in *As You Like It* and *Twelfth Night*," *Shakespeare Survey* 32 (1979), 63–72; Nancy K. Hayles, "Sexual Disguise in *Cymbeline*," *Modern Language Quarterly* 41 (1980), 231–47; Peter Hyland, "Shakespeare's Heroines: Disguise in the Romantic Comedies," *Ariel* 9 (1978), 23–39; and Peter B. Erickson, "Sexual Politics and the Social Structure in *As You Like It*," *Massachusetts Review* 23 (1982), 65–83. Hayles's argument ("Sexual Disguise in *As You Like It* and *Twelfth Night*") reflects the opinion of many critics today: "Shakespeare's use of sexual disguise shows a definite progression: whereas in the early plays he uses it to explore the implications of sexual role-playing, in the later plays he seems increasingly interested in the metaphysical implications of the disguise, using it as a means to investigate, and eventually resolve, the disparity between appearance and essence" (p. 63). My argument is that Shakespeare is equally interested in all these questions even in the earliest plays, and that there is no "resolution" to the disparity between appearance and essence in his comedies—there is, rather, a reveling in disparity and dislocation. In her essay on *Cymbeline*, Hayles makes the amazing claim that "what is missing in the early plays is any sustained exploration of the psychological possibilities of the disguise" (p. 232).

[2] For a useful introduction to the topic, see the essay by Mircea Eliade, "Mephistopheles and the Androgyne or the Mystery of the Whole," *The Two and the One* (New York: Harper & Row, 1965); and Carolyn Heilbrun, *Toward a Recognition of Androgyny* (New York: Knopf, 1973), especially her survey of literary history, pp. 3–45.

[3] Cf. Leo Salingar, *Shakespeare and the Traditions of Comedy* (Cambridge: Cambridge Univ. Press, 1974), p. 44.

[4] T. G., "The Rich Cabinet," in John Dover Wilson, *Life in Shakespeare's England* (1911; rpt. New York: Barnes & Noble, 1969), p. 174. The argument came, in part, from Deuteronomy 22:5: "A woman shall not wear anything that pertains to a man, nor shall a man put on a woman's garment; for whoever does these things is an abomination to the LORD your God."

[5] Phillip Stubbes, *Anatomy of the Abuses in England*, ed. F. J. Furnivall (London: N. Trubner, 1877–9; rpt. 1965), p. 73. For a comprehensive study of this aspect of antitheatricalism, see the fine recent study by Jonas Barish, *The Antitheatrical Prejudice* (Berkeley: Univ. of California Press, 1981), especially pp. 80–131; Barish notes that in the characters of Falstaff, Hamlet, Edgar, and Cleopatra at least, "Shake-

speare provides a positive version of the phenomenon of self-change, a glimpse into its transfiguring possibilities" (p. 130).

[6] My discussion of Rosalind rests on the prior general interpretations of the play by C. L. Barber, *Shakespeare's Festive Comedy* (Princeton: Princeton Univ. Press, 1959); John Russell Brown, *Shakespeare and His Comedies* (London: Methuen, 1962); Harold Jenkins, "*As You Like It,*" *Shakespeare Survey* 8 (1955), 40–51; Helen Gardner, "*As You Like It,*" *More Talking of Shakespeare,* ed. John Garrett (London: Longmans, Green, 1959); David Young, *The Heart's Forest* (New Haven: Yale Univ. Press, 1972); and Alexander Leggatt, *Shakespeare's Comedy of Love* (London: Methuen, 1974).

[7] The verb "translate," which is repeated as a comic threat by Touchstone against William ("translate thy life into death"—V.i.56), has been a key metamorphic term in several of the plays, especially *A Midsummer Night's Dream.*

[8] Arguing against the received critical tradition, Peter B. Erickson, "Sexual Politics and the Social Structure in *As You Like It,*" concludes, however, that Rosalind's involvement has a serious negative side, since she must eventually "resume a traditional female role in order to engage in love" (p. 71); her disguise is not truly transforming but merely "a protective device" (p. 70). The play, he concludes, "is primarily a defensive action against female power rather than a celebration of it" (p. 82). I argue, to the contrary, that the stereotypes of femininity have been invoked by Rosalind in order to be dismissed, and that a deeper energy which essentially transcends ordinary sex roles—which I still term "feminine," admittedly—is revealed throughout the play, and the other comedies of sexual disguise.

[9] See appendix to Arden edition, ed. Agnes Latham (London: Methuen, 1975), pp. 133–5.

Devon L. Hodges

ANATOMY AS COMEDY

As You Like It is a play constituted out of conflicting desires: the desire to escape the orders of language and society and the desire to celebrate them. It begins with an assertion of social and linguistic freedom against a repressive order, a movement of liberation or escape that C. L. Barber says is basic to the comic formula of "release to clarification."[1] "Release" is necessary because linguistic conventions constrain the creative energies of the lover and the poet; the patriarchal order represses women and youngest sons. But though Barber's formula implies that "clarification" is a consequence of "release," in *As You Like It* "release" seems to impede the construction of a comic unity. The subversive dynamic of "release," which opens up forms, also leaves the lovers unable to formalize their love in speech and marriage. At the end of the play, order is imposed on the emancipated characters in Arden to make this formalization possible—though even this happily clarified order cannot entirely satisfy the desire to reveal the "real" or "natural" that lies beyond form. Not everyone accepts a place in the comic order, some characters remain "out of doors," wandering in Arden, searching for something external to all man-made orders.

The mechanism of release in this play, of breaking through forms, is the method of anatomy. Shakespeare certainly had an "anatomy" in mind when he wrote *As You Like It:* the narrative source of the play is Thomas Lodge's *Rosalynde,* subtitled "Euphues golden legacie: found after his death in his cell at Silexdra."[2] The legacy is the antithetical style of Lyly's *Euphues: The Anatomy of Wit,* which Lodge adopted. His "euphuistic" narrative was produced by turning Lyly's anatomy inside-out: in *Rosalynde,* friendship is true and not feigning, "country amours" are opposed to "courtly fancies," and women and men are as good as they appear to be. This process of reversal turns Lyly's antiromantic anatomy into a romance. Yet a necessary discord underlies the harmonies of *Rosalynde* because Lodge uses Lyly's technique of antithesis to create his picture of unity. Lodge himself acknowledges the aggressiveness of his romance in a "Letter to Gentlemen Readers": "Heere you

From *Renaissance Fictions of Anatomy* (Amherst: University of Massachusetts Press, 1985), pp. 50–67.

may perhaps find some leaves of Venus mirtle, but heawen down by a souldier with his curtleaxe, not bought with the allurement of a filed tongue." The comic unity of *Rosalynde* bears the marks of a soldierly art—the marriage ceremony at its end is interrupted by a command that the men turn their "loves into lances."[3] In *As You Like It,* Shakespeare explores Lodge's anatomizing method of achieving order, a method of unification that requires the interruption of order.

A separation of the symbolic order from the plenitudes of truth and nature motivates any anatomy: there is no need to go beyond public forms to find a locus of meaning if forms are perceived as adequate representations of reality. In *As You Like It,* an attack on form is necessary because the realm ruled by Duke Frederick is inauthentic and unnatural. The duke has violated a fundamental law of feudal society, the law of primogeniture, by usurping the position of his older brother; Orlando and Adam tell us that "the service of the antique world" has been forgotten; and even the duke himself criticizes Oliver, Orlando's brother, for neglecting his familial obligations, the ancestral bonds that are the source of legitimacy for aristocratic family. Of course the duke's reason for upholding the standards of propriety is mercenary—he punishes Oliver by sending him "out of doors" and claims his house and lands—yet his mercenary actions make the point again that the public realm has become divorced from its moral foundations.

When forms appear to lack essential value, they point to a significance that lies outside them, silent and good. The People silenced in Duke Frederick's realm stand for all his realm is not. Orlando, for example, represents an archaic ethical order, "the spirit" of his father. In an opening speech, he rebels against a brother who excludes him from the public sphere: "The courtesy of nations allows you my better in that you are the first born, but the same tradition takes not away my blood were there twenty brothers betwixt us" (I.i.42–45).[4] Blood, the body itself, challenges the public order in words that strangely prefigure Edmund's:

> Wherefore should I
> Stand in the plague of custom, and permit
> The curiosity of nations to deprive me,
> For that I am some twelve or fourteen moonshines
> Lag of a brother?[5]

But Orlando's rebellion against his older brother, which parallels Duke Frederick's rebellion against the good Duke Senior, does not seem sinister because nature (blood, the forest of Arden) is the site of value in this play. Orlando is noble by nature ("he's gentle, never schooled and yet learned") but as a youngest son he has no position in society ("Only in this world I fill up a place"). And Rosalind is in an identical position. As the daughter of the legitimate duke she is truly noble, but as a young woman without family she has no place in society. She, like Orlando, has nothing except the power to signify what society excludes. They both exist in a negative relation to the symbolic order.

Duke Frederick articulates Rosalind's power to signify what has been banished from the public order. It is not what Rosalind says, but what she does not say, what she cannot say given the limits of what can be spoken, that is dangerous to his realm:

> Thus do all traitors.
> If their purgation did consist in words,
> They are as innocent as grace itself.
> Let it suffice thee that I trust thee not.   (I.iii.48–51)

Rosalind threatens his control over the symbolic order by indicating meanings he wants to censor. Her words are innocent—but her silence, filled with what cannot be said, is subversive: Rosalind's "very silence and her patience, / Speak to the people" (I.iii.74–75). By banishing her, Duke Frederick hopes to make his order manageable, to make it seem complete and legitimate.

What is banished by Duke Frederick finds a home in Arden. The inhabitants of the forest break through appearances, they reveal occluded matter—in other words, they conduct an anatomy of order to bring hidden contents to the surface. Arden is a kind of antiworld, a place where all that is repressed in the "working-day world" can be figured forth. In this world turned inside-out, women appear to be men, men busy themselves with idle love, and language has the freedom to speak everything and nothing. The symbolic order is renewed, filled with power by an explosion of language and of love. These two mysterious entities lack a stable identity—they are playful, changeable, excessive. In this, they re-semble the inhabitants of Arden who are wandering, transforming, displaced from home. Men and women, love and language, all participate in the dizzying freedom of Arden.

The disorienting center of the play, though it allows no one a secure place or identity, is a place of happiness because love is one of the things that is located beyond all order. True love "cannot be sounded," cannot be contained in a word or definition. Rosalind insists that attempts to formalize love are unnatural, as do Celia, Touchstone, and Jaques, in criticisms of Orlando's love poetry. His verses mar the trees they hang on, they reduce Rosalind to segments ("Helen's cheek, but not her heart, / Cleopatra's majesty, / Atalanta's better part . . ." [III.ii.139–41]), and they quench the fire of love in banal formulas: "what tedious homily of love have you wearied your parishioners withal, and never cried, 'Have patience, good people!' " (III.ii.149–51). The artifice of love falsifies its nature, makes love and the lover seem lifeless stereotypes—Jaques easily labels Orlando, he is "Signior Love." To release Orlando from convention, Rosalind "cures" him of love by leading him to its unorderable depths.

Her method of getting to those depths is an anatomy. As she explains to Orlando, her "cure" is a process of exposing and exacerbating her subject's disorder:

> He was to imagine me his love, his mistress; and I set him every day to woo me. At which time would I, being but a moonish youth, grieve, be effeminate, changeable, longing and liking, proud, fantastical, apish, shallow, inconstant, full

of tears, full of smiles; for every passion something and for no passion truly anything, as boys and women are for the most part cattle of this color; would not like him, now loathe him; then entertain him, then forswear him; now weep for him, then spit at him; that I drave my suitor from his mad humor of love to a living humor of madness, which was, to forswear the full stream of the world and to live in a nook merely monastic.   (III.ii.382–94)

The danger of her technique of teaching Orlando about love is that the portrayal of love's disorder can lead to the lover's separation from the orders of reason (a "living humor of madness") and society (life in a "nook merely monastic"). Fortunately, Orlando "would not be cured," for Rosalind's success would frustrate her desire for union. There is a risk involved in teaching Orlando the difference between love and false representations of it, just as there are dangers in a blindness to this difference, in Orlando's refusal to be cured.

Without Rosalind's lessons, Orlando could remain, like the shallow Phebe, infatuated with words when love is what escapes them. A love that defies all orders expresses itself only as endless contradiction:

I will be more jealous of thee than a Barbary cock-piegon over his hen, more clamorous than a parrot against rain, more newfangled than an ape, more giddy in my desires than a monkey. I will weep for nothing, like Diana in the fountain, and I will do that when you are disposed to be merry; I will laugh like a hyen, and that when thou are inclined to sleep.   (IV.i.136–42)

Here antithesis is a means of "release." When Rosalind puts on a mask, she does so to teach Orlando not to condemn her to one. She defines her "woman's wit" as an uncontainable energy: "Make the doors upon a woman's wit, and it will out at the casement; shut that, and 'twill out at the keyhole; stop that, 'twill fly with the smoke out at the chimney" (IV.i.148–51). Hers is an anatomizing wit, a wit that undermines forms. Rosalind adopts a role to subvert all roles, and displays her wit to announce that it is pledged to nothing. She tells Orlando that Rosalind has no consistent identity and so will appear to him in many forms, as an actress in many roles. In her demand for love's freedom and her own, she resembles Cleopatra—and also the skeptical Jaques.

As the comparison with Jaques indicates, Rosalind's radical doubt about the value of formalizing love could leave her, as well as her lover, in melancholy solitude. Love that is not communicated does not lead to the exchange of love that is basic to the union of lovers. When Rosalind sees that the debunking of roles and conventions has become an obstacle rather than a means to achieve her goal of marriage, she wearies of questioning and testing forms. The conflict between the indefinable nature of love and her desire to express it becomes apparent when she finds herself the only one of the lovers who cannot speak her love. The long passage in which Rosalind discovers herself caught between speech and silence deserves to be quoted in full:

PHEBE: Good shepherd, tell this youth what 'tis to love.
SILVIUS: It is to be all made of sighs and tears;
        And so am I for Phebe.
PHEBE: And I for Ganymede.
ORLANDO: And I for Rosalind.
ROSALIND: And I for no woman.
SILVIUS: It is to be all made of faith and service;
        And so am I for Phebe.
PHEBE: And I for Ganymede.
ORLANDO: And I for Rosalind.
ROSALIND: And I for no woman.
SILVIUS: It is to be all made of fantasy,
        All made of passion, all made of wishes,
        All adoration, duty, and observance,
        All humbleness, all patience, and impatience,
        All purity, all trial, all observance;
        And so am I for Phebe.
PHEBE: And so am I for Ganymede.
ORLANDO: And so am I for Rosalind.
ROSALIND: And so am I for no woman.
PHEBE: If this be so, why blame you me to love you?
SILVIUS: If this be so, why blame you me to love you?
ORLANDO: If this be so, why blame you me to love you?
ROSALIND: Why do you speak too, 'Why blame you me to
        love you?'
ORLANDO: To her that is not here, nor doth not hear.
ROSALIND: Pray you, no more of this; 'tis like the howling of
        Irish wolves against the moon.   (V.ii.78–104)

Rosalind's love, because it eschews form, is absent, "not here." Orlando says it "doth not hear" because it does not respond to his entreaties. To make itself present, love must use artifice, must repeat and repeat time-honored sentiments. If it remains silent, and true to its own inexpressibility, love can only announce itself by saying what it is not: Rosalind says her love is "for no woman." But isn't such a negative relation to form more attractive than the conventionality of the others? The discourse perpetuated by Orlando, Phebe, and Silvius turns love into a "howling," into a frenzy of words that can speak love, but only by announcing a love (a conditional one, "if this be so") separated from its object: "Why blame you me to love you?" Rosalind cannot speak her love; Orlando can speak his love only to announce his utter separation from Rosalind. Between the lovers stand a disguise, words, representation. Yet what stands between them also links them, allows them to be coupled. It is that alienating realm of speech that gives love form and places it in the symbolic order where marriages take place. In the end, Rosalind decides to rein in her anatomizing wit, accept a role as reality, and reassert the primacy of public forms of order. She does this by embracing conventions rather than by demystifying them. All is accomplished with the help of an "if," Touchstone's peacemaker. This "if" is an ironic, though useful, maker of order, and with it Rosalind can magically make forms but she cannot consecrate them. Hymen must be brought in to transfigure the new order because Rosalind's wayward wit puts it too much in question.

Rosalind's wit makes wandering and disruption an end rather than a means to an end. It is opposed to permanence, to closure, on the grounds that "the wiser, the waywarder" (IV.i.148). The association of her linguistic powers with magic is one sign of their uncanny and disorderly nature: in telling Orlando that her magic is "not damnable," Rosalind only reminds us that magic is diabolic and unlawful. Her mentor, "an old religious uncle" who "taught [her] how to speak" (III.ii.325–26) lives apart from society and from the laws that govern it. If Rosalind is in possession of his lawless and wonderful powers, she is also possessed by them. Word magic is hard to control—once the boundaries between illusion and reality have been blurred, it is hard to reestablish them.

In *Euphues,* John Lyly makes wit his field of research. He dissects "wit." At one point in the narrative he offers a commentary on the disruptive nature of his subject:

> Heere ye may beholde gentlemen, how lewdly wit standeth in his owne lyght, howe he deemeth no pennye good silver but his owne, preferring the blossome before the fruite, the budde before the flower, the greene blade before the ripe eare of corne, his owne witte before all mens wisedomes. Neyther is that geason, seeing for the most parte it is proper to all those of sharpe capacitie to esteeme of themselves, as most proper: if one bee harde in conceiving, they pronounce him a dowlte, if given to study, they proclayme him a duns, if merrye a jester, if sadde a Sainct, if full of wordes, a sotte, if without speach, a Cypher, if one argue with them boldly, then is he impudent, if coldely an innocent, if there be reasoning of divinitie, they cry *Quae supra nos nihil ad nos,* if of humanitie, *Sententias loquitur carnifex.*[6]

A wit, according to Lyly, is lewd, narcissistic, impatient, rebellious, and contrary. Lyly's own witty language is excessive, antithetical, and through its insistent use of the conditional "if," guarded against endorsing a truth. Rosalind's wit is equally "wayward," lewdly inconstant. In a demonstration of her wit, Rosalind tells Orlando she will have him and twenty other men as well, for "can one desire too much of a good thing?" (IV.i.110–11). Here words lead her beyond the bounds of propriety.

A language "out of all hooping," a lover's language, is always "either too much at once, or none at all" (III.ii.192). Celia tells Rosalind, "Cry 'holla' to thy tongue, I prithee; it curvets unseasonably" (III.ii.232–33). Intoxicated by love, Rosalind has been overcome by language: she is in danger of enjoying her wit more than Orlando. As Roland Barthes says in *A Lover's Discourse,* "The fulfilled lover has no need to write, to transmit, to reproduce."[7] As long as Rosalind is not fulfilled, she can demonstrate her magic by creating substitutes for Orlando—words, fictions, illusions. In getting pleasure this way, Rosalind reveals that wit has become an object of desire, not a means to reach someone else: wit "deemeth no pennye good silver but his owne." Erotic and licentious verbal encounters thus usurp the place of marriage and human reproduction. The freedoms of wordplay, however, offer pleasures that are not of the body. Orlando finally tells Ganymede, "I can live no longer by thinking" (V.ii.48). Rosalind replies: "I will weary you then no longer with idle talking" (V.ii.49–50). She stops the production of verbal substitutes by the same means that maintained it—magic. With another sleight of hand, order will appear. How can we trust that this is the real thing, not an illusion? Having waylaid order with her magical wit, Rosalind cannot successfully redeem it. Shakespeare must bring in a god, Hymen, to compel our belief in the solidity of the order established at the end of the play.

The masque is a traditional form for resolving contradictions and paradoxes.[8] Shakespeare uses it to transform the stage into a vision of order: verbal design is sanctioned by a transcendent authority and the fecundity of nature is captured in the social form of marriage. Hymen announces somewhat abruptly:

> Peace ho! I bar confusion:
> 'Tis I must make conclusion
>   Of these most strange events.
> Here's eight that must take hands
> To join in Hymen's bands,
>   If truth holds true contents.   (V.iv.119–24)

Hymen's "if" is unexpected and unsettling—it begins to decompose the order that has just been consecrated. His "if" causes a fissure between the form of truth and its contents that raises a question about the truthfulness of what appears true. Even without the subversive "if" there remains a tautology, one of the "vices of language."[9] In this instance, the tautology is an image of truth's inability to be other than itself, though ironically this image is logically false. Truth cannot be spoken truly because language is made up of signs that substitute for truth itself.

The celebration of the masque requires that all the participants give up their critical distance from external form and submit themselves to one in order to renew it. Enveloped in form, the celebrants lose their wit and their freedom, and the power to order passes from Hymen to Jaques, who is separate from the form of the masque. At this moment we are distanced from the structure of comic unity and forced to recognize that it is not inclusive—Jaques remains outside this supposed order created by an "if." Duke Senior beseeches him, "Stay, Jaques, stay." Jaques replies, "To see no pastime I" (V.iv.188–89).

By calling the celebration of marriage a "pastime" Jaques turns the comic resolution into a fiction, a form separate from serious truths that are to be found outside it. Throughout the play, he relentlessly attempts to negate forms—not to get at the truths of the body but to get at meanings uncorrupted by their physical casing. He is always searching for these pure and profound truths—Jaques remains in the forest to discover "matter to be heard and learned"—because he finds no body, no order that is a site of uncorrupted value. The inevitable contamination of worldly form provokes a desire for absolute "release." This radical form of "release" cannot be achieved so long as men are masked on the stage of the world or encased in the decaying flesh of the body.

Jaques is not the only one who questions the value of theatrical gestures of opening and discovering. Even in an early scene of the play, when "release" promises to take Orlando and Rosalind from "banishment to liberty," Oliver's attempts to reveal the hidden truth of Orlando put the efficacy of opening up forms into question. Denying responsibility for a self-serving exposé of his brother, Oliver says: "I speak but brotherly of him, but should I anatomize him to thee as he is, I must blush and weep, and thou must look pale and wonder" (I.i.143–45). His words reveal the theatrics of the anatomist, the anatomist's disgust at corruption, but nothing of the subject he desires to dismember. His anatomy, then, is not a technique of discovery but a technique of displacement. It is a circuitous method— by exposing others the anatomist exposes himself. When Jaques insists that "the wise man's folly is anatomized / Even by the squand'ring glances of the fool," Duke Senior responds:

Most mischievous foul sin, in chiding sin.
For thou thyself has been a libertine,
As sensual as the brutish sting itself;
And all th' embossèd sores and headed evils
That thou with license of free foot has caught,
Wouldst thou disgorge into the general world.   (II.vii.64–69)

In this passage, the duke points out how the process of exposing others reveals the anatomist. Instead of getting at reality, at the nature of things, the anatomist covers up the world with images of himself, with the debris of his own corrupt life.

Depicted in this way, anatomy is not a positive method for bringing the truth to light, but a mechanism of self-exposure. Arden is haunted by the possibility that there is no way to go beyond self to another, beyond forms to nature. Both Phebe and Orlando are in love with mirrors of themselves: Orlando learns to love Rosalind by courting another boy; Phebe loves her own femininity which is reflected in Ganymede's.[10] Such narcissistic love, born of a process that discovers the self in others, impedes love-in-marriage, the familiar ritual of comic resolution: Orlando cannot marry another boy, nor Phebe another woman. Fortunately Rosalind is both a mirror and something else—she is self and other. But these categories, of course, are quite unstable and the play between them encourages the kind of confusion that Rosalind must resolve.

Jaques's defense of his negating technique, for example, depends on a denial of the difference between self and other. He tells the duke that whether he reveals himself or others, the result is the same, he exposes the endless vanity of men. All men narcissistically promote themselves until their energy for self-dramatization, the energy of life itself, is exhausted:

> Why, who cries out on pride
> That can therein tax any private party?
> Doth it not flow as hugely as the sea
> Till that the weary very means do ebb?   (II.vii.70–73)

To cure men of their folly, Jaques must "through and through / Cleanse the foul body of th' infected world" (II.vii.59–60). This cleansing will negate all the bodies of the world, reduce them to rubble, in an effort to return the world to order. The world, it seems, must be dismantled to be restored.

Jaques's melancholy is a reflection of such a fragmented world without a coherent meaning. This melancholy, like Rosalind's love, is better defined by what it is not than by what it is;

> I have neither the scholar's melancholy, which is emulation; nor the musician's, which is fantastical; nor the courtier's, which is proud; nor the soldier's, which is ambitious; nor the lawyer's, which is politic; nor the lady's, which is nice; nor the lover's, which is all these: but it is a melancholy of mine own, compounded of many simples, extracted from many objects, and indeed the sundry contemplation of my travels, which, by often rumination, wraps me in a most humorous sadness.   (IV.i.10–18)

This description provokes Rosalind's antivoyaging remark: "I had rather have a fool to make me merry than experience to make me sad: and to travel for it too" (IV.i.24–26). But Touchstone, the fool, has a brain in much the same state: "And in his brain, / Which is as dry as the remainder biscuit / After a voyage, he hath strange places crammed / With observation, the which he vents / In mangled forms" (II.vii.38–42). Both brains are made from a process of dislocation and displacement, from a voyaging that anatomizes the voyager. The result of "travels" is a brain crammed with bits and pieces that have lost their native ground, and with it, the anchor of their meaning. People become like those bits and pieces when they renounce their home to go wandering. Because all the exiles in Arden are wanderers, they are all vulnerable to such a loss of coherent identity. Apparently, the mechanism of "release" can undo the self by transforming it into "mangled forms," or a thing "compounded of many simples." This transformation ruins forms rather than renewing them.

Jaques and Touchstone, two characters Shakespeare added to his version of Lodge's "Rosalynde," use their unstructuring energies to expose the artificiality of the "nature" of Arden. Jaques, says Orlando, is a "fool or a cipher" and Touchstone is both. A cipher is a figure that increases or decreases the value of other figures though it is nothing in itself. It is everything and nothing like Jaques's melancholy. A touchstone is a catalyst of no value in itself which tests the value and authenticity of other things. Touchstone and Jaques, like Rosalind and Orlando, thus have a negative relation to the symbolic order—only in the formers' case they have a negative relation to the symbolic order of *Arden.* The nature of Arden, as well as the nature of society, is apparently inauthentic and unnatural. The good Duke Senior kills the natural inhabitants of the forest so that Jaques swears he does "more usurp" than his brother. And the duke further veils natural reality by translating it into a civilized style, by finding "tongues in trees, books in the running brooks, / Sermons in stones, and good in everything" (II.i.16–17). I lis artificial means of representing nature does violence to nature—a "sweet style" usurps what it signifies.

The two "fools" point out the artificiality of the forest's inhabitants and devalorize the pastoral order so glorified by Duke Senior. William Empson has taught us what Jaques teaches in the forest ("most invectively he pierceth through the body of the country, city, court, yea, and of this our life, swearing that we are mere usurpers . . ."), that the pastoral world is an aristocratic invention tyrannically imposed on nature so that the court can claim the virtues of the simple life, the harmony between rich and poor, while keeping their distance from rustic life and smelly poverty.[11] Corin, the figure of this harsher nature, has hands that smell of tar not civet, and has known the cruelty of a churlish master. Jaques crows with delight when Touchstone cuts through the trappings of the pastoral ideal with his anatomizing wit and reveals an unidealized nature (itself a convention):

> . . . 'It is ten o'clock.
> Thus we may see,' quoth he, 'how the world wags.
> 'Tis but an hour ago since it was nine,
> And after one hour more 'twill be eleven;
> And so, from hour to hour, we ripe and ripe,
> And then, from hour to hour, we rot and rot;
> And thereby hangs a tale.'   (II.vii.22–28)

Touchstone reveals an ability to argue in "good set terms" juxtaposed with a belief that the world is sunk in meaningless matter. This cynical view seems to be a product of the self-conscious linguistic virtuosity that characterizes Touchstone and Jaques. Their sophisticated attention to rhetoric has taught them that words are dissociated from any absolute ground of meaning: the matter of words mirrors the matter of the world which ripens and rots. But though both Touchstone and Jaques expose the unnatural nature of the symbolic order, Rosalind distinguishes between them, and Touchstone is included in the comic order at the end of the play while Jaques remains outside it.

When Rosalind says to Jaques, "I had rather have a fool to make me merry than experience to make me sad," she indicates that the fool accommodates man to society in a way that Jaques does not. This seems odd at first because Touchstone is more skeptical than Jaques. He is not nostalgic for a golden age and claims no vision of moral perfection as the incentive for his mocking attacks on the inhabitants of the court and forest. Paradoxically, Touchstone's skepticism is exactly what makes him less disruptive than Jaques. Because he accepts all forms and models of reality as equally true or false, he anatomizes the world not to "cure" it but to provide entertaining proofs of the illogic of logical analysis. Touchstone makes reason as strange as madness, nature as absurd as courtly artifice. It is this unavoidable duplicity of our perceptions that redeems them. One cannot lie if one cannot speak the truth: "... if you swear by that that is not, you are not forsworn" (I.ii.70–71). He celebrates the topsy-turvy condition of the world in which "the truest poetry is the most feigning."[12] By radically separating the fictional order from "true" reality he releases us from the burden of trying to find the truth. Yet at the same time his "foolishness" gives other characters a "seriousness," a measure of reality. In this way, he prevents revelations about the artificial nature of the comic order from turning the play into a tragic exploration of the limits of symbolic order.

Touchstone finds the essential fictionality of the world a source of freedom, Jaques finds it a source of melancholy. When Jaques asks to be granted the role of fool, there is a proviso to his request:

> It is my only suit,
> Provided that you weed your better judgments
> Of all opinion that grows rank in them
> That I am wise. I must have liberty
> Withal, as large a charter as the wind,
> To blow on whom I please ...   (II.vii.44–49)

Jaques can only cleanse the "foul body of the infected world" by distancing himself from all the false forms that give shape to human experience; even the suit of the fool might constrain him. This movement of separation challenges the value of the refined comic order—and it undermines Jaques's own identity. Liberty from an external identity means a self scattered to the winds. By refusing any role, Jaques can have no stable identity; by refusing any single system of interpretation, he can find the world only in bits and pieces without relation or relevance. His very name, Jaques, is associated with "jakes," a privy, and the useless debris of man.

As far as Jaques is concerned, human forms are no more than such debris. From his melancholy perspective, the body is a locus of corruption, not of positive values. In his speech on the seven ages of man, Jaques conducts a dissection of the body of human life that gradually reduces it to nothing: "mere oblivion, / Sans teeth, sans eyes, sans taste, sans everything" (II.vii.165–66). Human reality is hollow, empty, because it is mere appearance: "All the world's a stage, / And all the men and women merely players" (II.vii.139–40). Through the equation of the world and the stage, life and representation are conflated into superficial matter.[13] The co-incidence of reality and the stage draws attention to the superficiality of Jaques's own language so his critique both loses some of its force and is strengthened by example: his melancholy posturing and verbal excesses, such as moralizing a spectacle into a "thousand similes," makes linguistic and theatrical representation seem unnatural and contrived. His anatomizing discourse is as limited and conventional as Orlando's love poetry—Orlando is "Signior Love," Jaques is another stereotype, "Monsieur Melancholy."[14] It is not "experience" or nature that has made Jaques sad, but books.[15] Orlando rebukes Jaques for his bookishness, saying, "I answer your right painted cloth, from whence you have studied your questions" (III.ii.261–62). R. Warwick Bond insists that *Euphues* is the book that determines Jaques's identity: "Jaques ... is simply Euphues Redivivus."[16] But Jaques also has much in common with Nashe—he negates forms (the bodies of country, city, court) to produce them. Jaques sucks life out of forms, as a "weasel sucks eggs" because the destruction of forms enables him to create new, fragmented ones.

If the decomposition of forms is a means of artistic production rather than a means of analysis, we might conclude that anatomy, or other means of "release," pose no real critique of the symbolic order. In a sense this is right, comedies mock the orders that serve for reality but also reinstate them as guarantors of community and proof of the existence of an irreducible meaning. But this comedy does not just pretend to desire "release" while actually firmly upholding the status quo. It is not enough to say that Jaques is merely a showman rather than a critic, and that Rosalind's effort to explore the depths is merely a ruse of language. Rosalind and Orlando insist that the social order of Duke Frederick is repressive; Jaques insists that man is encased in matter that separates him from the profound truth of things. And when the play ends, it is left to Jaques to expose the inadequacies of the "clarified" order of comic resolution. When he puts the characters in their places they begin to seem like empirical objects: they are "you," "you," "you," "you," and "you." By "you" he designates the Duke, Orlando, Oliver, Silvius, and Touchstone, who are all lost to a form that usurps their identity. The women are not designated at all. This comic form that envelops the characters is no more absolute than the one created by the usurping Duke Frederick; it will decay in time. Jaques tells Touchstone: "Thy loving voyage is but for two months victualled." What seems like a permanent order is yet another voyage.

Jaques's refusal to succumb to any one vision of order, no matter how compelling it is, seems misanthropic: he gives up participation in a community in order to inhabit the duke's abandoned cave. Yet the whole play has emphasized the affirmative power of negating forms and going into exile. A sign of "true love" is a man's separation from society: "if thou hast not broke from company / Abruptly . . . / Thou has not loved" (II.iv.37–39). Freedom is found in banishment, love in solitude, life in Arden is "more sweet / Than that of painted pomp" (II.i.2–3). As the lovers move back to court, new exiles inhabit the forest, and this means what it did in the beginning—the need for order is challenged by a desire to escape from its constraints. Admittedly Duke Frederick is oddly cast as a "convertite" (yet so is Oliver) and Jaques is a rather gloomy model of intellectual liberty. But though each man's antidote for idolatry is extreme, the play insists on the importance of subverting conventional orders, even affirmative conventions of ending.

Though Jaques's refusal to join the dance of marriage may seem to be a rejection of life, his renunciation gives expression to the comedy's central desire for "release," a desire whose ability to endanger comic order is now apparent. The tension we feel between the comic celebration of form and the desire to escape it is different from the *balance* between these two impulses that is found in *Euphues* and "Euphues golden legacie." A mark of this difference is its ability to produce tragedy. *As You Like It* is a point of departure for a voyage into the fragmented world of *King Lear*. Within the comic desire for a "clarified" order grows a desperate need to reveal the essence of love and truth that provokes and sustains the circular and disruptive anatomizing activity. Because an order "as you like it" is not the same as an order "as it really is" the play leaves us asking questions: Is man enslaved by false orders? Do these orders protect us from chaos? Can we anatomize these structures that bind us? Or should we?

NOTES

[1] C. L. Barber sets forth his theory of comedy in *Shakespeare's Festive Comedy: A Study of Dramatic Form in Relation to Social Custom* (Princeton: Princeton University Press, 1959). Barber's definition of comic form makes it difficult for him to address the tone of despair and anxiety that characterizes many of the late comedies.

[2] From the frontispiece of Thomas Lodge's *Rosalynde, Euphues golden legacie, The Complete Works of Thomas Lodge* (1883; reprint ed., London: Russell and Russell, 1963), vol. I.

[3] Ibid., pp. 7, 137.

[4] All citations from the plays are to *William Shakespeare: The Complete Works*, ed. Alfred Harbage (Baltimore: Penguin, 1970).

[5] *King Lear*, I.ii.2–6. In her article *"As You Like It"* (reprinted in *Shakespeare: The Comedies*, ed. Kenneth Muir [Englewood Cliffs: Prentice-Hall, 1965]), Helen Gardner discusses the elements that relate *As You Like It* to *King Lear*. See especially pp. 65–66.

[6] Lyly, *Euphues: The Anatomy of Wit*, in *The Complete Works of John Lyly*, ed. W. Warwick Bond (1902; reprint ed., Oxford: Clarendon Press, 1967), I:195.

[7] Roland Barthes, *A Lover's Discourse*, trans. Richard Howard (New York: Hill and Wang, 1978), p. 56.

[8] For an analysis of the masque see Angus Fletcher, *The Transcendental Masque: An Essay on Milton's Comus* (Ithaca and London: Cornell University Press, 1971). In his discussion of the ephemerality of the masque and its resort to magic, Fletcher reveals the ambiguous nature of this festive form.

[9] Miriam Joseph lists "tautology" as one of the vices of language in her *Shakespeare's Use of the Arts of Language* (New York: Columbia University Press, 1947), p. 302. She also mentions the Tudor rhetoricians' delight in anatomies, a delight shared by Shakespeare (see p. 369).

[10] Rosalind chides Orlando because he does not appear to love anyone but himself: "you are rather point-device in your accoustrements, as loving yourself than seeming the lover of any other" (III.ii.360–62).

[11] For my understanding of the pastoral I am indebted, as most of us are, to William Empson's *Some Versions of Pastoral* (London: Chatto and Windus, 1935).

[12] Touchstone, as has often been noted, here echoes Sir Philip Sidney's remark in *An Apologie for Poetry* that the poet "nothing affirms and therefore never lieth."

[13] Perhaps this critique of representation may tell us something about why there are no mothers in *As You Like It* or *King Lear*. Displacements, banishments, exiles can thematize an initial separation from the mother. They also may reveal a desire for such a separation—a desire to avoid natural reproduction and the death and corruption that all living images suffer. In *King Lear* the link between natural reproduction and the horrible fertility of decay underlies the play's most misogynist language.

[14] Bridget Gellert Lyons, in *Voice of Melancholy: Studies in Literary Treatments of Melancholy in Renaissance England* (New York: W. W. Norton, 1971), discusses the convention of melancholy in *As You Like It*. Jaques, she says, "gives expression, by his comments and his very existence, to some of the disharmonies of the forest" (p. 51).

[15] Harold Jenkins suggests a link between Jaques and the studious middle son of Rowland de Boys, also named Jaques. See his article *"As You Like It,"* in *Shakespeare Survey* 8, ed. Allardyce Nicoll (Cambridge: Cambridge University Press, 1955), pp. 40–51.

[16] R. Warwick Bond, "Introductory Essay," *Works of John Lyly*, p. 167.

Barbara J. Bono

MIXED GENDER, MIXED GENRE IN *AS YOU LIKE IT*

Does Shakespeare's preoccupation, especially in the comedies, with strong female characters and an underlying complex of "feminine" concerns—sexuality and familial and domestic life—provide evidence for what Juliet Dusinberre calls a "feminism of Shakespeare's time"?[1] Or does the same evidence indicate male projections of what women must be, what Madelon Gohlke terms a "matriarchal substratum or subtext within the patriarchal text" that "is not feminist," but rather "provide[s] a rationale for the structure of male dominance"?[2] Put more generally, does the literature and social practice of the early modern period exhibit, as Stephen Greenblatt and Natalie Zemon Davis suggest, a theatricality, a ready embrace of role playing and social inversion, that nonetheless functions most often to test and strengthen traditional authority?[3] And if, with Davis and, more tentatively, Greenblatt, we wish to argue that the subversion occasionally escapes its cultural containment, how does this escape occur, and in what does it, or our latter-day perception of it, consist? In this essay I seek to erect a framework of contemporary feminist theory around a traditional genre-based analysis of the heroic, romantic, and pastoral strains in Shakespeare's *As You Like It* in order to conjure a complex response to these questions.

Recently Nancy Chodorow has offered a powerful and influential new model for psychoanalysis and the sociology of gender that seems very useful for analyzing the representation of gender in literature as well.[4] In an object-relations account of identity formation that stresses the temporal primacy of the mother, Chodorow presses her analysis back beyond the oedipal phase to the preoedipal phase, significantly revising Freud's classic accounts of both masculinity and femininity.

Freud privileges the male sex in his account of gender identity, speaking of the oedipal castration fear of the boy child and the penis envy of the girl child. But by placing the mother as socializer at the heart of her account, Chodorow character-

From *Renaissance Genres: Essays on Theory, History, and Interpretation* (Harvard English Studies 14), edited by Barbara Keifer Lewalski (Cambridge, MA: Harvard University Press, 1986), pp. 189–212.

izes gender and sexual differentiation not "as presence or absence of masculinity and the male genital" but as "two different presences."[5] The male child defines himself in a tension-fraught opposition to his potentially engulfing mother, while the female child has the more complex and extended, if less extreme, task of simultaneously affirming a gender identity with the mother and an individual differentiation from her.[6] A girl child's "penis envy" is, then, not a recognition of a primary lack but a secondary, defensive reaction against maternal power and an attempted appropriation of what is seen as greater masculine autonomy from it. Chodorow argues that the events of the oedipal period must be understood against this preoedipal background that is itself more centrally a social than a biological experience: "In fact, what occurs for both sexes during the oedipal period is a product of this knowledge about gender and its social and familial significance, rather than the reverse (as the psychoanalytic accounts have it)."[7]

The strengths of Chodorow's clinically documented and tenaciously argued model seem to me many. Her stress on the early, preconscious psychological formation of these patterns in interaction with a female mother who is primary caretaker explains the seeming universality, rootedness, and strong elements of complicity in those arrangements through which women become the "second sex." Although the responsibility has often been diffused or configured somewhat differently, primary female mothering has been a cultural and historical constant. However, it need not be an inevitability. Chodorow's theory is genuinely anthropological and sociological in denying biological determinism and in noting considerable differences in the social practice of mothering, and it shares with thinkers like Dorothy Dinnerstein a revolutionary feminist belief in the possibility of change in our sexual arrangements based on changing the sexual division of labor into shared parenting.[8]

It also contains an embryonic historical dimension, for Chodorow notes that the emphasis on the single female mother has altered over time. She comments especially on the effects of modern capitalism in widening the sexual division of labor by separating home and workplace and institutionalizing within the workplace a division between largely female service occupations and the ideal of a male worker detached from prior community, eager to succeed, and highly malleable to organizational needs.[9] Certain features of this analysis seem relevant to the early modern period in England, during the rise of capitalism—the period when Shakespeare's plays were written. Then men, often no longer owners or caretakers of land in a feudal system, were sent out early for education or apprenticeship and took up entrepreneurial schemes in court and city, while patriarchal values kept women even more closely tied to the work of childbearing and motherhood.[10]

Coppélia Kahn has demonstrated the applicability of Chodorow's theory of gender formation to the representation of male personality in Shakespeare's plays, particularly *King Lear*. Arguing that Lear's unconscious male fear of maternal power is displaced into metaphoric expression, Kahn instances his loathing of his "pelican daughters" and his shame at his own woman's tears and "female" hysteria (the "climbing mother," the disorder of the wandering womb).[11] She might also have added the most inclusive metaphoric expression in the play of this threatening female power, the goddess-Mother Nature whom Edmund invokes to "stand up for bastards," and who proves Lear and his followers not ague-proof. The implication of this sexual metaphorization of landscape is that pastoral and antipastoral—"soft" and "hard" primitivism—may figure the opposite sides of the male crisis of individuation from the mother—nurturance or antipathy.

Kahn's methodological tactic supports Louis Montrose's excellent sociological reading of that pastoral play, As You Like It.[12] Focusing explicitly on the historically sensitive oedipal situation of brothers' rivalry over a paternal inheritance, Montrose rightly restores balance to the interpretation of the play by dwelling on the very engaging plot of Orlando's rise that frames Rosalind's androgynous disguising. He devotes the penultimate section of his essay on "the complex interrelationship of brothers, fathers, and sons in As You Like It" to a suggestive discussion of Rosalind and of the play's strategies for containment of the feminine. In Montrose's shrewd formulation, "The 'feminism' of Shakespearean comedy seems to me more ambivalent in tone and more ironic in form than such critics [those infatuated with Rosalind's exuberance] have wanted to believe."[13] Kahn's work suggests that from a male point of view both Rosalind and Arden are initially threatening but eventually beneficent manifestations of a nonfeminist maternal subtext. It is possible, then, that in Shakespeare's works both the explicitly threatening women of the tragedies and the seemingly benevolent women of the comedies operate within a "universe of masculinist assumptions" about the nature of women.[14]

Yet Chodorow's model would also argue for a positive female identity, although one severely handicapped by the perception of itself as culturally secondary. Kahn and Montrose do not inquire whether Shakespearean drama can plausibly represent this point of view, and if so, whether that drama can provide us with any tool for dislodging "the universe of masculinist assumptions" in which it is embedded. In what follows I would like to sketch both Orlando's and Rosalind's roles in the play on the basis of Chodorow's model for the formation of gender identity. I shall argue that the patriarchal, oedipal crisis of the first act of the play is displaced back onto its preoedipal ground in the nature of the forest of Arden—that place named suggestively after Shakespeare's own mother, Mary Arden, and the forest near his birthplace at Stratford-on-Avon.[15] There the play can represent both the male struggle for identity and a female "double-voiced" discourse—Elaine Showalter's term for one that simultaneously acknowledges its dependence on the male and implies its own unique positive value—within it.[16]

For this Shakespeare employs, of course, not a modern psychoanalytic or sociological vocabulary, but his period's vocabulary of genre, set within the consciously experimental frame of the mixed genre of pastoral.[17] Orlando's masculine heroic quest, couched simultaneously in the language of biblical typology and classical epic, is resolved within Arden's "sweet style." There Rosalind, fully acting out romance's conventions of disguise, transforms the social perception of woman from the Petrarchan conventions that both idealize and degrade them to a new convention of companionate marriage. Unlike Orlando's simpler quest, Rosalind's "double-voiced" discourse, criticizing the subject of which she is a part, can thus offer a method for cultural change. She performs *within* the text the critical task feminists today must perform *toward the text as a whole*. As Madelon Gohlke says, "For a feminist critic to deconstruct this discourse is simultaneously to recognize her own historicity and to engage in the process of dislocation of the unconscious by which she begins to affirm her own reality."[18]

But only begins. Rosalind's deconstructive efforts within her own text are one such beginning—a method, not an ideal end. Ironically, she resubordinates herself through marriage to masculine hierarchy, giving herself to her father to be given to her husband, and thus serves the socially conservative purpose of Shakespearean romantic comedy. And "she," of course, acts out a fiction of femininity on an exclusively male stage, her part played by a boy. The representation of women has, more often than not, functioned this way in literature, as in life—as an accommodating device within the dominant fictions of male identity.

Thus far I have emphasized Rosalind's critical role within the text and her eventual surrender of it. Nonetheless, the interaction in *As You Like It* between masculine heroic discourse and feminine romantic "double-voiced" discourse, which it is the burden of this essay to document, forms the dramatic "inside" to a metadramatic context or "outside" of more pure interpretative possibility. Rosalind's disguise, initially the most striking convention of romance implausability in this text that is so largely structured like an "old tale" (1.2.120), ultimately functions to create new possibilities for it. Her mutable action most fully demonstrates Touchstone's peacemaking "If" (5.4.97–103); Ganymede—the lovely boy whose rapture connected earth and heaven—predicates Hymen, the god of marriage who will "atone" all the elements of the play. In this play romance sustains the constructive, as well as the critical, aspects of pastoral. Arden and the audience addressed in the "Epilogue" function as the complementary environments of the play. Although, looking ahead to *Lear*, I shall characterize the pastoral environment of Arden as a sometimes harsh, sometimes nurturing "Mother Nature"; it is also, as Amiens hints to the Duke, a theater for literary and social criticism and change. For the culturally belated urban artists of the Renaissance, pastoral, which in theory promised a return to origins and a poetic apprenticeship, in practice often presented itself as a field for heightened reflexivity, itself criticizing the subject—the larger culture—of which it formed a part. The "Epilogue" to *As You Like It* freely acknowledges affect as in part constituting the meaning of a work of art: although we may never know what Shakespeare's audience made of the actor-playing-Rosalind's final address, we are licensed to make of it what pleases. At the close of this essay I shall offer a few tentative speculations on why Shakespeare himself, in his later career, made difficult or surrendered this "poco tempo silvano," this play-space of pastoral. But within *As You Like It*, at least, we and the forest are the final judges.

In Shakespeare's *As You Like It* both Duke Senior and Orlando are victims of parricidal rage. The anger of Orlando's brother Oliver is given biblical and classical archetypal overtones as their old family retainer Adam, a representative of the

Golden Age "When service sweat for duty, not for meed" (2.3.58), stands in place of their father to bemoan the loss of original "accord" and to denounce Oliver, that Cain figure, who has made "this house . . . but a butchery" (1.1.64; 2.3.27). Shakespeare heightens the at once fairy-tale and all-too-contemporary figure of the impoverished younger brother into an image of paradise lost, where the rising spirit of one's father threatens to turn into rankling bitterness.[19]

Orlando does not seek the patrimony. He desires only his "poor allottery" of "but poor a thousand crowns" (1.1.73; 2–3) and his due "breeding" in gentility. Ironically, he has only his physical strength, his wrestler's skill, to prove these largely immaterial claims, and even his victory over Charles is immediately frustrated by Duke Frederick's antipathy. As with Chodorow's oedipally fraught male child, these problems in the patriarchy open a greater void in his identity, a potential regression to a threatening maternal subtext. Orlando fears that his growth may prove, as Oliver says, "rank" (cf. 1.1.13 with 1.1.85–86). In the wrestling scene Charles taunts him with being, like Antaeus, "desirous to lie with his mother earth" (1.2.201). Although Orlando at first inverts the allusion by defeating Charles as the moral Hercules defeated Antaeus, he then assimilates some of its force when, in a "modest" displacement of Charles's incestuous image, he finds himself violently in love with Rosalind.[20] His formerly dignified speech before Rosalind is now shattered as the deepest dimension of his insecurity, his lack of good breeding, surfaces (cf. 1.2.165–193 and 245–260), and he fears exile in an inhospitable nature where he might have to beg, or, like Tom Jones, fall in with robbers (1.1.75; 2.3.31–35).[21]

When Orlando flees to the forest, he expects to encounter savagery. Instead, this young man struggling for gentility—"inland bred" (2.7.96)[22]—meets not brigands but a kindly, paternal, philosophic ruler, the exiled Duke: "Sit down and feed, and welcome to our table" (2.7.105). Shakespeare compresses in this brief exchange the ancient ideal of hospitality, those guest-rites most fully performed in the offering of a meal, the contemplative counterweight to epic's celebration of martial deeds and heroic adventure. And as with Odysseus at Alcinous's house or Aeneas at Dido's banquet, the gesture releases Orlando's pent-up memory and social desire. His deeply moving litany of the ceremonies of civilization is ritually echoed by the Duke:

> True is it that we have seen better days,
> And have with holy bell been knoll'd to church,
> And sat at good men's feasts, and wip'd our eyes
> Of drops that sacred pity hath engend'red;
> And therefore sit you down in gentleness,
> And take upon command what help we have
> That to your wanting may be minist'red.   (2.7.120–126)

The text expands momentarily into a calm reflective pool of noble pity—"sunt lacrimae rerum et mentem mortalia tangunt" ("here, too, there are tears for misfortune and mortal sorrows touch the heart," *Aeneid*, 1.462). A moment later Orlando visually contradicts Jaques's vivid but reductionistic image of the "seven ages of man" by entering with the frail old Adam, quite possibly borne on his shoulders, and thereby evoking that classical image of *pietas,* Aeneas carrying his father Anchises from burning Troy (2.7.139–168). Then, even while Amiens sings of man's ingratitude, the Duke discovers that Orlando is his beloved "good Sir Rowland's son" (2.7.191–192) and welcomes him to his new society.

The Duke's masculine governing identity has not been violently dislocated by exile. Unlike Lear, who feels the "climbing mother," gives way to women's tears, and, in a sharply discontinuous action marked by disjoint, raving speech, exposes himself to the raging elements, Duke Senior exercises seemingly benign verbal control over his environment. The balanced blank verse of his first speech moves to contain the sharp sensuous apprehension of difference: "the icy fang / And churlish chiding of the winter's wind, / Which ... bites and blows upon my body" is literally bracketed by his declaration that "Here feel we *not* the penalty of Adam" and his smiling philosophic conclusion (2.1.5–17, emphasis mine). The Duke tries to surround the threatening nature that had opened up with the failure of the patriarchy in the first act, controlling it so that Orlando, and to a large extent we, now experience it as the playfulness of Rosalind, rather than the threat of the unnurturing and devouring mother. His "kindly," "sweet" stylization—the words resonate with the high philosophic seriousness of the *dolce stil nuovo* and its ideals of gentility—now permits the growth of Orlando's romantic art.

Chodorow speaks of boys as having to "define themselves as more separate and distinct [from the mother], with a greater sense of rigid ego boundaries and differentiation," and thus resolving their oedipal crisis more rapidly, extremely, and definitively than girls. The resolution takes the form of "identification with his father ... the superiority of masculine identification and prerogatives over feminine" (in Freud's more extreme language, "What we have come to consider the normal male contempt for women"), and the eventual displacement of his primary love for his mother onto an appropriate heterosexual love object.[23] Orlando, after initial conflict with paternal figures—his older brother and Duke Frederick—which nearly culminates in archetypal tragedy, experiences nature as harshly threatening. He is saved from its ravages by a kindly father figure who thus metaphorically restores the archetypal line of paternal descent. With the confidence of that masculine relatedness he is able to play seriously at the civilized game of love without threatening his basic male heroic identity. Then Rosalind-as-Ganymede can work to refine his personality while being herself ultimately contained by an overt masculinist sexual ideology.

Meanwhile, similar social problems unfold differently in an aristocratic women's world. Instead of Orlando's importunate strivings, Rosalind at court displays a more diffuse melancholy, partially relieved by feminine confidences—Chodorow's female "self in relationship."[24] Rosalind's musings about the precarious social position of women in love—"[Fortune] the bountiful blind woman doth most mistake in her gifts to women" (1.2.35–36)—suggest that the Duke's exile, deeply felt though it is, is less important than her problematic femininity, especially without his protection. And the desultory and slightly forced nature of the talk portrays the extreme constraints on women's expression in such a setting. Even Touchstone's flat joke about the pancakes must be triggered by a reminder of their feminine lack of a beard (1.2.60–80)! Against this sense of inferiority and vulnerability the young women here have only ready wit.

Exiled by her tyrannous uncle, Rosalind assumes masculine disguise as a safeguard against female vulnerability in a threatening male world. Once she is safely installed in her cottage in Arden, however, there is in theory no need for her to maintain that role. Indeed, once she hears from Celia that young Orlando, who at court "tripp'd up the wrastler's heels and your heart, both in an instant" (3.2.212–213), is in the forest poeticizing her praises, she immediately exclaims, "Alas the day, what shall I do with my doublet and hose?" (3.2.219–220), and bursts forth with a stereotypically female torrent of questions and effusions, ending with "Do you not know I am a woman? when I think, I must speak" (3.2.249–250). She seems on the verge of throwing off her masculine attire and becoming the Renaissance total woman: witty, perhaps, but ultimately compliant.

At this moment, however, Orlando and Jaques enter in conversation. They implicitly raise the issue of women's dependence on men that Rosalind's exile from the court has merely transferred from the political to the psychological sphere. Orlando's "pretty answers," the love commonplaces that Touchstone has already parodied (2.4.46–56; 3.2.100–112) and that Rosalind herself has criticized as "tedious" and having "more feet than the verses would bear" (3.2.155, 165–166), are now attacked by the satiric Jaques, "Monsieur Melancholy." Although Orlando, "Signior Love," holds his own in this comic agon, it is not at all clear from the women's point of view that his disagreement with Jaques is anything more than a battle of wits masking potentially violent sexual appetite. As Jaques accuses, Orlando may be tritely copying his "posies" out of the inscriptions inside goldsmiths' rings. More ominously, he may have "conn'd" the "rings" themselves from the goldsmiths' wives, where the connotations "con" = "pudendum" and "rings" = "vagina" suggest seduction. As Celia warns, if you drink in this type of discourse uncritically, you risk putting a "man in your belly" (3.2.204). Hearing this affected and subtly threatening exchange prompts Rosalind to keep her doublet and hose, and what is more, to use them in exactly the sort of "double-voiced" discourse that, according to Showalter, has always characterized the relationship of female to male culture: "I will speak to him like a saucy lackey, and under that habit play the knave with him" (3.2.295–297). That is, she will adopt the "habit"—the clothing and habitual ways—of the dominant male culture, including its view of women, even while skewing it "saucily" toward self-consciousness and criticism, and maintaining a part of herself hidden and inviolate.

Nancy Vickers, in a recent article on Petrarchism, implies the defensive wisdom of this tactic.[25] This tradition imagines a chaste, inaccessible, Diana-like woman as the object of the male speaker's love, engendering in him a narcissistically luxuriant range of contradictory emotions that further objectify her, retributively fragmenting her body. Shakespeare continually documents and criticizes this pathology, from Romeo's bookish love for the chaste Rosaline, to Orsino's self-indulgent laments after the "cloistered" Olivia, to its *reductio ad absurdum* in Troilus' languishing after the parts of Cressida, soon to become nauseating "fragments, scraps, the bits and greasy relics / Of her o'er-eaten faith" (*Tro.*, 5.2.159–160). Within this self-generating fiction the only power that women seem to have is the defensive one of refusal, for then, at least, they may put off being consumed and discarded: as Cressida says: "Therefore this maxim out of love I teach: / Achievement is command; ungain'd beseech" (*Tro.*, 1.2.293–294). Orlando hymns a Diana-like Rosalind in a patently artificial language predicated on the Duke's philosophic sweet style; instead of finding "tongues in trees" (2.1.16), the eager new versifier vandalizes them: "these trees shall be my books, / And in their barks my thoughts I'll character" (3.2.5–6). Rosalind witnesses the hitherto uncultivated Orlando's burgeoning conventional love poetry, and by remaining a boy at first defensively distances herself from it.

But Rosalind ultimately accomplishes something more constructive through her pastoral disguise as Ganymede, that pretty boy beloved by Jove, alternately a figure of sexual degradation or of ecstasy.[26] By self-consciously retaining her superficially plausible disguise as a girlish boy—that is, by seeming to "be" Ganymede offering to "play" Rosalind—Rosalind simultaneously offers Orlando a chance to test "the faith of . . . [his] love" (3.2.428) within the relatively nonthreatening limits of supposed male discourse about women, and attempts to exorcise her own fears about giving herself into such a discourse.

In doing so she illustrates the greater social burden borne by women, in line with Chodorow's contention that the oedipus complex develops "different forms of 'relational potential' in people of different genders" and that "Girls emerge from this period with a basis for 'empathy' built into their primary definition of self in a way that boys do not."[27] Having suffered an oedipal crisis in the first act of the play because of the exile of her father and the opposition of Duke Frederick, Rosalind too is thrown back upon nature. Unlike Orlando, however, she does not experience this preoedipal nature as harshly threatening, nor does she require the immediate assurances of a restored father figure. Instead she arrives "weary" but resourceful; female ennervation in the court here translates into boyish pluck (2.4.1–8). As Chodorow says, "girls do not define themselves in terms of the denial of preoedipal relational modes to the same extent as do boys. Therefore, regression to these modes tends not to feel as much a basic threat to their ego."[28]

Chodorow's careful characterization of "a relational complexity in feminine self-definition and personality which is not characteristic of masculine self-definition or personality"[29] not only highlights the difference between Rosalind's and Orlando's reactions to Arden; it also helps explain why Rosalind/Ganymede behaves the way she/he does there. In Arden Rosalind discovers a female identity that will allow her to complete the difficult, triangulated resolution of a girl's typical oedipal crisis: differentiation from *and* continuity with the mother and transfer of affection from the father onto an appropriate heterosexual love object. She must act out her own involvement with this less threatening "Mother Nature" in a way that does not shatter Orlando's more fragile ego boundaries; having done so she may deliver herself to the restored patriarchy, giving herself to her father to be given by him in marriage to her husband.

Her interaction as Ganymede/Rosalind with Orlando thus functions from the male perspective as a form of accommodation and as a test. In the court Orlando had been tongue-tied before beautiful, young, aristocratic women; freed and newly confident in the forest he understandably blurts out clichés. Talk with an attractive boy about women can work to root and refine his discourse, as encounter with "the real thing" at this point could not. Orlando recovers his quietly dignified desire in conversation with Ganymede: "I am he that is so love-shak'd"; "I would not be cur'd"; "By the faith of my love" (3.2.367, 425, 428). Meanwhile, Rosalind/Ganymede tests "the faith of . . . [his] love" against the tradition of misogyny that the unrealistic idealism of Petrarchism could reinforce. As a young man supposedly educated by a sexually disillusioned and withdrawn "old religious uncle of mine" (3.2.344), she professes scepticism toward Orlando and cynicism toward women (3.2.369–371, 348–350), and in her succeeding therapy, proposing to cure love by counsel, she acts out for his benefit men's stereotypical expectations of women's fickleness and seeming cruelty

> in this manner. He was to imagine me his love, his mistress; and I set him every day to woo me. At which time would I, being but a moonish youth, grieve, be effeminate, changeable, longing and liking, proud, fantastical, apish, shallow, inconstant, full of tears, full of smiles . . . that I drave my suitor from his mad humor of love to a living humor of madness, which was, to forswear the full stream of the world, and live in a nook merely monastic.
>
> (3.2.407–412, 417–421)

In response to her trying poses, Orlando remains constant. The Orlando we see in the final act of the play is now appropriately sceptical of fanciful love at first sight and has painfully earned the "real" love he is given.

However, he does not develop a very much more sophisticated understanding of women's ambiguous position in the world. Throughout Rosalind's disguising, Orlando retains an essentially simple faith grounded in his newly secure identity in the Duke's service. He has an increasingly melancholy feeling that this interlude is just a game—that he may be wasting time—and he breaks off wooing to "attend the Duke at dinner" (4.1.180). Rosalind's action as Ganymede/Rosalind does not shock or void his identity in the way nature had earlier threatened to do; instead she leads him to revise his Petrarchan idealization of women—"The fair, the chaste, and unexpressive she" (3.2.10)—toward a desire for a chaste wife, and sets that desire within the dominant code of his male heroic identity.

Rosalind as Ganymede, however, transforms herself more thoroughly. As her words imply, she is not a dispassionate therapist: "Love is merely a madness, and I tell you, deserves as well a dark house and a whip as madmen do; and the reason why they are not so punish'd and cur'd is, that *the lunacy is so ordinary that the whippers are in love too"* (3.2.400–404, emphasis mine). Critics have always commented on Rosalind's control of decorum while in disguise, but in a play written almost contemporaneously with *Hamlet* her "holiday humor" (4.1.69), like his "antic disposition," is as much used to exorcise her own fears about love as it is to criticize or educate her lover. Rosalind's control lies in standing outside of amatory convention, but it is her action within these conventions that carries her, almost imperceptibly, into the "magic" of creating a new, and within the value judgments of this play, more adequate convention of companionate marriage.

This becomes clear in her interaction with Silvius and Phebe. During a frustrating break in her play with Orlando—he is late for his appointment with her—she slips from her earlier facile and uncritical sympathy for Silvius' mooning "shepherd's passion" (2.4.60) to a desire to *do* something, to enter their amusingly static and artificial pastoral "pageant" and "prove a busy actor in their play" (3.4.47–59). What she does there, quite to her surprise, is to become the sexually ambiguous means—a boyish "ripe sister" (4.3.87)—through which their hopelessly stalemated and conventional Petrarchan attitudes are softened toward reciprocal love. Silvius, who has previously been an utter fool in love, running off stage (as Orlando later does for Rosalind, cf. 3.2.9–10) exclaiming "O Phebe, Phebe, Phebe!" (2.4.43), assumes a sober fidelity under Ganymede's rebuke; the disdainful Phebe, having now felt the pang of love for Ganymede, is at least sorry for "gentle" Silvius (3.5.85). When Rosalind dissolves her disguise at the end of the play, they have seen each other through her, and Phebe assures Silvius that "Thy faith my fancy to thee doth combine" (5.4.150).

Rosalind-as-Ganymede's action within Silvius and Phebe's play has double relevance for her action within her own. It makes explicit her androgynous power, even while it implies her own subliminal desire to give herself to Orlando. In her next scene with Orlando she fulfills her earlier plan (4.1), acting as she thinks men expect women to do, alternately Lady Disdain and the threateningly promiscuous dark lady of the sonnets. The vehemence and verve of her acting here argues that she is now doing this as much for her own sake as for Orlando's. It is necessary for her to misuse her sex, to soil her own nest, as Celia half-jokingly puts it (4.1.201–204), in order to hide the "woman's fear" (1.3.119) in her heart. She must act out her ambivalence toward her social inscription as woman in order to participate in male privilege. Yet she has just sharply criticized such behavior in Phebe, urging her to "thank heaven, fasting, for a good man's love" (3.5.58), and in 4.1 she becomes confident enough in Orlando's faithful replies to stage a mock marriage. Temporarily empowered *within* Petrarchan love conventions, she has worked her way through to surrendering them in favor of a provisional trust in her partially tested lover. The imaginative space provided by the forest can take her this far—to an imagined wedding.

It takes an intrusion from outside the forest and a resurgence of male heroic force to turn the imagined wedding into a real one. The Duke's "kindness" and Rosalind-as-Ganymede's "play" have allowed Orlando to become a moral rather than merely a physical Hercules (see the wrestling match and Rosalind's cry at 1.2.210), and thus also a type of Christ.[30] Those inchoate energies which in the court could find expression only through wrestling Charles, in the forest focus on the picture of "A wretched ragged man, o'ergrown with hair" and menaced by a snake and a lioness (4.3.102–132). Suddenly Arden has grown threatening again, its postlapsarian state implied by the snake; its maternal peril implied by the Ovidian "suck'd and hungry lioness"; the masculine fear of return to nature emblematized as the supposed wild man. This threat presents itself to Orlando as a moral dilemma, for he recognizes the endangered man as his brother, his eldest brother, "that same brother . . . the most unnatural / That liv'd amongst men." The "old oak, whose boughs were moss'd with age / And high top bald with dry antiquity" and the "wretched ragged man, o'ergrown with hair" both suggest patriarchal and epic genealogy brought to the verge of savagery and decay by Oliver and Duke Frederick's actions: as Orlando earlier laments, "a rotten tree, / That cannot so much as a blossom yield" (2.3.63–64).[31] The description builds to a climax that Shakespeare will repeat near the end of *The Tempest*. To Rosalind's anxious query, "But to Orlando: did he leave him there, / Food to the suck'd and hungry lioness?" the stranger, like Prospero to Ariel (*Temp.*, 5.1.24–28), replies:

> . . . kindness, nobler ever than revenge,
> And nature, stronger than his just occasion,
> Made him give battle to the lioness,
> Who quickly fell before him . . .

Orlando redeems Eden, and the story bursts into present reality with all the force of its teller's awaking and sudden conversion to brotherly love: "in which hurtling / From miserable slumber *I* awaked" (emphasis mine).

The stranger is thus revealed as Orlando's eldest brother, Oliver. His conversion is emphasized by the dramatic introduction of the personal pronoun and the succeeding insistent play upon it (4.3.135–137). Oliver declares that his real identity surfaced from disguise through disguise; he states that his former unnaturalness has been "sweetly" transformed in the forest; he undergoes in a flash the experience of male bonding, of kinship, that his brother had found with the exiled Duke, to whose society Orlando now leads him (4.3.142–144).

The bloody napkin Oliver brings to Ganymede/Rosalind emblematizes the male adversarial experience of the world of nature. The sign of Orlando's wounding by the lioness, it intrudes the reality of death into Arden: *et in Arcadia ego*. Because of it Rosalind discovers how empathetically tied she is to Orlando: Oliver reports "he [Orlando] fainted, / And cried in fainting upon Rosalind," (4.3.148–149), and Ganymede also promptly swoons. She can now only lamely maintain her disguise; events have impelled her toward accepting this "reality," even with its implied threat to herself—for the "bloody napkin" will reappear in *Othello* as the strawberried handkerchief, a threatening emblem of the dangers of sexual consummation.

Things happen quickly after this. Orlando, now "estate[d]" with the patrimony by his grateful brother, readily gives consent to Oliver's marriage to Celia (5.2.1–15). The improbability of this marriage is satisfactorily glossed by Rosalind/ Ganymede's witty "pair of stairs to marriage" speech (5.2.29–41), which at once raises our objections to the suddenness of it and reminds us that it is her own protracted negotiation with Orlando that predicates our conditional acceptance of this love at first sight. Rosalind is having increasing difficulty maintaining her disguise as Oliver and Orlando's words seem to cut closer and closer to her real identity. Pressured by Orlando's emotional urgency—"I can live no longer by thinking"—Rosalind/Ganymede declares, "I will weary you then no longer with idle talking" (5.2.50–52). Persuaded now by Orlando's "gesture" (5.2.62), which I take to be as much his heroic action in saving his brother as his fidelity within their love discourse, Ganymede promises to produce Rosalind to marry Orlando in truth tomorrow.

In the final act of *As You Like It* Rosalind seemingly surrenders the play. She gives herself to the Duke her father so that he may give her to Orlando (5.4.19–20, 116–118). She thus reminds us that their initial attraction to each other was as much through their fathers—the old Sir Rowland de Boys whom Duke Senior loved as his soul (1.2.235–239)—as it was to their unmediated selves, and gives herself into the patriarchy toward which her defensive behavior all along has been in reference.

Yet in *As You Like It* a tissue of metadramatic discourse has been woven through and around this penultimate sublimation of the self-consciously fictive mode of romance to the redeemed biblical "realism" of its patrilinear plot that may help us suggest what "kind" of pastoral this play finally is. During the course of their comic wooing Audrey queries Touchstone, "I do not know what 'poetical' is. Is it honest in deed and word? Is it a true thing?" to which Touchstone replies, "No, truly; for the truest poetry is the most feigning, and lovers are given to poetry; and what they swear in poetry may be said as lovers they do feign" (3.3.17–22). Now Touchstone would dearly love to find Audrey a little more poetical, for then, despite her protestations, she might feign/fain (pretend/desire) to lie (to tell a falsehood/to copulate), and either way he might get to have sex with her. But more seriously, his reply and the play's constant allusions to the analogous powers of poetry and sexual relations to make something like, but other than, the previously existing reality have relevance to the metadramatic question of what its action produces in us, its audience. Is poetry merely a lie, or does it work to give apprehensible form to our desires? And what, we ask as feminist critics, are these desires?

As You Like It is the ultimately contextual play. Despite its very firm grounding in contemporary social realities and the conventions of romantic and heroic dis-course, the play remains conscious that its pastoral inside reflects a playful outside of continuing interpretation. Thus act 3, scene 2, the initial scene of pastoral ne-gotiation, is prefaced by a debate between Touchstone and Corin on the signifi-cance of "this shepherd's life," in which the old shepherd's simple and appropriate tautologies are circumscribed by Touchstone's courtly wit. Touchstone does not decenter the mysterious *esse* of Arden, any more than he discomposes Corin, but he does remind us that as sophisticated, postlapsarian auditors we will never be content to rest here. Structured as a debate in all its details and its major patterns, *As You Like It* also invites us to enter its debates, ourselves "busy actor[s] in their play" (3.4.56).

On the specific issue of the play's treatment of gender identity and sex roles, we need finally to move beyond Rosalind's defensive fears, her complex interaction as Ganymede/Rosalind, and her resubmission of herself to the restored patriarchy of her noble father and tested lover to consider the altered environment of the last movement of the play, including Rosalind's invocation of magic, and the play's metadramatic "Epilogue."

For all its self-conscious artfulness, its impositions and nuances of style, a part of this play remains beyond man's control and is discovered in action. As the play closes, that part, suddenly, and without explanation, turns benign: "the icy fang / And churlish chiding of the winter's wind" (2.1.6–7) turns to "spring time, the only pretty [ring] time" (5.3.19); Rosalind/Ganymede's fictional misogynistic "old religious uncle" (3.2.343–350) becomes an equally fictional but now romantically helpful "magician, most profound in his art, and yet not damnable" (5.2.60–61; see also 5.4.30–34); and from beyond any rational expectations that the text has established, the god Hymen comes to "atone" the play, wedding earth and heaven, country and town. Hymen's own words can serve as an hermeneutic for this final movement of the play: "Feed yourselves with questioning; / That reason wonder may diminish" (5.4.138–139). Rational interpretation and the conversations that the characters conduct beneath Hymen's nuptial lyric can explain in great part how these characters have come together. But though "reason wonder may diminish," it cannot cancel it altogether. The play has worked toward evoking an atmosphere of wonder and a promise of fresh beginnings that Touchstone's realism or Duke Frederick's and Jaques's contemplative withdrawals can anchor but not destroy. As You Like It transforms the problem of sexual relations insofar as it suggests a world of possibility for the continued negotiation of these differences.

In the metadramatic "Epilogue" the continued negotiation of sexual difference becomes the tentative metaphor for the most successful art. Here, for once, men bear the greater burden. The Elizabethan boy actor who played Rosalind conjures women to please themselves and men to play with women for mutual pleasure:

> My way is to conjure you, and I'll begin with the women. I charge you, O women, for the love you bear to men, to like as much of this play as please you; and I charge you, O men, for the love you bear to women (as I perceive by your simp'ring, none of you hates them), that between you and the women the play may please.   ("Epilogue," 11–17)

He thus inverts the sexological situation of the play itself, where Orlando had but to become assured in his male heroic identity, while Rosalind had had, through her disguise, her "double-voiced" discourse, to accommodate herself to him. This final inversion in this consummately playful play suggests that men and women can work together—albeit often awkwardly—to transform a world not deterministically bound by its cultural conventions.

Much of Shakespeare's later career suggests how difficult that is. As You Like It itself delicately skirts, with the Duke's sweet style, Orlando's simple heroism, and

Rosalind's self-restraint, the excoriating issue of the nonfeminist maternal subtext that will erupt in Shakespeare's tragedies. Although we may use Rosalind's double-voiced discourse and the final metadramatic openness of the play to decenter its patriarchal assumptions, Shakespeare's later plays gravitate around the threat to these values represented by a woman's projected infidelity, the "nothing" that is the source of her reproductive power.[32] In closing I can only hazard some of the symptoms and causes of this shift from comic playfulness to tragic anxiety about sexuality.

I believe that as Shakespeare perfected his romantic comedies and the movement toward marriage within them, he was compelled to face more directly the threat *within* marriage that coincides with the metaphysical and political crisis uncovered in his history plays. If, as the history plays suggest, there is no clear divine sanction for ruling, nor any untainted or disinterested human succession, you confront your origin in the female body, where no one really knows his father: "there," as Othello cries, "where I have garner'd up my heart, / Where either I must live or bear no life; / The fountain from the which my current runs / Or else dries up" (*Othello*, 4.2.57–60). Literary conventions such as the traditional chaste inaccessibility of the idealized lady and the use of boy actors to play female parts might shield Shakespeare for a time from this threat of the female body, allowing him, in the romantic comedies, to experiment with a dazzling series of sexual permutations that we may now appropriate for our own ends. But Shakespeare also deconstructs these literary conventions in the course of his plays in a way that brings him up against the new social realities of marriage and the family in early modern Europe, where decline of external religious authority, loss of feudal power, urban centralization, and nascent capitalism all function to alienate actual women while making their sexuality the focus of ever more anxious regard. Within Shakespeare's career *As You Like It* offers us a brief moment of tremulous poise before we sound those depths.[33]

NOTES

This essay is a revised and expanded version of a paper delivered at the 1984 Ohio Shakespeare Conference on "Shakespeare and Gender." It was first drafted during my 1982–83 tenure as a Junior Fellow at the Cornell Society for the Humanities. I am grateful to the Society and for the 1983–84 Harvard Mellon Faculty Fellowship that allowed me to continue work on it.
[1] Juliet Dusinberre, *Shakespeare and the Nature of Women* (London, 1975), p. 1.
[2] Madelon Gohlke, " 'I Wooed Thee with My Sword': Shakespeare's Tragic Paradigms," in *Representing Shakespeare: New Psychoanalytic Essays*, ed. Murray Schwartz and Coppélia Kahn (Baltimore, 1980), p. 180.
[3] Stephen Greenblatt, "Invisible Bullets: Renaissance Authority and Its Subversion," *Glyph*, 8 (1981), 40–61; Natalie Zemon Davis, *Society and Culture in Early Modern France* (Stanford, 1975), esp. "The Reasons of Misrule," pp. 97–123, and "Women on Top," pp. 124–151.
[4] Nancy Chodorow, *The Reproduction of Mothering: Psychoanalysis and the Sociology of Gender* (Berkeley and Los Angeles, 1978).
[5] Ibid., pp. 141–158, esp. p. 157.
[6] Ibid., p. 169: "Women's mothering, then, produces asymmetries in the relational experiences of girls and boys as they grow up, which account for crucial differences in feminine and masculine personality, and the relational capacities and modes which these entail ... From the retention of preoedipal attach-

ments to their mother, growing girls come to define and experience themselves as continuous with others; their experience of self contains more flexible or permeable ego boundaries. Boys come to define themselves as more separate and distinct, with a greater sense of rigid ego boundaries and differentiation. The basic feminine sense of self is connected to the world, the basic masculine sense of self is separate."

[7] Ibid., p. 151.

[8] Dorothy Dinnerstein, *The Mermaid and the Minotaur: Sexual Arrangements and Human Malaise* (New York, 1977).

[9] Chodorow, *Reproduction*, pp. 173–190.

[10] See, for example, Lawrence Stone, *The Family, Sex and Marriage in England, 1500–1800* (New York, 1977), pp. 123–218.

[11] Coppélia Kahn, "Excavating 'Those Dim Minoan Regions': Maternal Subtexts in Patriarchal Literature," *Diacritics,* 12 (1982), 37–41.

[12] Louis Adrian Montrose, " 'The Place of a Brother' in *As You Like It:* Social Process and Comic Form," *Shakespeare Quarterly,* 32 (1981), 28–54.

[13] Ibid., pp. 53, 52n.

[14] The phrase is Myra Jehlen's, "Archimedes and the Paradox of Feminist Criticism," *SIGNS,* 6 (1981), 576, as cited by Kahn, "Maternal Subtexts," p. 32.

[15] For the forest of Arden and Mary Arden, see Samuel Schoenbaum, *William Shakespeare: A Compact Documentary Life* (Oxford, 1977), pp. 4, 19–22.

[16] Elaine Showalter, "Feminist Criticism in the Wilderness," *Critical Inquiry,* 8 (1981), 201–204.

[17] Rosalie L. Colie, *Shakespeare's Living Art* (Princeton, 1974), pp. 243–261.

[18] Gohlke, "Shakespeare's Tragic Paradigms," p. 184.

[19] Shakespeare first evokes the ideal image of Arden—where echoes of Eden fuse with Hesiodic hints of "the golden world" and more local, English tales of social inversion (1.1.114–119)—within the socially oppressive opening scene, where Orlando complains that Oliver mars the *imago dei* and "the spirit of my father" within him (1.1.29–34 and 1.1.21–23, 46–51, 70–71). See Montrose, "Place of a Brother," pp. 45–47, for parallels between the biblical story of Cain and Abel and the contemporary problem of the patrimony and unequal inheritance. Throughout my essay I cite the text of *As You Like It* from *The Riverside Shakespeare,* ed. G. Blakemore Evans (Boston, 1974).

[20] See Montrose, "Place of a Brother," pp. 37–38, for a glossing of the significance of the fight, and Richard Knowles, "Myth and Type in *As You Like It,*" *ELH,* 33 (1966), 1–22, on the allusions to Hercules.

[21] *As You Like It* has often been compared with *Lear.* Some of the deepest filiations connect Orlando's vague misgivings about his breeding with Edmund's vigorous embrace of his bastardy as cause of his naturalistic villainy, and Orlando's fear of nature with Edgar's painful exposure on the heath as poor Tom. *As You Like It* avoids painful male confrontation with the threatening maternal subtext of nature through Orlando's own restraint and the benign paternal mediation of Duke Senior, but it remains a latent menace.

[22] See Madeleine Doran, " 'Yet Am I Inland Bred,' " *Shakespeare Quarterly,* 15 (1964), 99–114, for a discussion of the rich traditions of civility that inform the play.

[23] Chodorow, *Reproduction*, pp. 169, 94, 182.

[24] Ibid., p. 169; see also n.5 above.

[25] Nancy Vickers, "Diana Described: Scattered Woman and Scattered Rhyme," *Critical Inquiry,* 8 (1981), 265–280.

[26] For the myth of Ganymede as potentially degrading or exalting, see Erwin Panofsky, *Studies in Iconology: Humanistic Themes in the Art of the Renaissance* (New York, 1962), pp. 212–218. In *As You Like It* Ganymede offers a homoerotic bridge to Orlando's encounter with a "real" female other. Shakespeare's decision to highlight the dramatic fact that boy actors played women's parts may indicate that we are seeing an essentially male drama of power in which women are even further objectified as mere roles. But I think it also indicates the strain which that convention of representation was coming under, as Shakespeare's portrayal of women shifts from the already powerful girls of the romantic comedies to the explicitly threatening women of the tragedies. In the later plays, although boys still play the woman's part, the extra-dramatic referents of their play have become an imagined woman, not an excluded middle term: we move from the boy actor who plays Portia playing a young male lawyer in *The Merchant of Venice* to the boy actor who plays Cleopatra complaining that a boy actor will misplay her—"Some squeaking Cleopatra boy my greatness / I'th'posture of a whore" (*Antony and Cleopatra* 5.2.220–221)—and to the artifice-shattering resurrection of Hermione in *The Winter's Tale.*

[27] Chodorow, *Reproduction*, pp. 166–167.

[28] Ibid., p. 167.

[29] Ibid., p. 93.

[30] Knowles, "Myth and Type," pp. 14–18.

[31] See Montrose, "Place of a Brother," pp. 50–51, for the female sexual threat of the snake and the lioness, and p. 43 for the genealogical significance of the description of Oliver. The lioness probably descends from the lioness who mauls Thisbe's mantle with her bloody mouth in Ovid's story of Pyramus and Thisbe, *Metamorphoses,* bk. 4, a story that we know from the rude mechanicals' play in *A Midsummer Night's Dream* was much on Shakespeare's mind. I am grateful to B. Cass Clarke for suggesting its relevance here. The genealogical tree is one of the *topoi* of epic, invoked to establish the text's relationship to the past; see, for example, Homer, *Odyssey,* 23.173–204; Vergil, *Aeneid,* 4.437–449; Dante, *Divine Comedy,* "Purgatorio," 31.70–75.

[32] This issue has received two recent impressive formulations: "I am reading the development from the comedies through the problem plays and the major tragedies in terms of an explosion of the sexual tensions that threaten without rupturing the surface of the earlier plays" (Gohlke, "Shakespeare's Tragic Paradigms," p. 174); "Possibilities for conflict latent in earlier writings are released in the violent action of tragedy, where boundaries previously provided by separation of genre are broken through, and the drama takes into itself the entire range of family-based conflict in Shakespeare" (Richard Wheeler, *Shakespeare's Development and the Problem Comedies: Turn and Counter-Turn* [Berkeley and Los Angeles, 1981], p. 156).

[33] For *As You Like It* as a work of exquisite balance, see the classic essays by Helen Gardner, *"As You Like It,"* in *More Talking of Shakespeare,* ed. John W. P. Garret (London; New York, 1959), pp. 17–32, and Ann Barton, *"As You Like It* and *Twelfth Night:* Shakespeare's Sense of an Ending," in *Shakespearean Comedy,* ed. Malcolm Bradbury and D. J. Palmer, Stratford-upon-Avon Studies 14 (1972), pp. 160–180.

Marjorie Garber

THE EDUCATION OF ORLANDO

When Rosalind learns from Celia that Orlando is in the Forest of Arden, she cries out in mingled joy and consternation, "Alas the day, what shall I do with my doublet and hose?" (3.2.219–20).[1] Members of the audience might perhaps be pardoned were they to answer her, not in the "one word" she demands, but with the familiar chant of the burlesque house, "Take it off!"—either literally (if she has been provident enough to bring a change of clothing with her to Arden) or figuratively, by identifying herself to him at once as Rosalind, rather than continuing the fiction that she is a youth named Ganymede, a native of the forest. Indeed Celia makes a suggestion along these lines, when she hears Rosalind—as Ganymede—abusing the reputations of women when she talks to Orlando about the nature of love. "You have simply misus'd our sex in your love-prate," says Celia. "We must have your doublet and hose pluck'd over your head, and show the world what the bird hath done to her own nest" (4.1.201–4). There is in fact very little risk to her should she do so, except perhaps from a blast of the "winter wind" about which Amiens sings so feelingly (2.7.174). She is perfectly safe. Clearly there are no outlaws in the forest, or other predatory men; they have all been left behind at court. Moreover, she is assured of Orlando's love for her, since both she and Celia have read the poems with which he has festooned Arden's otherwise blameless trees. In short, there is apparently no reason for her to remain clad as a boy. Why then does she do so?

In other Shakespearian comedies, women dressed as men have compelling reasons for remaining in disguise. Julia in *The Two Gentlemen of Verona* is trapped in her male attire because of the perfidy of her erstwhile lover, Proteus. She initially disguises herself for the same reason Rosalind gives: "for I would prevent / The loose encounters of lascivious men" (2.7.40–41), but she fully intends to reveal herself once she reaches her "loving Proteus" (7). When to her chagrin she finds him in the act of offering his love to Silvia instead, she retains her male guise, enlists

From *Comedy from Shakespeare to Sheridan: Change and Continuity in the English and European Dramatic Tradition*, edited by A. R. Braunmuller and J. C. Bulman (Newark: University of Delaware Press, 1986), pp. 102–12.

herself in Proteus's service, carries his love tokens to Silvia, and only reveals her true identity in the final scene, when she fears that Valentine will make good on his extraordinary promise to give Proteus "all that was mine in Silvia" (5.4.83). At this point Julia swoons (or pretends to swoon), produces a ring given her by Proteus, and acknowledges that her "immodest raiment" is a "disguise of love" (106–7). Her costume is essential to the working out of the plot.

The same is true in *Twelfth Night*. Shipwrecked in Illyria, Viola initially wishes to gain employment with the Countess Olivia in her own shape as a woman, though without disclosing her name and station. "O that I serv'd that lady," she tells the sea caption who rescues her, "And might not be delivered to the world / Till I had made mine own occasion mellow, / What my estate is" (*Twelfth Night*, 1.2.41–44). It is only because Olivia's mourning makes a suit to her impossible that Viola determines to "conceal me what I am" (53) and seek service with Duke Orsino in the guise of the youth Cesario. Like Julia she is then trapped in her disguise when she falls in love with the man she serves and is sent by him to plead his love to Olivia. Here the disguise is even more central to the plot than in *Two Gentlemen*, since it is the means by which Olivia meets and marries Sebastian, and Orsino discovers his own love for Viola.

Portia is not trapped in her role as the wise young judge Balthasar, but it is essential that she should be dressed as a man in order to free Antonio, confound Shylock, and—ultimately—teach her husband a lesson about the nature of generosity and love. And Imogen, too, is forced by circumstance to retain her male disguise. Dressed as a boy, and fleeing like Julia after her departed lover, she thinks she has found him dead and therefore enlists as "Fidele" in the service of the Roman general. Her disguise and subsequent adventures lead directly to the restoration of Cymbeline's sons, as well as to her reunion with her beloved Posthumus.

All these women must retain their disguises because of exigencies of the plot. But what is Rosalind's rationale? What if she were to step forward in act 3, scene 2, not like a "saucy lackey" (296) but like herself, and declare that she is the "Heavenly Rosalind" Orlando has been seeking? There would of course be one unfortunate repercussion, since the play would effectively come to an end in the middle of the third act (as would have occurred if Cordelia had answered at once when Lear asked her how much she loved him). But beyond that, would anything be lost? Can Shakespeare be keeping Rosalind in disguise merely to prolong his play, or is there another purpose in her decision not to unmask herself.

Many reasons have been advanced for the continued existence of Ganymede after Orlando comes on the scene. G. L. Kittredge quotes one Lady Martin, writing in *Blackwood's Magazine* for October, 1884, who offers the opinion that "surely it was the finest and boldest of all devices, one of which only a Shakespeare could have ventured, to put his heroine into such a position that she could, without revealing her own secret, probe the heart of her lover to the very bottom, and so assure herself that the love which possessed her own being was as completely the master of his." In a rather ungentlemanly fashion Kittredge then goes on to demolish Lady Martin: "This amiable and eloquent observation," he notes, "is typical of many that have been mistakenly made upon details of Shakespeare's plots. The 'device' is not Shakespeare's, but Lodge's."[2] Subsequent critics have been willing to recognize that Shakespeare was capable of changing what he did not wish to retain from his sources and have tended to theorize somewhat along Lady Martin's lines. C. L. Barber, for example, remarks that when disguised "Rosalind is not committed to the conventional language and attitudes of love, loaded as these inevitably are with sentimentality,"[3] and Anne Barton suggests that as Ganymede "she learns a great deal about herself, about Orlando, and about love itself which she could not have done within the normal conventions of society."[4] A recent feminist critic, Clara Claiborne Park, carries the argument for Rosalind's independence and self-knowledge a step further, pointing out that "male garments immensely broaden the sphere in which female energy can manifest itself. Dressed as a man, a nubile woman can go places and do things she couldn't do otherwise, thus getting the play out of the court and the closet and into interesting places like forests or Welsh mountains. Once Rosalind is disguised as a man, she can be as saucy and self-assertive as she likes."[5] Those critics interested in the question seem in general to agree that disguise is a freeing action for Rosalind and that her double role allows her to be at once caustic and caring, tender and tough.

I do not wish to quarrel with these sensible observations, but I would like to suggest a slight change of emphasis. As the lessons she gives to Orlando immediately testify, Rosalind does not have to learn much, if anything, about love, or about the quality and depth of her own feelings. Nor, as I have already mentioned, does she really need assurance (*pace* Lady Martin) that Orlando loves her. What she does need, and what the play needs, is an Orlando who knows "what 'tis to love" (5.2.83). He is the one who has immersed himself in a pseudo-Petrarchan fantasy world, hanging "tongues . . . on every tree" (3.2.127) in unconscious fulfillment of Duke Senior's attitudinizing ("tongues in trees, books in the running brooks, / Sermons in stones, and good in every thing" [2.1.16–17]). What Barber calls the "conventional language and attitudes of love," with their attendant "sentimentality," are pitfalls for Orlando much more than for Rosalind.

H. B. Charlton comments that "Rosalind, disguised as Ganymede, pretends to be herself in order to teach Orlando to woo."[6] This is certainly true, but it is not, I think, the whole truth. For what Rosalind is teaching is not so much technique as substance. Her disguise as Ganymede permits her to educate him about himself, about her, and about the nature of love. It is for Orlando, not for Rosalind, that the masquerade is required; indeed the play could fittingly, I believe, be subtitled "The Education of Orlando." Whether we agree with Ms. Park that "she is twice the person he is" or not,[7] it seems clear that in *As You Like It,* as in so many of Shakespeare's comedies, the woman is superior to her man in self-knowledge and in her knowledge of human nature. The degree to which Orlando is successfully educated, and the limits of his final understanding, can be seen by examining their various encounters in the court and in the forest and by considering what happens as a result of those encounters.

In act 1, scene 2 Rosalind and Orlando meet at the wrestling match and fall in

love at first sight. The following scene, which begins with Rosalind's acknowledge-
ment of her passion to Celia, ends with her banishment, and Celia's resolution to
accompany her to the Forest of Arden. The two events are psychologically related;
Rosalind's advancement toward maturity by falling in love is in a sense the same act
as her banishment from the palace of Duke Frederick. Banishment is a rite of
passage here; a threshold moment that leads both lovers to the forest. The whole
scene is beautifully modulated, as the young women's discussion of Orlando leads
naturally into some playful observations on the paternal generation and the relationship between his father and theirs.

> ROSALIND:The Duke my father lov'd his father dearly.
> CELIA: Doth it therefore ensue that you should love his son dearly?
>   By this kind of chase, I should hate him, for my father hated
>   his father dearly; yet I hate not Orlando.
> ROSALIND: No, faith, hate him not, for my sake.
> CELIA: Why should I not? Doth he not deserve well?
>   *Enter* DUKE [FREDERICK] *with* LORDS.
> ROSALIND: Let me love him for that, and do you love him because I do.
>   Look, here comes the Duke.
> CELIA: With his eyes full of anger.
> DUKE FREDERICK: Mistress, dispatch you with your safest haste,
> And get you from our court.   (1.3.29–43)

The shift from prose to verse with Duke Frederick's first speech underscores the
sudden change from intimacy to formality. Rosalind's act of falling in love is itself a
rebellion against patriarchal domination and the filial bond. Since she is living under
the foster care of her jealous and unloving uncle, her sundering from his protection
is abrupt and harsh, but some such separation would have been inevitable. Her
love, as much as his hatred, banishes her to Arden.

Meanwhile Orlando, who has also fallen in love, is likewise banished from
home. His tyrannical older brother, Oliver, has usurped his patrimony and stands
in a relationship to him that is structurally analogous to that between Duke Frederick and Rosalind. Although he is the youngest son, Orlando bears his father's
name ("Rowland de Boys" translates readily as "Orlando of the forest"), and in the
play's opening scene he asserts that "the spirit of my father, which I think is within
me, begins to mutiny against this servitude" (1.1.22–24). Orlando's banishment, like
Rosalind's, is a step toward independence and maturity. It is interesting to note that
in the first scene he complains about the quality of his upbringing; Oliver, he says,
"mines my gentility with my education" (21). The education he does not receive at
home he will find in the forest, with "Ganymede" for his teacher. Carrying old
Adam on his shoulders like Aeneas bearing his father Anchises, Orlando enters the
forest (where, as he matures, the father-figure Adam disappears from the plot),
and shortly begins to post his love poems on the trees.

When she learns that it is indeed Orlando who has written these poems in her
praise, Rosalind asks Celia a crucial question: "But doth he know that I am in this

forest and in man's apparel?" (3.2.229–30). Deception is already in her mind. If he does not know who she is, she will not at this time reveal herself to him. Instead she declares her intention to "speak to him like a saucy lackey, and under the habit play the knave with him" (295–97).

What is her motivation for doing so? In seeking to answer this question, we should note that there are three distinct stages in Orlando's development as a lover. When he first meets Rosalind after the wrestling match he is tongue-tied, unable to speak. She has presented him with a chain, but he can find no words to acknowledge her gift: "Can I not say, 'I thank you'? My better parts / Are all thrown down, and that which here stands up / Is but a quintain, a mere lifeless block" (1.2.249–51). Rosalind abandons maidenly modesty to approach him ("Did you call, sir?" [253]), but he remains speechless, struck dumb by love: "What passion hangs these weights upon my tongue? / I cannot speak to her, yet she urged conference" (257–58). This is the first stage, that of ineffability; for the match to succeed he must somehow learn to communicate his feelings.

He does this initially through the medium of his love poems, but while the poems are an advance upon total speechlessness, they do not constitute a wholly satisfactory mode of communication. For one thing, they are one-sided, monovocal; Orlando has no reason to expect that Rosalind will ever see or hear of them. For another thing, as Touchstone dryly points out, they are simply not very good poems. "The very false gallop of verses" (3.2.112) is his sardonic verdict, and even Rosalind acknowledges that they offer a "tedious homily of love" (155–56) with "more feet than the verses would bear" (165–66), and lame ones at that. Hackneyed, conventional, derivative, ineloquent, Orlando's poems announce an emotion but fail to go further than that; they do not attain the condition of discourse. One of Rosalind's tasks, therefore, will be to make him speak to her in the natural language of men and women. The method she adopts to do so—remaining in a disguise that will make him less ill at ease than he was at their first meeting—is somewhat comparable to the plot of Goldsmith's She Stoops to Conquer, in which the bashful young Marlow is able to make love to Miss Hardcastle because he thinks she is a servant in a country inn, not the well-bred daughter of a wealthy man. Rosalind, too, stoops to conquer, by retaining her doublet and hose.

Orlando's love poems also suggest a psychological state of self-absorption that accords with Erik Erikson's description of adolescent love: "an attempt to arrive at a definition of one's identity by projecting one's diffused self-image on another and by seeing it thus reflected and gradually clarified."[8] The first time Rosalind sees him in the forest he is deep in conversation with Jaques, the play's epitome of self-love, and there are resemblances between them, despite their mutual antipathy (and perhaps contributing to it). Both are obsessed with their own feelings. Orlando successfully teases Jaques with the old joke of the fool in the brook, but there is a sense in which he himself is also a Narcissus, seeking his own reflection. His mock-Petrarchan poetry, like that of the lords in Love's Labour's Lost, indicates a lack of maturity and a failure of other-directedness. Like Phebe, he is in love with love and with the image of himself as a lover. Rosalind seems to sense this when, in the character of Ganymede, she points out that he is not dressed in the true lover's traditional disarray: "you are no such man; you are rather point-device in your accoustrements, as loving yourself, than seeming the lover of any other" (3.2.381–84). Orlando needs time—time to grow from an infatuated youth to a man who knows the real nature of love, from a boy who pins poems on trees to a man whose love token is a "bloody napkin" (4.3.138). By not revealing her true identity Rosalind gives him that time. From their first encounter in the forest she becomes his teacher.

Time is, indeed, the first subject that they touch upon in the course of that encounter—time and its relativity. Pretending she does not know who he is, Rosalind is able to mention the hypothetical presence of a "true lover in the forest" (3.2.302) and to comment upon the eagerness of "a young maid between the contract of her marriage and the day it is solemniz'd" (313–15). She thus usurps and desentimentalizes the topic of love that Orlando has elaborately established as his own. Jaques had addressed him contemptuously as "Signior Love," and I think we may see his insistence on playing the part of the lover as an aspect of his adolescent posturing. He will now be required to prove his love by acts of constancy and by the quick use of his wits—very different from the self-glorifying practice of posting love poems for all to see. Dialogue and interplay have already begun to replace the sterile and stereotypical intercourse between a man and his pen. Orlando is no longer in command of the love theme—if, indeed, he ever was. The focus and the creative energy are instead to be found in "Ganymede"—or rather, in "Ganymede" as "he" will take up the part of "Rosalind."

It is a convention of Shakespearian comedy that husbands and lovers do not recognize their ladies when those ladies are dressed in male attire. Bassanio fails to see through Portia's disguise, and Posthumus cannot recognize Imogen. But both of these men are distracted by important events taking place concurrently. Bassanio is overwhelmed with gratitude by the salvation of Antonio, and Posthumus is convinced that his wife is dead and that he has found her murderer. Orlando, by contrast has his mind wholly on Rosalind, yet he does not see her as she stands before him. "Let no face be kept in mind," he wrote, "But the fair of Rosalind" (3.2.94–95). He is now gazing into that face and does not recognize it. This is particularly striking because of the nature of the dialogue that takes place between them. Consider some of the peculiarities of diction in the following exchange:

> ORLANDO: Where dwell you, *pretty* youth?
> ROSALIND: With this shepherdess, my sister; here in the *skirts* of the forest, like fringe upon a *petticoat.*
> ORLANDO: Are you native of this place?
> ROSALIND: As the *cony* that you see dwell where *she* is kindled.
>
> (334–40; emphasis mine)

Given the dramatic situation, such a collection of sex-linked words is bound to call attention to itself. Orlando's word "pretty" probably carries the primary meaning, now obsolete, of "clever, skillful, apt" (OED II.2a), referring to the witty conversation that has just taken place. But the word *pretty* in Shakespeare is almost always used to describe either women or children; it is interesting to note that the only reference to "pretty youth" in any of Shakespeare's other plays is addressed to Julia in *Two Gentlemen* when she is masquerading as a boy (4.2.58). Moreover, a few scenes later in *As You Like It* the infatuated shepherdess Phebe also uses the phrase "pretty youth" (3.5.113). She is cataloguing "Ganymede's" verbal and physical charms, and her word "pretty" could refer to either, though she will shortly speak of "a pretty redness in his lip" (120). The phrase "pretty youth" is not conclusive evidence that Orlando somehow senses the woman beneath the doublet and hose, but it is suggestive, especially in view of what follows. For Rosalind's key words in this exchange are unambiguously female: "skirts" and "petticoat"—both garments she is not wearing but should be—and the image of a female rabbit rather than a male one with whom to compare herself. "Skirts" meaning "borders" is a word in common usage, appearing both later in this play (5.4.159) and in *Hamlet* (1.1.97), as well as in the works of many of Shakespeare's contemporaries, but in combination with "petticoat" it is plainly mischievous, a witty and pointed literalizing of the implicit metaphor. "Petticoat" itself is often a synonym for woman, as in Rosalind's own earlier exclamation as the travelers entered the Forest of Arden: "I could find in my heart to disgrace my man's apparel and to cry like a woman; but I must comfort the weaker vessel, as doublet and hose ought to show itself courageous to petticoat" (2.4.4–7). As to "cony," which in the forest context means "rabbit," in Shakespeare's time it was also a term of endearment for a woman. For Orlando as well as for the audience these words are clues to her real identity, though clues he is too dense to follow up. This part of the scene should, I think, be extremely funny on the stage—but funny at Orlando's expense.

Since the Elizabethan actor playing Rosalind would of course have been a boy, presenting the Chinese box syndrome of a boy playing a girl playing a boy playing a girl (actor-Rosalind-"Ganymede"-"Rosalind"), some periodic hints or asides would have been dramaturgically helpful in keeping the audience cognizant of what they were supposed to be seeing. *As You Like It* is particularly playful in this regard, ringing the changes on these changes throughout the play and especially in the epilogue. But the proliferation of such sly hints in the first conversation between Orlando and the disguised Rosalind is of considerable interest. "I thank God I am not a woman," she remarks (3.2.347–48), and again there is a broad wink to the audience—but perhaps also a small nudge in the ribs to Orlando. Yet he is so determined to be lovesick that he does not recognize the object of his love.

ORLANDO: Fair youth, I would I could make thee believe I love.
ROSALIND: Me believe it? You may as soon make her that you love believe it, which I warrant she is apter to do than to confess she does: that is one of the points in the which women still give the lie to their consciences.
(385–91)

Here Rosalind is wrestling with the same maidenly dilemma that troubled Juliet and Cressida—what are the social risks for a woman who tells her love? But like those women, she is in a sense telling her love now—if only Orlando had the wit to listen. Yet by the end of the scene he is still addressing her as "good youth" (433). "Nay," she replies, "you must call me Rosalind" (434).

Their fictive courtship, with its badinage, wooing lessons, and play-acted "marriage," threatens to go on forever in the timelessness of Arden. Under the guise of Ganymede, Rosalind teaches Orlando not only the rules of love and its nature, but the uses of language—and even, to her everlasting credit, the gentle arts of irony and self-deprecation. But two events intervene to bring the fiction to an end: Orlando's rescue of his brother Oliver from a lioness, and the instant mutual passion of Oliver and Celia.

I have elsewhere discussed at length the incident of the lioness and the "bloody napkin" Orlando sends as a love token "unto the shepherd youth / That he in sport doth call his Rosalind" (4.3.155–56).[9] Let me merely say briefly here that I regard this as an initiation ritual, both in martial and in sexual terms, and that I see the gift of the bloody napkin as a curiously but appropriately displaced version of the ceremonial "showing of the sheets" by which in some cultures a newly married woman demonstrates her virginity and fidelity to her husband. The napkin is thus a love token of a very different kind from the superficial love poems Orlando has earlier sent to Rosalind in testimony of his love. For the education of Orlando, however, the love match between his brother and Celia is even more germane, because it brings an end to the fictional world in which Orlando has lived with his "Rosalind." "O, how bitter a thing it is to look into happiness through another man's eyes!" he exclaims (5.2.43–45), and Rosalind asks, "Why then, tomorrow I cannot serve your turn for Rosalind?" (48–49). Orlando's reply is the single most important turning point in his development: "I can live no longer by thinking" (50). In the language of education we have been using, this is both a graduation and a commencement, a change and a new beginning. Imagination and play, which have brought him to this point, are no longer enough to sustain him. And as if he has said the magic words—as indeed he has—Rosalind now promises to produce his true beloved, "to set her before your eyes to-morrow, human as she is, and without any danger" (66–68). The significant phrase here is "human as she is." The real Rosalind is not the paper paragon of Orlando's halting sonnets but a woman of complexity, wit, and passion. This will be Orlando's final lesson.

Readers of the play are occasionally as nonplussed as Orlando by the rapidity with which Oliver and Celia fall in love.[10] "Is't possible that on so little acquaintance you should like her? that but seeing, you should love her? and loving, woo? and wooing, she should grant? And will you persever to enjoy her?" (5.2.1–4). Our amazement is the more because all of this wooing takes place offstage, between acts 4 and 5. Compared with the protracted courtship of Orlando and Rosalind, which has constituted virtually the entire action of the play, this manifestation of bethrothal-at-first-sight is potentially unsettling, especially because we have no particular reason to like Orlando before he appears in the forest and because we have been led by Rosalind to believe that some extended education is necessary to develop a true and enduring love. Orlando, too, liked and loved at first sight, but he is still learning "what 'tis to woo," and is—or so he thinks—very far from having his lady grant his suit.

Oliver describes his transformation from tyrant to lover as a "conversion." "I do not shame / To tell you what I was," he explains to Celia, "Since my conversion / So sweetly tastes, being the thing I am" (4.3.135–37). His is the alternative path to Rosalind's gradualist mode of education, an instantaneous Pauline reversal that fills the erstwhile nay-sayer with the spirit of love. Oliver's "conversion" accords with the Christian doctrine of salvation; like the late-arriving laborers in the vineyard (Matt. 20:1–16) his reward is made equal to that of his apparently more deserving brother, and the two courtships, one so lengthy and the other so swift, are, in Hymen's words, "earthly things made even" (5.4.109).

Conversion is in fact a recurrent theme in the final scene of the play. We learn that Duke Frederick, advancing on the forest with malign intent, has encountered "an old religious man" and "after some question with him, was converted / Both from his enterprise and from the world" (5.4.160–62). Like Oliver he offers to abdicate his lands and position in favor of the brother he had formerly sought to kill. At this point Jaques decides to join him, observing that "Out of these convertites / There is much matter to be heard and learn'd" (184–85). The emphasis upon instruction and discourse here is significant, offering a pertinent analogy to the love lessons Rosalind has been giving Orlando. But while Duke Frederick's conversion removes him from society, Oliver's socializes him. Learning to love his brother, he finds himself, more or less in consequence, capable of falling in love with Celia.

As we have seen, the lightning love affair of Oliver and Celia acts as a catalyst for Orlando, moving him to make the crucial transition from play acting to reality. His declaration, "I can live no longer by thinking," makes possible Rosalind's change of roles, from teacher to "human" lover. The lessons, and the need for them, are over. But how much has Orlando really learned? Throughout the play Rosalind has offered clues to her real identity, double-edged hints that she is in fact the very woman she is pretending to be. Orlando's failure to take those hints was, for the audience as well as Rosalind, an indication that he was not yet prepared to have the truth thrust upon him. When he finally feels ready to choose the real, despite its inherent dangers, over the make-believe, we have some reason to think that he has profited from the unsentimental education he has received. Yet even after "Ganymede" promises to set Rosalind before his eyes, Orlando makes one significant error in interpretation that makes it clear he is, in one sense at least, no match for Rosalind. The issue is subtle—some might say finical—but it is also, as is Rosalind's way, instructive, for the audience in the theater if not for Orlando.

In the course of that same first conversation in the forest with which we have been so much concerned, Orlando inquiries as to whether the "youth" he addresses is native to the forest. "Your accent," he observes, "is something finer than you could purchase in so remov'd a dwelling" (3.2.341–42). Once again he hovers on the brink of discovery. But Rosalind has a ready reply, one that touches on "Ganymede's" own education. "An old religious uncle of mine taught me to speak, who was in his youth an inland man; one that knew courtship too well, for there he fell in love" (345–47). The former courtier who finds purity and peace in the countryside is a commonplace of pastoral literature; Spenser's Melibee is only one member of a hoary and numerous tribe, who, had they all inhabited England's forests in Elizabeth's time, would have jostled one another uncomfortably for lack of room. Rosalind's invention thus has just the right degree of verisimilitude to take in Orlando, and just the right degree of triteness to amuse the listening audience. Orlando readily accepts this explanation, moving eagerly on to the more tempting topic of love, and the matter is dropped. Or so it seems.

Much later in the play, when the spectacle of Celia and Oliver in love has incited him to abjure "thinking" for action, Orlando is vouchsafed another item of information about the supposed education of "Ganymede." "Believe then if you please," the disguised Rosalind tells him,

> that I can do strange things. I have, since I was three years old, convers'd with a magician, most profound in his art and yet not damnable. If you do love Rosalind so near the heart as your gesture cries it out, when your brother marries Aliena, shall you marry her. I know into what straits of fortune she is driven, and it is not impossible to me, if it appear not inconvenient to you, to set her before your eyes tomorrow, human as she is, and without any danger.
> ORLANDO: Speak'st thou in sober meanings?
> ROSALIND: By my life, I do, which I tender dearly, though I say I am a magician.
> (5.2.58–71)

Orlando accepts this windfall without question and confides his good luck to Duke Senior, who willingly agrees to give Rosalind to him in marriage. On the following day "Ganymede" approaches both Orlando and the Duke to make sure their minds are constant. Receiving the appropriate assurances, "he" exits the stage, and the Duke turns immediately to Orlando to offer one of those observations that so often herald the clearing of the skies at the close of Shakespearian comedy: "I do remember in this shepherd boy / Some lively touches of my daughter's favor" (5.426–27). We are very close to the truth here. Yet Orlando, characteristically, confuses rather than clarifies the matter, so sure is he that he is in possession of the facts.

> My lord, the first time that I ever saw him
> Methought he was a brother to your daughter.
> But, my good lord, this boy is forest-born,
> And hath been tutor'd in the rudiments
> Of many desperate studies by his uncle,
> Whom he reports to be a great magician,
> Obscured in the circle of the forest.   (28–34)

It is Orlando himself who is obscured here, in the circle of the forest. For notice what he has done. He has conflated the two tales Rosalind told him, identifying the "old religious uncle" who ostensibly taught young Ganymede to speak, with the profound magician with whom Ganymede has conversed from the age of three. This inference makes perfect sense, but it is wrong, and wrong in an important way. "I am a magician," she told him, plainly. And plainly the magician with whom Rosalind has conversed from the voluble age of three is no one but Rosalind herself, the only begetter of the magic that will produce Orlando's beloved before his eyes and reveal to the Duke and all the lovers her true identity, and their true partners.

Rosalind's role as a magician is emphasized in the epilogue, when she announces to the audience "My way is to conjure you" (Epilogue, 10–11). As she herself remarks, "It is not the fashion to see the lady the epilogue" (1–2), but in this play the lady has earned her place. Hand in hand with Orlando she danced in celebration of her wedding, and then, with the other couples, departed the stage. But she returns, and she returns alone. Her reappearance underscores the degree to which she has directed events in Arden from her first encounter with Orlando to the successful performance of four marriages. "Human as she is" she has played two parts throughout the play and, in the process, transformed Orlando from a tongue-tied boy to an articulate and (relatively) self-knowledgeable husband. If he is not entirely her equal, it is hard to fault him for that. For Rosalind stands alone among Shakespeare's comic heroines as clearly as she stands alone on the stage for the Epilogue. Like Prospero, whom in many ways she prefigures, she tempers her magic with humanity, and were she to divest herself of her doublet and hose, she might justifiably address them as Prospero addresses his "magic garment": "Lie there, my art" (*Tempest*, 1.2.24).

NOTES

[1] References are to *The Riverside Shakespeare*, ed. G. Blakemore Evans et al. (Boston: Houghton Mifflin, 1974).

[2] *As You Like It*, ed. George Lyman Kittredge (Boston: Ginn and Co., 1939), pp. 149–50.

[3] C. L. Barber, *Shakespeare's Festive Comedy* (Princeton: Princeton University Press, 1959), p. 233.

[4] Anne Barton, Introduction to *As You Like It*, in *The Riverside Shakespeare*, ed. Evans, p. 366.

[5] Clara Claiborne Park, "As We Like It: How a Girl Can Be Smart and Still Popular," in *The Woman's Part: Feminist Criticism of Shakespeare* (Urbana: University of Illinois Press, 1980), p. 108.

[6] *Shakespearian Comedy* (1938: reprint, London: Methuen, 1973), p. 282.

[7] Ibid., p. 109.

[8] Erik Erikson, *Identity: Youth and Crisis* (New York: W. W. Norton, 1968), p. 132.

[9] Marjorie Garber, *Coming of Age in Shakespeare* (London: Methuen, 1981), pp. 145–48.

[10] I say "readers" because audiences in the theater tend to be so swept by the energies of the plot that they do not stop to analyze the improbability here. My students, however, have occasionally been perturbed by it.

Camille Paglia

SHAKESPEARE AND DIONYSUS

In his treatment of sex and personality, Shakespeare is a shape-shifter and master of transformations. He returns dramatic impersonation to its ritual origins in the cult of Dionysus, where masks were magic. Shakespeare recognizes that western identity, in its long pagan line, *is* impersonation. Kenneth Burke calls role in drama "salvation via change or purification of identity (purification in either the moral or chemical sense)."[1] The pattern of chemical breakdown, remixture of elements, and composition of new personality is clear in *King Lear,* where the protagonist is set to the boil on a stormy heath. Alchemy, which began in Hellenistic Egypt, entered the Middle Ages through Arabic texts and remained influential throughout the Renaissance. Its esoteric symbolism was a matter of literate common knowledge down to the seventeenth century, when science took over its terms and techniques. There is debate about how much alchemical lore survived the Renaissance and was transmitted to the founders of Romanticism. That Coleridge was influenced by German commentary on the subject seems certain.

Alchemy, like astrology, has been stigmatized at its worst rather than remembered at its best. It was not just a mercenary scrabble for a formula to turn lead to gold. It was a philosophical quest for the creative secrets of nature. Mind and matter were linked, in the pagan way. Alchemy is pagan naturism. Titus Burckhardt says alchemy's spiritual aim was "the achievement of 'inward silver' or 'inward gold'—in their immutable purity and luminosity."[2] Jung speaks of alchemy as not only "the mother of chemistry" but "the forerunner of our modern psychology of the unconscious."[3] Jack Lindsay sees alchemy prefiguring all scientific and anthropological "concepts of development and evolution."[4] The alchemical process sought to transform the *prima materia,* or chaos of mutable substances, into the eternal and incorruptible "Philosopher's Stone." This perfected entity was depicted as an androgyne, a *rebis* ("double thing"). Both the primal matrix and the finished product were hermaphroditic, because they contained all four basic elements, earth, water,

From *Sexual Personae: Art and Decadence from Nefertiti to Emily Dickinson* (New Haven: Yale University Press, 1990), pp. 198–212.

air, and fire. The self-contained magnum opus of alchemical process was symbolized by the uroboros, the self-begetting, self-devouring serpent. The synthesis of contraries in the watery "bath" of the *opus* was a *hierosgamos* or *coniunctio* ("sacred marriage" or "union"), a "chymical wedding" of male and female. This pair appeared as brother and sister in incestuous intercourse. The terminology of incest is everywhere in alchemy, betraying its implicit pagan character. Romanticism's incest themes may bear this ancient history.

The alchemists gave the name "Mercurius" to an allegorical hermaphrodite constituting all or part of the process. Mercurius, the god and planet, is liquid mercury or quicksilver, the elixir of transformations. Arthur Edward Waite says, "*Universal Mercury* is the animating spirit diffused throughout the universe."[5] Mercurius is my name for one of the most fascinating and restless western sexual personae. We earlier traced the idea of the "mercurial" to crafty, wing-footed Hermes. My Mercurius, first conceived by Shakespeare, is the androgynous spirit of impersonation, the living embodiment of multiplicity of persona. Mercurius possesses verbal and therefore mental power. Shakespeare's great Mercurius androgyne is the transvestite Rosalind and after her the male-willed Cleopatra. The main characteristic is an electric wit, dazzling, triumphant, euphoric, combined with rapid alternations of persona. Lesser examples are Goethe's Mignon, Jane Austen's Emma, and Tolstoy's Natasha. Lady Caroline Lamb, Byron's tempestuous mistress, will be our real-life example of the negative or afflicted Mercurius. At their most stagy and manipulative, Katharine Hepburn as Tracy Lord in *The Philadelphia Story* and Vivien Leigh as Scarlett O'Hara in *Gone with the Wind* are the riveting Mercurius. Above all is Patrick Dennis' breezy Auntie Mame, lavish practitioner of multiple personae, whose cult status among male homosexuals is the unmistakable sign of her cross-sexual character.

Shakespeare is the most prolific single contributor to that parade of sexual personae which is western art. The liberated woman, I said, is the symbol of the English Renaissance, as the beautiful boy is of the Italian. In Shakespeare, liberated woman speaks, irrepressibly. Wit, as Jacob Burckhardt suggests, is a concomitant of the new "free personality" of the Renaissance.[6] Western wit, culminating in Oscar Wilde, is aggressive and competitive. It is an aristocratic language of social maneuvering and sexual display. The English and the French jointly created this hard style, for which there are few parallels in the Far East, where cultivated humor tends to be mild and diffuse. *The Faerie Queene*'s arms and armour turn into wit in Shakespeare's Renaissance Amazons. Rosalind, the young heroine of *As You Like It* (1599–1600), is one of the most original characters of Renaissance literature, capsulizing the era's psychological changes. The play's source is Thomas Lodge's prose romance, *Rosalynde or Euphues' Golden Legacy* (1590), which contains most of the plot. But Shakespeare makes the story a fantasia upon western personality. He enlarges and complicates Rosalind's character by giving her wit, audacity, and masculine force. Rosalind is Shakespeare's answer to Spenser's Belphoebe and Britomart, whom he spins into verbal and psychological motion. Rosalind is kinetic rather than iconistic. She too is a virgin. Indeed, her exhilarating freshness depends on that virginity. But Shakespeare removes Amazonian virginity from its holy self-sequestration and puts it into social engagement. Rosalind, unlike the high-minded Belphoebe and Britomart, has fun. She inhabits newly reclaimed secular space.

In her transvestite adventure, Rosalind seems to resemble Viola of Shakespeare's *Twelfth Night*, but temperamentally, the two women are completely unalike. In her authority over the other characters, Rosalind surpasses all of Shakespeare's comic heroines. Productions of *As You Like It* rarely show this. Intrepid Rosalind is usually reduced to Viola, and both parts are marred by summer-camp pastoral sentimentality. Rosalind's whole meaning is lyricism of personality *without* sentimentality. These roles, written for boy actors, have ambiguities of tone which modern actresses suppress. The androgynous Rosalind is prettified and demasculinized. Shakespeare's Portia is momentarily transvestite in *The Merchant of Venice*, where she wears a lawyer's robe for one act. But Portia's is not a complete sexual persona; that is, the play's other characters do not respond to him/her erotically. Rosalind and Viola are sexual instigators, the cause of irksome romatic errors. In many tales available to Shakespeare, a disguised woman inspires another woman's unhappy love. Most such stories were Italian, influenced by classical models, like Ovid's Iphis. The Italian tales, like their English prose counterparts, imitate the droll Ovidian manner of sexual innuendo. *As You Like It* and *Twelfth Night* depart from their sources in avoiding bedchamber intrigue. Shakespeare is interested in psychology, not pornography.

Both Rosalind and Viola adopt male clothing in crisis, but Viola's predicament is grimmer. She is orphaned and shipwrecked. Rosalind, on the other hand, banished by her usurper uncle, elects a male persona as whim and escapade. Both heroines choose sexually ambiguous alter egos. Viola is Cesario, a eunuch, and Rosalind Ganymede (as in Lodge), the beautiful boy kidnapped by Zeus. Rosalind is brasher than Viola from the start, arming herself with swashbuckling cutlass and boarspear. Viola, with her frail court rapier, makes a girlish and delicate boy at best. She is timid and easily terrorized. Rosalind relishes trouble and even creates it, as in her malicious meddling in the Sylvius-Phebe romance. When Olivia falls in love with her, Viola feels compassion toward this victim of her sexual illusion. But Rosalind is incapable of compassion where her own direct interest is not at stake. She can be hard, disdainful. Rosalind's lack of conventional feminine tenderness is part of her lofty power as a sexual persona. There is intimidation in her, uncaught by modern productions. Unlike Viola, Rosalind acts and conspires and laughs at the consequences.

Twelfth Night's plot resolution depends on the mechanistic device of twins. Viola surrenders her uncomfortable male role to a convenient brother, who uncomplainingly steps into her place in Olivia's affections. *As You Like It*, however, is centered on the more ambiguous Rosalind, who subsumes both twins within her nature. Viola is melancholy, recessive, but Rosalind is exuberant and egotistical, with a flamboyant instinct for center stage. The difference is clearest at play's end. Viola falls into long silence, keeping the joy of reunion to herself. Her decorous self-removal is the opposite of Rosalind's lordly capture of the finale of *As You Like It*.

Dominating her play better than her father has dominated his own realm, Rosalind asserts her innate aristocratic authority.

Shakespeare rings his double-sexed heroines with rippling circles of sexual ambiguity. Olivia's infatuation with Viola/Cesario is as suspicious as that of Spenser's Malecasta with Britomart, for the disguised Viola strikes everyone as feminine in voice and appearance. *Twelfth Night* begins with Duke Orsino savoring his sexual submission to the indifferent Olivia, whom he describes with outmoded Petrarchan metaphors of coldness and cruelty. Since the narcissistic Orsino is of dubious masculinity, Viola's ardor for him is problematic. In both *Twelfth Night* and *As You Like It*, the transvestite heroines fall for men far inferior to them. Even feminine Viola has sexual peculiarities. L. G. Salingar says of Viola and her precursors in the play's Roman and Italian sources, she is "the only one to fall in love *after* assuming her disguise."[7] So Viola falls in love not as a woman but as an androgyne. That she senses and esteems Orsino's half-feminine state is suggested in a covert confession of love where she casts him fleetingly as a woman (II.iv.23–28). Conveying Orsino's masochistic endearments to the arrogant Olivia, Viola is an androgyne bearing a hermaphroditic message from one androgyne to another. Viola transports Orsino's residual maleness before Olivia, where it radiates as an amatory promise seeming to come from Viola herself. Thus Viola's official mission further masculinizes her. Richard Bernheimer speaks of personality as a vehicle of representation by diplomats and attorneys: in "the fascination of his presence," deputy may eclipse employer.[8] The fetching Viola is a conflation of sexual representations. She represents Orsino but also, as Cesario, she represents a male. *Twelfth Night* relativizes gender and identity by this masque-like succession of representations. The principal characters become androgynous echoes of one another.

Like his counterpart in *Twelfth Night*, the male lead of *As You Like It* has severe dramatic shortcomings. Orlando, with whom Rosalind instantly falls in love, is adolescent-looking, barely bearded. Shakespeare undercuts his athletic prowess by making him the butt of constant jokes. The slow-witted Orlando is an unimpressive exponent of his sex in a play ruled by a vigorous heroine. Bertrand Evans calls him "only a sturdy booby."[9] Like Orsino, Orlando is more manipulated than manipulating. There may be a homoerotic element in his prompt consent to Rosalind/Ganymede's transsexual game. In *As You Like It*, Shakespeare reduces the Renaissance prestige of male authority to maximize his heroine's princely potency. Rosalind is intellectually and emotionally superior, sweeping all the characters into her sexual orbit. There is a lesbian suggestiveness in Phebe's infatuation with the disguised Rosalind, whose prettiness she dwells on and savors (III.v.113–23). Rosalind as a boy is, in Oliver's words, "fair, of female favor" (IV.iii.86–87). Her maleness is glamorously half-female.

The childhood liaison of Rosalind and Celia is also homoerotic. Shakespeare puts the girls into emotional alignment from the first moment Rosalind is mentioned and before she has even appeared. "Never two ladies loved as they do"; they have been "coupled and inseparable," even sleeping together (I.i.109, iii.71–74). This amorously exclusive friendship functions in the first act as a structural counterpoise to the adult marriages of the last act, which ends in a vision of the wedding god. In an essay on the use of "you" and "thou" in As You Like It, Angus McIntosh remarks that "you" often carries "an overtone of disgust and annoyance." After they encounter Orlando in the Forest of Arden, Celia, with "a note of huffiness," begins to "you" Rosalind, indicating "'the intrusion of Orlando into the cosiness of their hitherto undisturbed relationship."[10] I find evidence of Celia's jealousy even in the first act, when Rosalind hangs back to compliment Orlando and Celia says sharply, "Will you go, coz?" (I.ii.245). In the forest, Rosalind tries to get Celia to play the priest and marry her to the duped Orlando. "I cannot say the words," Celia replies (IV.i.121). She must be prodded three times before she can bring herself to give away the bride. That Shakespeare intends this subtext of sexual tension seems proved by the fact that in his source in Lodge it is the Celia character who merrily invents and urges on the sham wedding ceremony.

Because of the premodern prestige of virginity, the union of Rosalind and Celia is surely emotional and not overtly sexual. Their intimacy is that female matrix I found in Britomart's bond to her nurse. In As You Like It the matrix is an early stage of primary narcissism from which emerge the adult heterosexual commitments of the finale. Midway through the play, Rosalind exclaims, "But what talk we of fathers when there is such a man as Orlando?" (III.iv.35–36). Family and childhood alliances must yield to the new world of marriage. This is a characteristic English Renaissance movement: exogamy reinforces the social structure. Rosalind undergoes a process of increasing sexual differentiation. She splits from Celia by psychic mitosis. Their friendship is an all-in-all of gender, a solace for that motherlessness which Shakespeare curiously imposes on his maidens, leaving them defenseless in Hamlet and Othello. At the end of As You Like It, Rosalind and Celia sacrifice their relationship to take up the fixed sex roles of marriage. A choice is made, not necessarily inevitable. Hugh Richmond was, to my knowledge, the first critic to freely admit Rosalind's "capacity for bisexuality."[11] Unlike Viola, Rosalind is borderline. She could go either way. One of the unnoticed themes of As You Like It is Rosalind's temptation toward her outlaw male extreme and her overcoming of it to enter the larger social order. She is distinctly flirtatious in her prank with Phebe. Rosalind as Ganymede pretends to be a rakish lady-killer and, at her assumption of that sexual persona, actually becomes one. A superb language of arrogant command suddenly flows from her (III.v.35ff.). She is all sex and power. It is a complex psychological response to erotic opportunity, which she may or may not consciously recognize. In the scene in Spenser where she romances the dismayed Amoret, Britomart's actions are divorced from her thoughts, which are on her future husband. So Spenser and Shakespeare prefigure the modern theory of the unconscious, which Freud said was invented by the Romantic poets. Britomart and Rosalind drift into an involuntary realm of lesbian courtship. Male disguise elicits wayward impulses from the socially repressed side of their sexual nature.

Are there any fixed coordinates for masculinity and femininity in Shakespeare's transvestite comedies? Commentary on sex-differences can be fatuous, as in Orsino's pontifications. Rosalind's maxims on the sexes are usually satirical. In these plays, clothes make the man. By fixing the social persona, costume transforms thought, behavior, and gender. The one distinction between male and female seems to be combat ability. Viola is afraid to duel, and Rosalind faints at the sight of blood. Viola's twin, Sebastian, on the other hand, is hot-tempered and slaps people around. So Shakespeare gives men a physical genius that will out. Aside from this, Shakespeare seems to view masculinity and femininity as masks to put on and take off. He makes remarkably few allusions to sexual anatomy here: in the two plays I find one explicit remark and two or three puns. Viola, quailing at a duel, cries, "A little thing would make me tell them how much I lack of a man" (III.iv.313–15). Man minus "little thing" equals woman. Rosalind's resolve to "suit me all points like a man" hints at the obvious qualification that one male point isn't ordinarily available to army supply (I.iii.114). A clown parodies Orlando's love verse: "He that sweetest rose will find / Must find love's prick, and Rosalind" (III.ii.111–12). To consummate his love for Rosalind, the moping Orlando must recover his manly autonomy. Like Artegall in drag, he must straighten up and take charge. Second, Rosalind as rose is both flower and thorn. Disguised as an armed male, she has dual sexual attributes, the phallic "love's prick" as well as the female genital "rose." One expects more bawdiness in cross-dressing Renaissance imbroglios. In a source of Twelfth Night, Barnabe Rich's Of Apolonius and Silla (1581), Silvio, Viola's precursor, reveals her sex at the end by "loosing his garments down to his stomach," showing "his breasts and pretty teats." An arresting moment in boudoir reading, ill fit for the stage! Shakespeare's treatment of sexual ambiguity is remarkably chaste.

Shakespeare's characters often fail to read the correct sex of their colleagues or even to recognize their own lovers onstage. The motif of twins mistaken for one another comes from Plautus and Terence, who took it from Greek New Comedy. But in classical drama, the twins are the same sex. The Renaissance, with its attraction for the androgynous, altered the theme to opposite-sex twins. As if sparked by the zeitgeist, Shakespeare managed to father boy-and-girl twins. The use of virtuoso boy actors in all female roles conditioned Elizabethan playgoers to a suspension of sexual disbelief. The textual ambiguities of the transvestite comedies would be heightened by the presence of boys in the lead roles. The epilogue to As You Like It, which some think not by Shakespeare, demands audience recognition of the theatrical transsexualism. The actor playing Rosalind comes forward in female dress and addresses the audience: "If I were a woman, I would kiss as many of you as had beards that pleased me." A touch of male homosexual coquetry. At the end of performance, modern female impersonators similarly step out from the dramatic frame, revealing their real sex by tearing off wig and brassiere or emerging in tuxedo. Male portrayal of female roles in Elizabethan theater was inherently more homoerotic than the same custom in Greece or Japan. Greek actors wore wooden masks; Japanese Kabuki employs heavy schematic makeup. Greek and Japanese actors could be any age. But Elizabethan theater used beardless boys, probably with wigs and some makeup. But there were no masks. A boy had to be facially feminine enough to pass as a woman. The erotic piquancy must surely have led to claques of groupies, like those dogging the castrati of Italian opera.

Earlier, I spoke of the androgynous beauty of adolescent boys and the religious purity of their singing voices. The boy-angel inhabiting the stage Rosalind added his own hermaphroditism to an already sexually complex role. *As You Like It* and *Twelfth Night* played by boys would be shimmering spectacles of the mystery of gender. The quality of spectacle is evident in the last act of *Twelfth Night*, where the twins protract the traditional recognition scene to hypnotic length, a technique of cinematic slow motion I found in Shakespeare's *Rape of Lucrece*. London's National Theatre attempted an all-male production of *As You Like It* in 1967, the costumes Sixties mod. The director sought "an atmosphere of spiritual purity."[12] The episode where Rosalind as Ganymede induces Orlando to mock-woo her would specially benefit from such idealizing treatment, for it is a dazzling series of impersonations: we see a boy playing a girl playing a boy playing a girl. A reviewer said this production was "as simple, stylised and, in fact, as cold as a Noh play." Still, these actors were young adults, not boys. Roger Baker claims boys as Rosalind and Viola would be "really unnerving": "Boys can act with a natural gravity and grace."[13] Transvestite boys, we saw, led the Greek sacred procession of the Dionysian Oschophoria. Their unmasked presence on the Elizabethan stage reproduced the archaic ritualism and cultism of early drama.

Like Michelangelo's poetry, Shakespeare's sonnets are addressed to two love-objects, a baffling forceful woman and a beautiful boy. The unidentified fair youth was evidently highly androgynous in appearance. Shakespeare calls him "angel," "sweet boy," "beauteous and lovely youth" (144, 108, 54). Most blatant is Sonnet 20, where Shakespeare calls the youth his "master mistress" and says he has "a woman's face" and "a woman's gentle heart." Meaning him to be a woman, Nature "fell a-doting" and mistakenly added a penis. This is like Phaedrus' drunken Prometheus getting human genitals wrong. Sonnet 20 anticipates modern hormonal theory, where a fetus with male genitalia may retain female brain chemistry, producing an inner conviction of womanhood and a longing to change sex. The youth of Sonnet 20 is a hermaphrodite, facially and emotionally female but with the sexual superfluity of a penis—from which Shakespeare explicitly abstains. I suspect Shakespeare, like Michelangelo, was a Greek homosexual idealist who did not necessarily seek physical relations with men. G. Wilson Knight says Shakespeare's sonnets express "the recognition in his adored boy of a bisexual strength-with-grace" and identifies this view with Plato's, calling it "the seraphic intuition." Knight writes brilliantly about erotic idealism, which transforms libidinal energy into aesthetic vision, "a flooded consciousness": "You must have a maximum of ardour with a minimum of possible accomplishment, so that desire is forced into eye and mind to create."[14]

The beautiful boy belongs to the sonnets and must remain there. He cannot enter the plays. Rosalind is the beautiful boy reimagined in social terms. References to homosexuality are rare in Shakespeare's plays. There may be homosexual overtones to Iago's behavior in *Othello* and Leontes' in *The Winter's Tale* or to

Antonio's devotion to Sebastian in *Twelfth Night* and Patroclus' to Achilles in *Troilus and Cressida*. But Shakespeare never dwells on homosexuality or constructs a play or major character around it like his contemporary Marlowe, who opens *Dido, Queen of Carthage* with Jupiter "dandling Ganymede upon his knee" and *Edward the Second* with the king's male lover reading a mash note in the street. That play ends with the anal execution of the homosexual king with a red-hot poker.

I see in Shakespeare a segregation by genre, which diverts homosexuality into lyric and keeps it out of drama. I spoke of the Greek-invented beautiful boy as an Apollonian androgyne, silent and solipsistic. He is an objet d'art, brought into being by the admirer's reverent eye. Silence is a threat to drama, which thrives by voice. Northrop Frye speaks of "the self-enclosed world of the unproductive and narcissistic beautiful youth of Shakespeare's sonnets, a 'liquid prisoner pent in walls of glass.'"[15] Frye is using an alchemical image from Sonnet 5, where summer flowers are distilled into an alembic of perfume, like love and beauty transformed into art. The beautiful boy of the sonnets is asocial, self-absorbed. Shakespeare exhorts him to marry and beget heirs lest his patrician line end (Sonnets 1–17). Ironically, as I see it, if the youth were to make the social commitment of marriage, he would immediately lose his glamourous narcissistic beauty, which is produced by his removal from time and community. I have stressed that the Apollonian mode is harsh, absolutist, and separatist. Apollonian beings are incapable of Dionysian participation: they cannot "take part," since Apollonianism is coldy unitary, indivisible. The transvestite Rosalind inherits the marriage obligation of the fair youth, whose refusal of social integration confines him to the sonnets. A beautiful boy in the plays would seem shallow and small. In Shakespeare's drama, the only Ganymede is a woman. In Rosalind, the beautiful boy makes the choice for others rather than self.

Shakespeare's reflections upon androgynous personae were inspired by the Renaissance ferment in sex roles, which hit England later than Italy. The distance between these national phases of the Renaissance is illustrated by the fact that Shakespeare and Marlowe were born the same year Michelangelo died at age eighty-nine. Puritan preachers of the Elizabethan and Jacobean period inveighed against effeminate men and masculine women wearing men's clothes. Thus Shakespeare's transvestite comedies address a public issue and take a liberal position on it. Unlike Botticelli, who allowed Savonarola to destroy his pagan style, Shakespeare never yielded to Puritan pressure. In fact there is a turn toward decadence rather than away from it in his Jacobean plays. Shakespeare continued to believe in sexual personae as a mode of self-definition. This theme is treated in different ways in his two principal genres. His sonnets circulated in manuscript among an aristocratic coterie of Apollonian exclusiveness. But the plays were for the mixed social classes of the Globe Theatre, the democratic "Many" whom Plutarch identifies with Dionysus. Hence the psychic metamorphoses of Shakespeare's androgynes were in analogy to the rowdy pluralism of his audience.

That boy actors played girls is consistent with *As You Like It*'s claim that boys and women are emotionally alike. Rosalind as Ganymede claims she cured a man of love by pretending to be his beloved: "At which time would I, being but a moonish youth, grieve, be effeminate, changeable, longing and liking, proud, fantastical, apish, shallow, inconstant, full of tears, full of smiles; for every passion something and for no passion truly anything, as boys and women are for the most part cattle of this color" (III.ii.400–06). There are intimations here of the charming vexations of pederasty. Vergil's Mercury says, "Woman is forever various and changeable" (*Aen.* IV.569–70). Verdi's duke agrees: "La donna è mobile." Woman is mobile, changeable, fickle. Boys are moonish, as Rosalind puts it, because their mercurial inconstancy of mind resembles the ever-altering phases of the feminine moon, ruler of women's lives. Shakespeare is speaking of adolescents, more proof that Van den Berg is wrong to say adolescence was never noticed and therefore did not exist before the Enlightenment. Rosalind's speech is a catalog of rapid shifts of persona, that giddy free movement among mood-states which I identify with the fun-loving but deceitful Hermes/Mercury. Are boys and women volatile by hormonal alchemy? Some male artists and writers have the nervous sensibility and delicate trembling fingers of women. Sensitivity begins in the body, which mind and vocation follow.

Shakespeare elsewhere broadens his model of androgynous volatility to include special men or men in special situations. "The lunatic, the lover, and the poet / Are of imagination all compact": artists and lovers are like lunatics, literally moon-men (*Midsummer* V.i.7–8). To love "is to be all made of fantasy." The true lover is "unstaid and skittish in all motions" save the beloved's image. The lover should wear "changeable taffeta," for his mind is "a very opal" (*AYLI* V.ii.93; *Twelfth* II.iv.17–20, 73–75). Love dematerializes masculinity. Things are glimmering, wavering, liquefied. Art and love dissolve social habit and form, a Dionysian fluidity. Shakespeare's clowns also inhabit a déclassé world of androgynous freedom. The medieval fool or jester had licensed access to satiric commentary and multiple personae. In *King Lear* Shakespeare gives the asexual fool Zen-like maxims of ultimate truth, toward which the pompous king makes his painful way. In *Romeo and Juliet* the jester role is played by the ill-starred nobleman Mercutio, named for his unruly mercurial temperament. His speech is a mad rush of images, metaphors, puns. Woman, boy, lunatic, lover, poet, fool: Shakespeare unites them emotionally and psychologically. They share the same fantastical quickness and variability. They are in moonlike psychic flux, which becomes manic-depressive instability in the frantic Mercutio. As a poet, Shakespeare belongs to this invisible fraternity of mixed sex. Inwardly, he too is a mercurial androgyne. Sonnet 29 charts one of his crushing mood-swings—low, lower, then up and away with the lark of sunrise.

Rosalind, the alchemical Mercurius, symbolizes comic mastery of multiple personae. Viola and Rosalind discipline their feelings, while the minor characters are full of excess and self-indulgence. Both women patiently maintain their male disguise in situations crying out for revelation. They differ, however, in their speech. Viola is discreet and solicitous, Rosalind aggressive, mischievous, bantering, railing. Riffling through her endless personae with mystical ease, Rosalind seems conscious of the fictiveness of personality. She theatricalizes her inner life. She stands mentally outside her role and all roles. Rosalind's characteristic tone is roguish self-satire: "Make the doors upon a woman's wit, and it will out at the casement; shut that, and 'twill out at the keyhole; stop that, 'twill fly with the smoke out at the chimney" (IV.i.154–57). Her own darting wit is this gusty draft in the closed household of Renaissance womanhood. Rosalind turns words to smoke, a spiritualistic emanation of her restless motility of thought. Her performance in drag is high camp—a useful if passé homosexual term. The essence of camp is manner, not décor. Rosalind fulfills Christopher Isherwood's definition of camp: she mocks something, her love for Orlando, which she takes seriously. Her supreme moment of high camp is the wooing scene, where she pretends to be what she really is—Rosalind.

The Mercurius and androgyne has the reckless dash and spontaneity of youth. Despite our racy modern bias, if Rosalind were to keep her male disguise, she would cease to grow as a character. Shakespeare's plays, I said, esteem development and process, Dionysian transformation. Rosalind transforms herself by going to the forest, but she would stagnate if she stayed there. Her valiant Amazon personality would be diminished and trivialized. She would turn into Shakespeare's other mercurial androgyne, the cavorting sky-spirit Ariel, who is all shape-shifting and speed, changing himself to Harpy and sea-nymph. Ariel, the trickster Till Eulenspiegel, and J. M. Barrie's Peter Pan (a boy played by an actress), demonstrate the feminizing effects of psychic mutability on males. This reverses the principle I found in Michelangelo, where monumentality masculinizes women. Rosalind must put an end to her proteanism and rejoin the Renaissance social order. Modern productions completely miss the severe pattern of ritualistic renunciation in *As You Like It*. Rosalind is not Peter Pan, nor is she Virginia Woolf's reckless, cigar-smoking Sally Seton. Rosalind is never madcap or flippant. Behind her playfulness of language and personae is a pressure of magisterial will. Multiplicity of mood tends toward anarchy. Shakespeare's Renaissance wisdom subordinates that multiplicity to social structure, containing its exuberant energies in marriage. In the Renaissance as now, play must be part of a dialectic of work, or it becomes decadent.

At the climax of *As You Like It*, Rosalind constructs a ceremony of farewell to her androgynous self. It is her moment of maximum wit or creative intelligence. The play's romantic entanglements are in total confusion. Rosalind proclaims that by "magic" she will deliver to each person his or her heart's desire. The revelation of her own identity and gender is the key: *As You Like It* ends in an alchemical experiment where Rosalind, as the hermaphroditic Mercurius, transmutes the play's characters and destinies, including her own. The magnum opus begins with a chant, a spell or litany of erotic fixation and frustration. The lines go round and round in circle magic, rings of the alchemical uroboros (V.ii.82–118, iv. 116–24). The play proposes a riddle, as snarled as the Gordian knot. Rosalind's personality, self-displayed, resolves these dismaying intricacies. When she appears undisguised, Rosalind is the surprise conclusion to an elegant sexual syllogism. Her shamanistic epiphany reorders the erotic chaos of the play. This Sphinx answers her own riddle. Oedipus' reply, "Man," works again, for Rosalind is the *anthropos* or perfected man of alchemy.

Rosalind's hybrid gender and perpetual transformations are the quicksilver of the alchemical Mercurius, who had the rainbow colors of the peacock's tail. Jung says Mercurius as quicksilver symbolizes "the 'fluid', i.e., mobile, intellect." Mercurius, like Rosalind, is "both material and spiritual."[16] Rosalind's spirituality is her purity, purpose, and romantic fidelity; her materiality is her realism and mordant pragmatism. An alchemical treatise of the early seventeenth century is called *Atalanta Fugiens,* "Atalanta in flight." It makes the swift huntress a metaphor for "the strength of the volatile Mercury."[17] *As You Like It* compares Rosalind to Atalanta and identifies wit with speed: "All thoughts . . . are winged" (III.ii.147; IV.i.135; III.ii.273–74). In her emotional reserve and verbal agility, Rosalind is an Atalanta *fugiens.* The Philosopher's Stone or hermaphroditic *rebis* of alchemy often has wings, which Jung interprets as "intuition or spiritual (winged) potentiality."[18] Both masculine and feminine, Rosalind is a Mercurius of swift, sovereign intelligence. Speed as hermaphroditic transcendance: we see this in Vergil's Amazon Camilla and Giambologna's ephebic Mercury in ecstatic flight.

Rosalind is the catalyst of *As You Like It,* the magic elixir transmuting base into noble metals. The editor of *Atalanta Fugiens* remarks, "Mercurius is the mercury in which the metals have to be dissolved, reduced to the primary matter before they can become gold."[19] The *rebis,* we noted, is often shown as incestuous brother and sister. Shakespeare alters the forest roles of Lodge's Rosalynde and Aliena (Celia) from page and mistress to brother and sister, as if to facilitate an alchemical analogy. This change does not preclude eroticism, in view of the lesbian tinge to Rosalind and Celia's friendship. As first cousins, they too risk incest. The primary transactions undertaken by Shakespeare's Mercurius are the Sylvius-Phebe romance (which turns triangle) and the bamboozling of the lovelorn Orlando. These alchemical experiments, in the closed glass retort of the play, succeed. Like Nero, Rosalind experiments with person and place. But hers is white rather than black magic, leading to love and marriage rather than debauchery and death. Lodge's Rosalynde claims to have a friend "deeply experienced in necromancy and magic," but Shakespeare's Rosalind boldly arrogates these occult powers to herself. Rosalind is both producer and star of the finale. Her hierarchically most commanding moment is paradoxically the one where she ritually lays aside her hermaphroditism to take up the socialized persona of obedient wife to Orlando. Her incantatory speech in female dress ceremonially restores heterosexual normality to the play. In it she names and cleanses her major social relationships, then reifies them. A new social structure is being constructed, with her father reinvested with his ducal authority. "Ducdame, ducdame, ducdame," sings Jaques in the forest, a nonsense word bemusing scholars (II.v.49). I say, the duke is a dame. Rosalind, as much as her uncle, has usurped her father's manhood. Now she surrenders what is not hers to reclaim her own sex.

Rosalind's magic is real, for she produces Hymen, the marriage spirit who enters with her in the last scene. Hymen is a prominent figure in court masque, but he is conspicuously out of place in a Shakespeare play. He is an embarrassment to modern commentators on the play, who ignore him whenever possible. Why this allegorical invasion of the naturalistic *As You Like It?* First of all, Hymen symbolizes the mass marriages which end Shakespearean comedy. He is reconciliation and social harmony, knitting the classes and leading the banished characters back to the redeemed city. But Hymen is also a by-product of the play's psychoalchemy. The alchemical operation had two parts: distillation and sublimation. Hymen, traditionally depicted as a beautiful young man, is a sexual sublimate. He is the emanation or double of Rosalind herself. He is the ghost of her maleness, exorcised but lingering on to preside over the exit from Arden. Shakespeare's technique here is allegorical repletion, the term I invented for Leonardo's *The Virgin with St. Anne.* Hymen's odd doubling of Rosalind is like Leonardo's awkward photographic superimposition of two female figures. Sexual personae flood the eye. The characters of *As You Like It* stand startled. Hymen is their collectively projected mental image of the transvestite Rosalind, now only a memory. Hymen is a visible distillation of her transsexual experience. In her romantic conspiracies, Rosalind has impersonated Hymen and hence evoked his presence. As the Mercurius who overcomes sexual duality and perfects base materials, she possesses the magnetic power of concord, ensuring the integrity of Renaissance social order.

Rosalind is, to borrow a phrase from Paracelsus, "a fiery and perfect Mercury extracted by Nature and Art."[20] She reinterprets the classical Amazon, making physical prowess intellectual. Rosalind is Shakespeare's version of Spenser's glamourous androgynes. Britomart's flashing armour and flaming sword become Rosalind's unanswerable wit. Shakespeare's transvestite heroine has masculine pride, verve, and cool aristocratic control—scarcely to be found in today's simplistic, innocuous Rosalinds. The ideal Rosalind must have both lyricism and force. There must be intelligence, depth, spontaneity, something quick and vivacious, with a hint of the wild and uncontrolled. The girl-boy Rosalind is in Atalanta-flight from mood to mood, an adolescent skittishness. The closest thing I have ever seen to Shakespeare's authentic Rosalind is Patricia Charbonneau's spirited performance as a coltish Reno cowgirl in Donna Deitch's film *Desert Hearts* (1985), based on a lesbian love story by Jane Rule.

Rosalind as Mercurius has a quick smile and mobile eye. Shakespeare's view of woman is revolutionary. Unlike Belphoebe or Britomart, Rosalind has a jovial inner landscape. It is not Spenser's grim arena of virtue's battle with vice. This landscape is airy and pleasant, full of charm and surprise. Rosalind's self-pleasuring is not like Mona Lisa's. No daemonic fog of solipsism hangs over her. Rosalind has an invigorating alertness. She is not smugly half-asleep, like Leonardo's Renaissance woman. Mona Lisa still has the baleful Gorgon eye of archaic archetype. She burns us with her glance. The daemonic eye sees nothing but its prey. It seeks power, the fascism of nature. But Rosalind's socialized eye *moves to see.* It takes things in. Hers are not the lustful rolling eyes of Spenser's femmes fatales, which slither, pierce, and possess. Rosalind's eye honors the integrity of objects and persons. Its mobility signals a mental processing of information, the visible sign of western intelligence. In Spenser, we saw, the virtuous eye is rigidly controlled. Until our century, a respectable woman kept her eyes modestly averted. Shakespeare legitimizes bold mobility of the female eye and identifies it with imagination. Rosalind's eye is truly perceptive: it both sees and understands. Shakespeare's great heroine unites multiplicity of gender, persona, word, eye, and thought.

NOTES

[1] *The Philosophy of Literary Form: Studies in Symbolic Action* (New York, 1957), 249.
[2] *Alchemy,* trans. William Stoddart (London, 1967), 13.
[3] *Collected Works,* trans. R. F. C. Hull (Princeton, 1967), 13:189.
[4] *The Origins of Alchemy in Graeco-Roman Egypt* (New York, 1970), 258.
[5] In Paracelsus, *Hermetic and Alchemical Writings,* ed. Arthur Edward Waite (New Hyde Park, N.Y., 1967), 2:374.
[6] *The Civilization of the Renaissance in Italy,* trans. S. G. C. Middlemore (New York, 1958), 1:143, 163.
[7] "The Design of *Twelfth Night,*" *Shakespeare Quarterly* 9 (1958): 121.
[8] *The Nature of Representation: A Phenomenological Inquiry* (New York, 1961), 124.
[9] *Shakespeare's Comedies* (Oxford, 1960), 93.
[10] *"As You Like It:* A Grammatical Clue to Character," *A Review of English Literature* 4, No. 2 (1963): 74, 76–77.
[11] *Shakespeare's Sexual Comedy* (New York, 1971), 137.
[12] Quoted on Roger Baker, *Drag: A History of Female Impersonation on the Stage* (London, 1968), 240.
[13] Ibid., 242, 240, 87.
[14] *The Mutual Flame* (London, 1955), 112. *Neglected Powers* (London, 1971), 49. *Mutual Flame,* 219, 155, 139.
[15] *A Study of English Romanticism* (New York, 1968), 140.
[16] *Collected Works,* 12:69; 13:237.
[17] Michael Maier, *Atalanta Fugiens,* ed. H. M. E. De Jong (Leiden, 1969), 316. First published 1617. The phrase appears in the epigraph on Maier's title page.
[18] *Collected Works,* 12:202.
[19] *Atalanta Fugiens,* 9n.
[20] *Hermetic and Alchemical Writings,* 1:66.

CONTRIBUTORS

HAROLD BLOOM is Sterling Professor of the Humanities at Yale University and Henry W. and Albert A. Berg Professor of English at the New York University Graduate School. He is a 1985 MacArthur Foundation Award recipient, served as the Charles Eliot Norton Professor of Poetry at Harvard University (1987–88), and is the author of nineteen books, the most recent being *The Book of J* (1990). Currently he is editing the Chelsea House series Modern Critical Views and The Critical Cosmos, and other Chelsea House series in literary criticism.

HAROLD C. GODDARD was head of the English department at Swarthmore College from 1909 to 1946. In addition to *The Meaning of Shakespeare* (1951), he published *Studies in New England Transcendentalism* in 1908 and edited a 1926 edition of the essays of Ralph Waldo Emerson.

C. L. BARBER was Professor of English at the University of California–Santa Cruz until his death in 1980. *Shakespeare's Festive Comedy* was published in 1959, and two further works, *The Whole Journey: Shakespeare's Power of Development* (1986) and *Creating Elizabethan Tragedy: The Theater of Marlowe and Kyd* (1988), have been edited and completed by Richard P. Wheeler.

WALTER R. DAVIS is Professor of English at Brown University. He has written *Idea and Act in Elizabethan Fiction* (1969) and *Thomas Campion* (1987) and edited the works of Thomas Campion (1967). He has also edited the anthology *Twentieth Century Interpretations of* Much Ado About Nothing (1969).

EDWARD I. BERRY, Dean of the Humanities at the University of Victoria (Victoria, British Columbia), is the author of *Patterns of Decay: Shakespeare's Early Histories* (1975) and *Shakespeare's Comic Rites* (1984).

CHARLES R. FORKER is Professor of English at Indiana University at Bloomington. Among his works are Henry V: *An Annotated Bibliography* (1983; with Joseph Candido), *Skull beneath the Skin: The Achievement of John Webster* (1986), *Fancy's Images: Contexts, Settings, and Perspectives in Shakespeare and His Contemporaries* (1990), and an edition of James Shirley's *The Cardinal* (1964).

R. CHRIS HASSEL, JR., Professor of English at Vanderbilt University (Nashville, TN), has written *Renaissance Drama and the English Church Year* (1979) and *Faith and Folly in Shakespeare's Romantic Comedies* (1980).

WILLIAM C. CARROLL is the author of *The Great Feast of Language in* Love's Labour's Lost (1976) and *The Metamorphoses of Shakespearean Comedy* (1985). He is Professor of English at Boston University.

DEVON L. HODGES is Professor of English at George Mason University (Fairfax, VA). She has written *Renaissance Fictions of Anatomy* (1985) and *Nostalgia and Sexual Difference: The Resistance to Contemporary Feminism* (1987; with Janice Doane).

BARBARA J. BONO is Associate Professor of English at SUNY–Buffalo. She is the author of *Literary Transvaluation from Vergilian Epic to Shakespearean Tragicomedy* (1984).

MARJORIE GARBER, Professor of English at Harvard University, has written *Dream in Shakespeare: From Metaphor to Metamorphosis* (1974), *Coming of Age in Shakespeare* (1981), and *Shakespeare's Ghost Writers: Literature as Uncanny Causality* (1987), and edited *Cannibals, Witches, and Divorce: Estranging the Renaissance* (1987).

CAMILLE PAGLIA, Associate Professor of Humanities at the University of the Arts (Philadelphia, PA), is the author of *Sexual Personae: Art and Decadence from Nefertiti to Emily Dickinson* (1990).

BIBLIOGRAPHY

Adelman, Janet. "Male Bonding in Shakespeare's Comedies." In *Shakespeare's "Rough Magic":
   Renaissance Essays in Honor of C. L. Barber,* edited by Peter B. Erickson and Coppélia
   Kahn. Newark: University of Delaware Press, 1985, pp. 73–103.

Anderson, Linda. "Romantic Comedies." In *A Kind of Wild Justice: Revenge in Shakespearean
   Comedies.* Newark: University of Delaware Press, 1987, pp. 57–125.

Bamber, Linda. *Comic Women, Tragic Men: A Study of Gender and Genre in Shakespeare.*
   Stanford: Stanford University Press, 1982.

Barnet, Sylvan. "Strange Events: Improbability in *As You Like It.*" *Shakespeare Studies* 4
   (1968): 119–31.

Barton, Anne. "*As You Like It* and *Twelfth Night:* Shakespeare's Sense of an Ending." In
   Shakespearean Comedy, ed. Malcolm Bradbury and David Palmer. (Stratford-upon-
   Avon Studies 14.) London: Edward Arnold, 1972, pp. 160–80.

Beckman, Margaret Boerner. "The Figure of Rosalind in *As You Like It.*" *Shakespeare
   Quarterly* 29 (1978): 44–51.

Belsey, Catherine. "Disrupting Sexual Difference: Meaning and Gender in the Comedies."
   In *Alternative Shakespeare,* edited by John Drakakis. London: Methuen, 1985, pp.
   166–90.

Bergren, Paula S. " 'A Prodigious Thing': The Jacobean Heroine in Male Disguise." *Philological
   Quarterly* 62 (1983): 383–402.

Bloom, Harold, ed. *William Shakespeare's* As You Like It. New York: Chelsea House, 1988.

Bracher, Mark. "Contrary Notions of Identity in *As You Like It.*" *Studies in English Literature
   1500–1900* 24 (1984): 225–40.

Braunmuller, A. R. and J. C. Bulman. "Introduction" to *Comedy from Shakespeare to Sheri-
   dan: Change and Continuity in the English and European Dramatic Tradition: Essays in
   Honor of Eugene M. Waith,* edited by A. R. Braunmuller and J. C. Bulman. Newark:
   University of Delaware Press, 1986, pp. 13–23.

Brooks, Charles. "Shakespeare's Heroine-Actresses." *Shakespeare Jahrbuch* (Heidelberg) 96
   (1960): 134–44.

Brown, John Russell. "Love's Order and the Judgement of *As You Like It.*" In *Shakespeare
   and His Comedies.* London: Methuen, 1957, pp. 124–59.

Brown, Steve. "The Boyhood of Shakespeare's Heroines: Notes on Gender Ambiguity in the
   Sixteenth Century." *Studies in English Literature 1500–1900* 30 (1990): 243–63.

Carlson, Susan. "Women in *As You Like It.*" *Essays in Literature* 14 (1987): 151–69.

Cirillo, Albert R. "*As You Like It:* Pastoralism Gone Awry." *ELH* 38 (1971): 19–39.

Colie, Rosalie L. "Perspectives on Pastoral: Romance, Comic and Tragic: *As You Like It* and
   The Winter's Tale." In *Shakespeare's Living Art.* Princeton: Princeton University Press,
   1974, pp. 243–85.

Daley, A. Stuart, "Where Are the Words in *As You Like It?*" *Shakespeare Quarterly* 34
   (1983): 172–80.

Draper, R. P. "Shakespeare's Pastoral Comedy." *Etudes Anglaises* 11 (1958): 1–17.

Dusinberre, Juliet. "Women and Education: Disguise and the Boy Actor." In *Shakespeare and
   the Nature of Women.* London: Macmillan, 1975, pp. 231–71.

Erickson, Peter B. "Sexual Politics and the Social Structure in *As You Like It.*" *Massachusetts
   Review* 23 (1982): 65–83.

Estrin, Barbara L. "The Dream of a Better Life in *As You Like It* and *Antony and Cleopatra.*"

In *The Raven and the Lark: Lost Children in Literature of the English Renaissance.* Lewisburg, PA: Bucknell University Press, 1985, pp. 143–58.

Evans, Bertrand. "Approach to the Summit: *As You Like It.*" In *Shakespeare's Comedies.* Oxford: Clarendon Press, 1960, pp. 87–98.

Fiedler, Leslie A. "The Woman as Stranger: or 'None but women left. . . .'" In *The Stranger in Shakespeare.* New York: Stein & Day, 1972, pp. 43–81.

Fineman, Joel. "Fratricide and Cuckoldry: Shakespeare's Doubles." In *Representing Shakespeare: New Psychoanalytical Essays,* edited by Murry M. Schwartz and Coppélia Kahn. Baltimore: Johns Hopkins University Press, 1980, pp. 70–109.

Fortin, René E. "'Tongues in Trees': Symbolic Patterns in *As You Like It.*" *Texas Studies in Literature and Language* 14 (1973): 569–86.

Gardner, Helen. *"As You Like It."* In *More Talking of Shakespeare,* edited by John Garrett. New York: Theatre Arts Books, 1959, pp. 17–32.

Green, Douglas E. "The 'Unexpressive She': Is There Really a Rosalind?" *Journal of Dramatic Theory and Criticism* 2, No. 2 (Spring 1988): 41–52.

Greenblatt, Stephen. "Fiction and Friction." In *Reconstructing Individualism: Autonomy, Individuality, and the Self in Western Thought,* edited by Thomas C. Heller et al. Stanford: Stanford University Press, 1986, pp. 30–52.

Hale, John K. "'Will Strive to Please You Every Day': Pleasure and Meaning in Shakespeare's Mature Comedies." *Studies in English Literature 1500–1900* 21 (1981): 241–55.

Halio, Jay L. "Introduction" to *Twentieth Century Interpretations in* As You Like It. Englewood Cliffs, NJ: Prenctice-Hall, 1968, pp. 1–13.

———. "No Clock in the Forest." *Studies In English Literature 1500–1900* 2 (1962): 197–207.

———, and Barbara C. Millard, ed. As You Like It: *An Annotated Bibliography 1940–80.* New York: Garland, 1985.

Harley, Marta Powell. "Rosalind, the Hare, and the Hyena in Shakespeare's *As You Like It.*" *Shakespeare Quarterly* 36 (1985): 335–37.

Hayles, Nancy K. "Sexual Disguise in *As You Like It* and *Twelfth Night.*" *Shakespeare Survey* 32 (1979): 63–72.

Hedrick, Donald K. "Merry and Weary Conversation: Textual Uncertainty in *As You Like It.* II.iv." *ELH* 46 (1979): 21–34.

Hyland, Peter. "Shakespeare's Heroines: Disguise in the Romantic Comedies." *Ariel* 9, No. 2 (April 1978): 23–39.

Jackson, Russell. "'Perfect Types of Womanhood': Rosalind, Beatrice and Viola in Victorian Criticism and Performance." *Shakespeare Survey* 32 (1979): 15–26.

Jamieson, Michael. "Shakespeare's Celibate Stage: The Problem of Accommodation of the Boy-Actors in *As You Like It, Antony and Cleopatra,* and *The Winter's Tale.*" In *Papers, Mainly Shakespearean,* edited by I. L. Duthie. Aberdeen: University of Aberdeen Press, 1964, pp. 21–39.

Jardine, Lisa. "Female Roles and Elizabethan Eroticism." In *Still Harping on Daughters: Women and Drama in the Age of Shakespeare.* Brighton: The Harvester Press, 1983, pp. 9–36.

Jenkins, Harold. *"As You Like It."* *Shakespeare Survey* 8 (1955): 40–51.

Johnson, Samuel. *"As You Like It."* In *Johnson on Shakespeare.* Edited by Bertrand H. Bronson with Jean M. O'Meara. New Haven: Yale University Press, 1986, pp. 98–106.

Kahn, Maura Slattery. "Much Virtue in *If.*" *Shakespeare Quarterly* 28 (1977): 40–50.

Kelly, Thomas. "Shakespeare's Romantic Heroes: Orlando Reconsidered." *Shakespeare Quarterly* 24 (1973): 12–24.

Kimbrough, Robert. "Androgyny Seen Through Shakespeare's Disguise." *Shakespeare Quarterly* 33 (1982): 17–33.

Knowles, Richard. "Myth and Type in *As You Like It.*" *ELH* 33 (1966): 1–22.

Latham, Agnes. "Introduction" to *As You Like It.* London: Methuen, 1975, pp. ix–xci.

Levine, Laura. "Men in Women's Clothing: Anti-Theatricality and Effeminization from 1579–1642." *Criticism* 28 (1986): 121–43.

MacCary, W. Thomas. "The Comic Significance of Transvestism in Plautus, Shakespeare and Beaumarchais." *Letterature Comparate* 1 (1981): 293–308.

McFarland, Thomas. "For Other Than for Dancing Measures: The Complications of *As You Like It.*" In *Shakespeare's Pastoral Comedy.* Chapel Hill: University of North Carolina Press, 1972, pp. 98–121.

Martz, William J. "Rosalind and Incremental Development of Character in Comedy." In *Shakespeare's Universe of Comedy.* New York: David Lewis, 1971, pp. 84–99.

Maus, Katharine Eisaman. "Playhouse Flesh and Blood." *ELH* 46 (1979): 595–617.

Mincoff, Marco. "What Shakespeare Did to *Rosalynde.*" *Shakespeare Jahrbuch* (Heidelberg) 96 (1960): 78–89.

Montrose, Louis Adrian. "'The Place of a Brother' in *As You Like It:* Social Process and Comic Form." *Shakespeare Quarterly* 32 (1981): 28–54.

Mowat, Barbara A. "Images of Woman in Shakespeare's Plays." *Southern Humanities Review* 11 (1977): 145–57.

Muir, Kenneth. "Maturity: *As You Like It.*" In *Shakespeare's Comic Sequence.* Liverpool: Liverpool University Press, 1979, pp. 84–91.

Nevo, Ruth. "Existence in Arden." In *Comic Transformation in Shakespeare.* London: Methuen, 1980, pp. 180–99.

Novy, Marianne. "*Daniel Deronda* and George Eliot's Female Re-Vision of Shakespeare." In *Women's Re-Visions of Shakespeare,* edited by Marianne Novy. Urbana: University of Illinois Press, 1990, pp. 89–107.

Nuttall, A. D. "Two Unassimilable Men." In *Shakespearean Comedy,* ed. Malcolm Bradbury and David Palmer. (Stratford-upon-Avon Studies 14.) London: Edward Arnold, 1972, pp. 210–40.

Orgel, Stephen. "Nobody's Perfect: Or Why Did the English Stage Take Boys for Women?" *South Atlantic Quarterly* 88 (1989): 7–29.

Palmer, D. J. "*As You Like It* and the Idea of Play." *Critical Quarterly* 13 (1971): 240–43.

Park, Clara Claiborne. "As We Like It: How a Girl Can Be Smart and Still Popular." *American Scholar* 42 (1973): 262–78.

Parrott, Thomas Marc. "The Master Craftsman: *As You Like It.*" In *Shakespearean Comedy.* New York: Oxford University Press, 1949, pp. 164–78.

Parry, P. H. "The Boyhood of Shakespeare's Heroines." In *Shakespeare Survey* 42 (1990): 99–109.

Pierce, Robert B. "The Moral Languages of *Rosalynde* and *As You Like It.*" *Studies in Philology* 68 (1971): 167–76.

Rackin, Phyllis. "Androgyny, Mimesis, and the Marriage of the Boy Heroine on the English Renaissance Stage." *PMLA* 102 (1987): 29–41.

Richman, David. "Moods." In *Laughter, Pain, and Wonder: Shakespeare's Comedies and the Audience.* Newark: University of Delaware Press, 1990, pp. 121–46.

Rickey, Mary Ellen. "Rosalind's Gentle Jupiter." *Shakespeare Quarterly* 13 (1962): 365–66.

Schwartz, Robert B. "Puritans, Libertines and the Green World of Utopia in *As You Like It.*" *Shakespeare Jahrbuch* (Heidelberg) 123 (1987): 66–73.

Scoufos, Alice-Lyle. "The *Paradiso Terrestre* and the Testing of Love in *As You Like It.*" *Shakespeare Survey* 14 (1981): 215–27.

Sen Gupta, S. C. "Middle Comedies." In *Shakespearean Comedy.* Calcutta: Oxford University Press, 1950, pp. 129–73.

Shaw, John. "Fortune and Nature in *As You Like It.*" *Shakespeare Quarterly* 6 (1955): 45–50.

Smidt, Kristian. "All Even in Arden?: Notes on the Composition of *As You Like It.*" *English Studies* 70 (1989): 490–503.

Smith, James. *"As You Like It."* In *Shakespearean and Other Essays.* Cambridge: Cambridge University Press, 1974, pp. 1–23.

Stanton, Kay. "The Disguise of Shakespeare's *As You Like It.*" *Iowa State Journal of Research* 59 (1985): 295–305.

Stockholder, Kay. "The Paths of True Love." In *Dream Works: Lovers and Families in Shakespeare's Plays.* Toronto: University of Toronto Press, 1987, pp. 26–39.

Taylor, Don Ervin. " 'Try in Time in Despite of a Fall': Time and Occasion in *As You Like It.*" *Texas Studies in Literature and Language* 24 (1982): 121–36.

Thompson, Karl F. "The Globe Plays." In *Modesty and Cunning: Shakespeare's Use of Literary Tradition.* Ann Arbor: University of Michigan Press, 1971, pp. 97–148.

Traci, Philip. "*As You Like It:* Homosexuality in Shakespeare's Play." *CLA Journal* 25 (1981): 91–105.

Vickers, Brian. "Gay Comedy." In *The Artistry of Shakespeare's Prose.* London: Methuen, 1968, pp. 179–239.

Waddington, Raymond B. "Moralizing the Spectacle: Dramatic Emblems in *As You Like It.*" *Shakespeare Quarterly* 33 (1982): 155–63.

Westlund, Joseph. "*As You Like It:* Serene Autonomy." In *Shakespeare's Reparative Comedies: A Psychoanalytic View of the Middle Plays.* Chicago: University of Chicago Press, 1984, pp. 69–91.

Whall, Helen M. "*As You Like It:* The Play of Analogy." *Huntington Library Quarterly* 47 (1984): 33–46.

Williamson, Marilyn L. "The Comedies of Courtship: Men's Profit, Women's Power." In *The Patriarchy of Shakespeare's Comedies.* Detroit: Wayne State University Press, 1986, pp. 25–53.

———. "The Masque of Hymen in *As You Like It.*" *Comparative Drama* 2 (1968–69): 248–58.

Wilson, Rawdon. "The Way to Arden: Attitudes Towards Time in *As You Like It.*" *Shakespeare Quarterly* 26 (1975): 16–24.

Woodbridge, Linda. *Women and the English Renaissance: Literature and the Nature of Womankind 1540–1620.* Urbana: University of Illinois Press, 1984, pp. 152–83.

Young, David. "Earthly Things Made Even: *As You Like It.*" In *The Heart's Forest: A Study of Shakespeare's Pastoral Plays.* New Haven: Yale University Press, 1972, pp. 38–72.

ACKNOWLEDGMENTS

" 'No Clock in the Forest': Time in *As You Like It*" by Jay L. Halio from *Studies in English Literature 1500–1900* 2, No. 2 (Spring 1962), © 1962 by Rice University Press. Reprinted by permission of *Studies in English Literature 1500–1900.*

"Shakespeare's Bitter Arcadia" by Jan Kott from *Shakespeare Our Contemporary* by Jan Kott, translated by Boleslaw Taborski, © 1964, 1965, 1966 by Panstwowe Wydawnictwo Naukowe and Doubleday, a division of Bantam Doubleday Dell Publishing Group, Inc. Reprinted by permission of Doubleday, a division of Bantam Doubleday Dell Publishing Group, Inc.

"Rosalind, Helena, and Isabella: The Descent to Sexual Realities" by Hugh M. Richmond from *Shakespeare's Sexual Comedy: A Mirror for Lovers* by Hugh M. Richmond, © 1971 by The Bobbs-Merrill Company, Inc. Reprinted by permission of the author.

" 'Ganymede' on the Elizabethan Stage: Homosexual Implications of the Use of Boy-Actors" by Gordon Lell from *Aegis* 1, No. 1 (Fall 1973), © 1973 by the Editors of *Aegis*. Reprinted by permission of the author.

"The Player in the Play" by Leo Salingar from *Shakespeare and the Traditions of Comedy* by Leo Salingar, © 1974 by Cambridge University Press. Reprinted by permission of Cambridge University Press.

"Counsels of God and Grace: Intimate Conversations between Women in Shakespeare's Plays" by Carole McKewin from *The Woman's Part: Feminist Criticism of Shakespeare*, edited by Carolyn Ruth Swift Lenz, Gayle Greene, and Carol Thomas Neely, © 1980 by the Board of Trustees of the University of Illinois. Reprinted by permission.

"The Dramatization of Double Meaning in Shakespeare's *As You Like It*" by Wolfgang Iser from *Theatre Journal* 35, No. 3 (October 1983), © 1983 by University and College Theatre Association of the American Theatre Association. Reprinted by permission of The Johns Hopkins University Press.

" 'As You Smile Not, He's Gagged': Mutuality in Shakespearean Comedy" by Marianne L. Novy from *Love's Argument: Gender Relations in Shakespeare* by Marianne L. Novy, © 1984 by The University of North Carolina Press. Reprinted by permission of The University of North Carolina Press.

"Magic versus Time: *As You Like It* and *Twelfth Night*" by Karen Newman from *Shakespeare's Rhetoric of Comic Character: Dramatic Convention in Classical Renaissance Comedy* by Karen Newman, © 1985 by Karen Newman. Reprinted by permission of Routledge.

"The Forest of Arden" by Peter Lindenbaum from *Changing Landscapes: Anti-Pastoral Sentiment in the English Renaissance* by Peter Lindenbaum, © 1986 by the University of Georgia Press. Reprinted by permission of the University of Georgia Press.

"*As You Like It*" by Robert Ornstein from *Shakespeare's Comedies: From Roman Farce to Romantic Mystery* by Robert Ornstein, © 1986 by Associated University Presses, Inc. Reprinted by permission of Associated University Presses, Inc.

"Feminine Disguise in Comedy" by James L. Calderwood from *Shakespeare and the Denial of Death* by James L. Calderwood, © 1987 by The University of Massachusetts Press. Reprinted by permission of The University of Massachusetts Press.

"Elizabeth" by Leah S. Marcus from *Puzzling Shakespeare: Local Reading and Its Discontents* by Leah S. Marcus, © 1988 by The Regents of the University of California. Reprinted by permission of The University of California Press.

"Travesty and Transgression: Transvestism in Shakespeare, Brecht, and Churchill" by Anne Herrmann from *Theatre Journal* 41, No. 2 (May 1989), © 1989 by The Johns Hopkins University Press. Reprinted by permission of The Johns Hopkins University Press.

"As You Like It" by Harold C. Goddard from *The Meaning of Shakespeare* by Harold C. Goddard, © 1951 by The University of Chicago. Reprinted by permission of The University of Chicago Press.

"Seriousness and Levity in *As You Like It*" (originally titled "The Alliance of Seriousness and Levity in *As You Like It*") by C. L. Barber from *Shakespeare's Festive Comedy: A Study of Dramatic Form and Its Relation to Social Custom* by C. L. Barber, © 1959 by Princeton University Press. Reprinted by permission of Princeton University Press.

"The Histrionics of Lodge's *Rosalynde*" (originally titled "Masking in Arden: The Histrionics of Lodge's *Rosalynde*") by Walter R. Davis from *Studies in English Literature 1500–1900* 5, No. 1 (Winter 1965), © 1965 by William March Rice University. Reprinted by permission of *Studies in English Literature 1500–1900*.

"Rosalynde and Rosalind" by Edward I. Berry from *Shakespeare Quarterly* 31, No. 1 (Spring 1980), © 1980 by The Folger Shakespeare Library. Reprinted by permission of *Shakespeare Quarterly*.

"Multiple Perspectives in Arden" (originally titled " 'All the World's a Stage': Multiple Perspectives in Arden") by Charles R. Forker from *Fancy's Images: Contexts, Settings, and Perspectives in Shakespeare and His Contemporaries* by Charles R. Forker, © 1990 by the Board of Trustees, Southern Illinois University. Reprinted by permission of *Iowa State Journal of Research* and the author.

"The Folly of the Lovers" by R. Chris Hassel, Jr., from *Faith and Folly in Shakespeare* by R. Chris Hassel, Jr., © 1980 by the University of Georgia Press. Reprinted by permission of the University of Georgia Press.

" 'Forget to Be a Woman' " by William C. Carroll from *The Metamorphoses of Shakespearean Comedy* by William C. Carroll, © 1985 by Princeton University Press. Reprinted by permission of Princeton University Press.

"Anatomy as Comedy" by Devon L. Hodges from *Renaissance Fictions of Anatomy* by Devon L. Hodges, © 1985 by The University of Massachusetts Press. Reprinted by permission of The University of Massachusetts Press.

"Mixed Gender, Mixed Genre in *As You Like It*" (originally titled "Mixed Gender, Mixed Genre in Shakespeare's *As You Like It*") by Barbara J. Bono from *Renaissance Genres: Essays on Theory, History, and Interpretation* (Harvard English Studies 14), © 1986 by the President and Fellows of Harvard College. Reprinted by permission of the Department of English, Harvard University.

"The Education of Orlando" by Marjorie Garber from *Comedy from Shakespeare to Sheridan: Change and Continuity in the English and European Dramatic Tradition* edited by A. R. Braunmuller and J. C. Bulman, © 1986 by Associated University Presses, Inc. Reprinted by permission of Associated University Presses, Inc.

"Shakespeare and Dionysus" by Camille Paglia from *Sexual Personae: Art and Decadence from Nefertiti to Emily Dickinson* by Camille Paglia, © 1990 by Yale University. Reprinted by permission of Yale University Press.

INDEX

Macbeth, 14, 24, 54–56
Macbeth (*Macbeth*), 55
Macbeth, Lady (*Macbeth*), 14, 24, 54–56
Machiavelli, Niccolò, 51
McIntosh, Angus, 182
Malecasta (*The Faerie Queene*), 181
Malvolio (*Twelfth Night*), 38
Marivaux, Pierre Carlet de Chamblain de, 31
Marlow (*She Stoops to Conquer*), 171
Marlowe, Christopher, 28, 130, 171; and *As You Like It*, 3–5
Martext, Sir Oliver, 108, 135
Martin, Lady, 168–69
Marvell, Andrew, 45, 81, 108
Marxism, 1
Matthew, 175
Measure for Measure, 41, 126
Melibee (*The Faerie Queene*), 176
Menaphon (Pandosto), 85
Merchant of Venice, The, 21, 52–54, 56, 180
Mercurius, 179, 186–87
Mercury, 130, 186, 188–89
Mercury (*Aenead*), 186
Mercutio (*Romeo and Juliet*), 24, 186
Meredith, George, 5, 66
Metamorphoses (Ovid), 27–28, 129–30
Metaphysicals, the, 81
Michelangelo Buonarrati, 184–85, 187
Midsummer Night's Dream, A, 40, 42, 65, 121, 129, 135, 186
Montanus (*Rosalynde*), 87–89
Montrose, Louis, 63, 153, 165n.20, 166n.31
Mother Nature, 153–54, 158
Much Ado About Nothing, 42, 52, 80, 102, 120
"Mutabilitie Cantos" (Spenser), 111

Narcissus, 171
Nashe, Thomas, 28, 82, 149
Neptune, 85
Nerissa (*The Merchant of Venice*), 53
Nero, 188
New Inn, The (Jonson), 85
New Testament, 134
North, Thomas, 28

Oberon (*A Midsummer Night's Dream*), 76
Odysseus, 155

Oedipus, 197
Oehlenschläger, Adam Gottlob, 10
Of Apolonius and Silla (Rich), 183
"Old religious uncle (man)," 143, 175–77
Oliver, 9, 29, 33, 37, 39, 41, 49, 60–61, 65, 103, 123, 129, 134–35, 139, 149, 155, 161–62, 170, 174–76
Olivia (*Twelfth Night*), 38–39, 77, 158, 168, 180–81
Orlando: character of, 10–12, 15–16, 22–24, 30, 32–39, 41, 43, 47–48, 51–52, 60–61, 67–69, 73–74, 79, 95, 97–98, 101–2, 104, 107–8, 114, 117, 120, 123, 128, 131–34, 139, 141–42, 145–46, 149, 154, 158–63, 168–77, 182, 184; as childlike, 11; and fallibility, 123; and gender, 155; and gentility, 155; and homoeroticism, 62; and masculinity, 60, 118–19; and patriarchy, 156; and religion, 103; as "Signior Love," 18, 101, 140, 148, 157, 172; and time, 16–17, 43–44; wooing of, 174–77
Orlando Furioso (Ariosto), 85
Orpheus (*Metamorphoses*), 27–28
Orsino, Duke (*Twelfth Night*), 38–39, 49–50, 124, 129, 157–58, 168, 181–82
Othello, 15, 161, 164, 182, 184
Othello (*Othello*), 15, 164
Ovid (P. Ovidius Naso), 27–28, 129–30, 161, 180

Palmer, D. J., 117, 124
Pandarus (*Troilus and Cressida*), 81
Pandosto (Greene), 85
Panofsky, Erwin, 165n.26
Paracelsus, Philippus Aureoluis, 189
Paris, 87
Park, Clara Claiborne, 169
"Passionate Shepherd to his Love, The" (Marlowe), 4
Patroclus (*Troilus and Cressida*), 185
Paul, St., 22
Paulina (*The Winter's Tale*), 41
Petrarch (Francesco Petrarca), 34–36, 44–45, 78, 103, 109, 118, 121, 124, 159–60, 169, 171, 181
Petronius (T. Petronius Arbiter), 23